T5-BPY-343

THE PUNITIVE OBSESSION

BY THE SAME AUTHOR

MY FATHER'S SON

KEAN

SINGAPORE GOES OFF THE AIR

THE HEART OF FAME

THE LITTLE TOUR
(*with Constantine FitzGibbon*)

THE OFFENDERS
(*with Derrick Sington*)

CRIME, PUNISHMENT AND CURE
(*with Derrick Sington*)

THE PRODIGY

SIX STUDIES IN HYPOCRISY

THE PUNITIVE OBSESSION

An unvarnished history of the English prison system

by

Giles Playfair

Vindictive and frivolous as we are, we are not absolute fiends, as we should be if our prison system had been deliberately invented and constructed by us all in one piece. It has grown upon us, and grown evilly, having evil roots; but its worst developments have been well meant, for the road to hell is paved with good intentions, not with bad ones . . .

G. BERNARD SHAW

LONDON
VICTOR GOLLANCZ LTD
1971

ISBN 0 575 00611 0

PRINTED IN GREAT BRITAIN
BY EBENEZER BAYLIS & SON LIMITED
THE TRINITY PRESS, WORCESTER, AND LONDON

D. A. S.

In Memoriam

ACKNOWLEDGEMENTS

I am grateful to the below-listed authors, editors and publishers for giving me permission to reproduce copyright material from the following books: *Low Company* by Mark Benney (Peter Davies, 1936); *The Verdict of You All* by Rupert Croft-Cooke (Secker & Warburg, 1955); *The English Prison System* by Lionel Fox (Routledge & Kegan Paul, 1952); *Prison Discipline* by M. L. Gordon (Routledge & Kegan Paul, 1922); *Prison Governor* by B. D. Grew (Herbert Jenkins, 1958); *Prison Screw* by L. W. Merrow Smith (Herbert Jenkins, 1962); *Paterson on Prisons* by Alexander Paterson, ed. S. K. Ruck (Frederick Muller, 1951); *Shades of the Prison House* by Stuart Wood (Williams & Norgate, 1932); *Invisible Bars* by Phoebe Willets (Epworth Press, 1963); *Recollections of a Prison Governor* by C. E. F. Rich (Hurst & Blackett, 1932); *Walls have Mouths* by Wilfred Macartney (Victor Gollancz, 1936); *Who lie in Gaol* by Joan Henry (Victor Gollancz, 1952); *Prison* by Michael Wolff (Eyre & Spottiswoode, 1967).

An extract from an article by William McConnachie which appeared in *The Sunday Telegraph* of 9th April 1967 is reproduced by permission of that newspaper; and an extract from an article by Michael Whitaker which appeared in *The Sunday Times* Magazine of 29th March 1970 is reprinted by kind permission of the author.

Professor Anatol Hold's letter about the murder of his daughter is reproduced by permission of *The Philadelphia Evening Bulletin*, where the letter was originally published in 1959.

CONTENTS

	Preface	9
1	Deterrence and Extermination	11
2	The Reformative Idea	22
3	The Millbank Experiment	30
4	The Prison Hulks	43
5	The Pentonville Experiment	59
6	The Common Gaols Under Local Government	71
7	Local Prisons Under Central Government	93
8	Penal Servitude	117
9	Women and Children	146
10	The Gladstone Committee	155
11	Alexander Paterson and After	177
12	The Penal Heritage	220
	Footnote	251
	Notes	253
	Bibliography	269
	Index	277

PREFACE

To write a popular and unvarnished history of the English Prison System might tax the capacity of the most gifted tale-spinner. It is not, after all, that sort of subject.

However, one could doubtless avoid making the story positively unpopular, if one were able to present it in such a way that it offered some interested group encouragement and hope for the future: the members of the Howard League, say, or at the other extreme, the Tory ladies who advocate the restoration of flogging. But this, it seems to me, the facts forbid, for they suggest that there is no way in which the Prison System can ever be made to serve, or serve sufficiently well, either of the two major purposes for which it was created and supposedly exists: deterrence and reform. Ideas for increasing its "effectiveness", whether they have emanated from Right or Left, seem to have revolved rather than progressed. And, as may be noted, while dealing with the past, I have repeatedly found myself jolted into the present; and *vice versa*.

Just over thirty years ago, Harold Nicolson stated in the House of Commons: "The real development is not one from cruelty or insensitiveness to humanitarianism. It is from muddle-headedness to intelligence. The development is really one from the broad aggregation of criminals to discrimination between criminals; and the whole process of penal reform in this country is this idea of segregation."

Harold Nicolson was, I fear, exactly wrong. There had been, when he spoke, a real advance towards humanitarianism—or at least from a greater to a lesser degree of cruelty and insensitiveness. But the advance from muddle-headedness to intelligence was, except in so far as means had been found to replace imprisonment, illusory. "This idea of segregation", which Nicolson appeared to regard as a contemporary inspiration, is now roughly two centuries old. We have toyed with it off and on throughout that period; we have yet to make it work or prove it workable.

"Our existing system is a mass of confusion, as all must be when the means are not appropriate to the end, and it is as idle to labour for reform of the numerous abuses in detail as to correct a sum figure by figure when it is wrongly stated."

So *The Spectator* wrote in 1842. This history points, cannot avoid pointing, to the same conclusion in 1970.

I

DETERRENCE AND EXTERMINATION

IF CRIME PREVENTION were considered to be simply a problem of how best to deal with people who show themselves unwilling or unable to conform to society's laws, and who consequently disturb society's peace, we should probably be more than ready by this time to renounce what Havelock Ellis once called the "antiquated blunderbuss of punishment." We should certainly be engaged in a frantic search for a better defence against a mounting crime rate than punitive imprisonment, which was founded a little over a century and a half ago with the declared objective of teaching (or forcing) criminals to mend their ways and which, despite varying changes of look, if not of basic character, has consistently failed to achieve its purpose. Though it may not have proved quite the most abortive social experiment in history, it has surely proved the costliest. In 1933, we spent a total of £1,286,617 on prisons. For the year ended 31 March 1968 (the latest information available at the time of writing) we spent £37,219,000: a vast increase and one that is out of all proportion to the rise in the cost of living during the same period.[1]

But the reason we dare not call a halt to this reckless investment, stop throwing good money after bad and cut our losses, is because we cannot bring ourselves to suspend belief in deterrent theory: in the idea that the mass of the citizenry (particularly the less privileged among them) would commit crimes if they dared to, and can only be restrained from doing so by the threat of sufficiently unpleasant legal consequences. For this reason, too, though we do not worry much about the fact that hundreds, if not thousands, of unreformed prisoners are released every year to prey upon society anew, we become deeply upset when a notorious prisoner "cheats the law" by getting out before he has served his sentence in full.

Admittedly, we like to pretend, and may even imagine, that

escapes pose an extraordinary threat to our safety. But in reality they threaten it far less than discharges, if only because they are and always have been comparatively very rare. So far as one knows, Charles Wilson, the train robber, committed no further offences while he was at large, and anyhow was obliging enough to absent himself in Canada. It would have been highly irrational to invest untold police time and money in hunting him down there and bringing him back here to serve the remainder of his sentence, at an eventual minimum cost to ourselves of £10,000 in maintenance charges, if his "dangerousness" had been the true grounds for doing so. But it wasn't, of course. The gargantuan sentence of 30 years had been passed on him in order to demonstrate to unknown others with similar criminal ambitions that the "game", as the trial Judge put it, "was not worth the most alluring candle." We were not prepared, if we could possibly help it, to allow him to make a mockery of that message.

No scientific attempt has ever been made to test the validity of deterrent theory—possibly, because neither the great majority among us who accept it nor the tiny minority who reject it are intellectually interested in an answer that might conflict with their respective emotional prejudices.[2] Undeniably, however, punishment fails in its deterrent purpose to the extent that crimes are actually committed, and today when the crime rate is very much higher and prison conditions supposedly a great deal easier than they were before the second world war, many of us insist that there must be a causal connection between the two.

If this is true, it is unproven; and what may lead one to doubt it is that there has never been a time when voices were not being raised in protest against the "softness" of punishment. Thus in 1967, Mr Duncan Sandys said: "Prisons are becoming more and more like rest homes."[3] In 1938, Lord Justice Greer warned in a letter to *The Times* of a grave danger of "leaving out of account the victim, when pitying the criminal."[4] In 1932, a prison governor wrote: "Our Prison Service was the best in the world, but impractical idealists have messed it up."[5] In 1901, *The Times* remarked that there was a "fine archaic flavour" in references to "humanity mongers who were lavish of their pity for the criminal and had none for the victim."[6] In 1877, *The Spectator* wrote: "The chief fault . . . of our treatment of prisoners is probably that it is too lenient." In 1863, Lord Chief Justice Cockburn noted "too great a tendency to forget that the protection of society should be the first consideration of the lawgiver", and by way of illustrating the point went on to observe: "Moderate labour, ample diet, substantial gratuities, with a remission of a fixed part of the punishment are hardly calculated to produce on the mind of the criminal that salutary dread of the recurrence of punishment that may be the means of deterring him."[7] In 1850, Lord Denman perceived "in some of the theories of benevolent men such a mode of administering the law as to encourage instead of deterring crime."[8] In 1831, a Gaoler remarked: "There has been a sort of ultra philanthropy towards prisoners, which has made them feel that they are the aggrieved party."[9] One could continue indefinitely with these sorts of example.

Yet, paradoxically, if they have been representative of majority opinion, as pretty certainly they have been, society as a whole has become less and less willing to apply deterrent theory with full logical force. Admittedly, as we shall see, there have been repeated shifts in emphasis in the history of imprisonment from reformative to deterrent purposes, and back again. Today, moreover, the restoration of the death penalty for murder still seems conceivable. On the other hand, the restoration of the pillory or the stocks is unimaginable. Nor would anybody in a responsible position, least of all a proponent of capital punishment, dare propose a return to the brutish kind of prison conditions that Lord Cockburn in his time considered already too lenient.

But Lord Cockburn recognized that the severity of legal penalties was subject to civilizing limitations. "Punishment," he said, "should be made as rigorous as is compatible with due regard for humanity, and consistent with the health of body and mind of those subjected to it."

Nor was that proviso, though a great deal less restrictive than it has since become, nearly as unrestrictive as it had been a hundred years earlier, when common criminals, from murderers to petty thieves, were all liable to be hanged. Yet by then society had grown far too civilized to practise deterrent theory without any regard at all for humane considerations.

In 1785, a House of Commons Select Committee regretfully reported that the "late increase in the number of public executions" had "produced no other effect than the removal of the offenders in question" and that crimes continued to "multiply in defiance of the severest exercise of justice."[10] By the "severest exercise of justice" the Committee meant, of course, public hanging, for though there was one severer punishment that remained on the statute books, it was only applicable to treason: an offence which the law regarded as uniquely heinous. Traitors were liable to be cut down from the rope alive, disembowelled, decapitated and quartered.

If Parliament at the time in question had had the courage of deterrent theory, it might have considered adopting the treason penalty for common criminals and retrieving some even more fearsome punishment from the dark ages, such as burning at the stake or boiling in oil, to frighten off potential traitors. But though Parliament was, in fact, to retain hanging, drawing and quartering as a defence against treason for nearly another half century, and was only to abandon it at last in defiance of dire warnings from the judiciary about the resultant menace to the nation's security, it had already begun to question the moral propriety of executing criminals indiscriminately. Illogically, therefore, it was encouraged by the evident ineffectiveness of the death penalty as a deterrent to introduce a new form of punishment, which was likely, on the face of it, to be much less, not more severe; namely reformative imprisonment. In the preamble to an Act of 1779, which authorized the building of government-run penitentiaries, Parliament declared that if criminals "were ordered to solitary imprisonment, accompanied by well regulated labour and religious instruction, it might be the means, under Providence, not only of deterring others from the commission of like crimes, but also of reforming the individuals, and inuring them to habits of industry."

This was the initial legislative move towards acceptance of a revolutionary principle that led, by several different routes, to the eventual establishment of a new penal system, under which the great majority of criminals were no longer to be permanently removed from the community, by means either of the rope or transportation to overseas colonies, but instead were to be taught how to live peaceably within the community during fixed periods of isolation in punitive institutions at home. But though a growing moral revulsion against indiscriminate hangings was one motive for Parliament's action, it was not the only one, and in fact the dismantling of this rough-and-ready method of dealing with the undeterred proved to be a slow and long-drawn-out process.

There were still no fewer than 205 capital offences left when the first quarter of the 19th century was over, though by then executions had become very much less frequent than they might have been and convictions for capital offences rarer than the courts wished them to be. For one thing, juries were showing themselves increasingly disinclined to put people in jeopardy of the gallows, with the result that many capital offenders were being found not guilty, no matter how strong the evidence against them might be, and a huge and widening gap between committals and convictions was mocking justice. For another thing, the Executive, doubtless in response to popular pressure, was making remarkably wide use of the royal prerogative of mercy to commute death sentences to transportation (often on the recommendation of the Judges), so that even those offenders whom the courts were able to convict and condemn had a far better than even chance of being reprieved.

In 1825, for example, only 50 of the 1,036 criminals, whom the courts sentenced to death, were actually executed, though, oddly enough, this number included eight of the 165 condemned horse-thieves. In 1831, the year before Parliament abolished capital punishment for cattle-stealing among various other minor kinds of larceny, there were proportionately still fewer death sentences put into effect—52 out of 1,601. This time all the condemned horse-thieves (they numbered 125) escaped the rope. So did 13 of the 14 sodomites, ten of the 25 arsonists and four of the 16 murderers.

By 1861, the only two offences that in effect remained capital were murder and treason. Four years later, a Royal Commission was appointed to consider, among other things, the advisability and practicability of total abolition.[11] At this point a debate began which has monotonously been repeating itself ever since in and out of Parliament.

As a means of punishing actual offenders, as opposed to deterring potential offenders, the death penalty was manifestly reduced to an anachronism, for transportation had been formally ended in 1857 and the old exterminatory penal system was now fully replaced by the supposedly reformative prison system. This historical truth was better understood by the witnesses who gave evidence before the Royal Commission than it is apt to be understood by present-day participants in the capital punishment dispute, and it was stated with particular clarity by Mr Justice Hill: "I agree with Lord Russell," he said, "in thinking that the punishment of death might have been expedient in past ages, furnishing as it does the most perfect form of 'incapacitation'. At a period in our history . . . when criminals were regarded with no feelings but scorn and hatred, or at best with absolute indifference to their sufferings, and when their reformation was undreamed of, it was by comparison humane to put them to a speedy and merciful death, such as that by the halter undoubtedly is."

Mr Justice Hill went on to say that criminals, far from being hated still, were for the most part deeply pitied; and though this was a hyperbolic and perhaps implicitly disapproving way of putting the point, the very existence of the prison system undoubtedly meant that, for better or worse, the public had recognized and accepted a moral obligation to consider the future welfare of criminals at the risk of being imperfectly protected from them. Under such a system, Mr Justice Hill concluded, there was no place left for the death penalty, and he recommended its total abolition: a recommendation, incidentally, that was eventually to be endorsed by a minority of the Commission, including John Bright.

But Mr Justice Hill specifically rejected deterrent theory. He did not believe, he said, that anybody who formed the intention of committing a crime bothered about the legal consequences or was capable of taking them into account. This, of course, was a heresy; and it was shared by none of his fellow members of the judiciary. "As the object of punishment is to prevent crime," Baron Bramwell told the Commission, "we must consider as our object, not how to punish the greatest number of persons, but how to prevent the greatest number of murders." In the majority view, this object could not possibly be fulfilled unless death remained the penalty for murder, though, curiously enough, Baron Bramwell himself thought that it could and should be dispensed with in the case of treason.

Still, there was no pretence that the presumed deterrent worth of a punishment was in itself a sufficient justification for retaining it. Indeed, a retired Judge, Lord Wensleydale, openly stated that he favoured hanging, not because he regarded it as a peerlessly powerful deterrent, but because he knew it to be the severest, and therefore the most effectively preventive punishment that society would consider tolerable. "Imprisonment for life," he said, "would be a punishment of greater severity, if rigidly carried into effect, but it never would be. The criminal . . . would in course of time become an object of pity, and the public sympathy being excited, the sentence would ultimately be remitted . . . I think there are punishments which are capable of a much greater deterrent effect than death, but they are punishments which the public would not for a moment endure, such as mutilation, cutting off of all a man's members, depriving him of his eye-sight, depriving him of his power of hearing, cutting off his limbs, confining him in a small place without the light of day, and so on. Punishments of that kind would deter much more than the taking away of life, but I am sure that the public would not endure them."

It may well have been a moot question in Lord Wensleydale's mind whether even the death penalty would continue to be endured by the public; and certainly neither he nor any of its other apologists dared recommend its restoration for lesser crimes than murder, although they were by no means ready to admit that wholesale hangings had proved practically abortive as a means of deterrence. James Fitzjames Stephen, the celebrated jurist, testified to his belief that the threat of the rope had "prevented many people from stealing sheep."

But the new penal system was inextricable from refinements of both deterrent theory and practice. For just as wholesale hangings were no longer morally permissible, so it had become morally imperative to deal with criminals more or less severely according to the gravity of their offence or their so-called "deserts." Thus while it was still maintained that punishment served to prevent crime in proportion to its severity, it was now held that the worse the crime, the severer the punishment which society needed (and was justified in using) to prevent it, and vice versa.

The case for retaining the death penalty for murder was, therefore, largely based on the argument that because murder was an especially heinous crime, an especially severe punishment was required to deter people from committing it. The propounders of this argument had logically to contend that though many people may have been prevented from stealing sheep by their fear of the rope, the reason why some sheep-stealers had not hesitated to commit murder was because of their awareness that they could be hanged only once. This, however, like virtually everything else that has been said in support of deterrent theory, was mere assertion; and, in the case of a crime more naturally associated with homicide than sheep-stealing, its implications appeared to be contradicted by statistical evidence. For while there had been no change in the murder rate (which remained consistently low) after rape ceased to be a capital offence in 1841, the incidence of rape itself had, if the figures did not lie, risen sharply; from 83 convictions during the ten years immediately preceding abolition to 514 convictions during the ten years following, and much more significantly, considering the growing reluctance that jurors had shown under the exterminatory system to convict anyone accused of a capital offence, from 514 to 1,303 committals during the same respective periods.

The assumption that hanging was needed to prevent a large number of people from committing murder whom it had not prevented from committing lesser crimes may anyway seem highly implausible in retrospect. But, historically, the deterrent case for retaining the death penalty rests on that assumption, and, a hundred years ago, this fact was too apparent to be evaded.

However, there was then, as there still is, a secondary retentionist argument. This was based on retributive theory, and one calls it secondary, because, to judge from the weight of legal opinion, retribution is in itself of secondary importance to deterrence, though there have been, and are, jurists who take the opposite view, including the present Master of the Rolls, Lord Denning. In any case, retribution and deterrence have always been closely connected objects of punishment in the law's estimation, and, with the advent of the prison system, both required the same sort of modifications for the same fundamental reason.

According to retributive theory, punishment is a means of expressing society's detestation of legal transgressions. So long as the exterminatory penal system lasted, this principle was applied on the assumption, which eventually turned out to be false, that society detested nearly all crimes equally—sheep-stealing no less than homicide. The retributive argument for continuing to hang murderers and traitors, after it had become obligatory to show other offenders graded degrees of mercy, was that the death penalty alone could provide a sufficient expression of society's extreme detestation of murder and treason. Lord Denning, when he gave evidence before the Gowers Commission on Capital Punishment,[12] was to re-iterate the point in this way: "The punishment for grave crimes should adequately reflect the revulsion felt by the majority of the citizens for them. It is a mistake to consider the object of punishment as being deterrent or reformative or preventive and nothing else. The ultimate justification of any punishment is not that it is a deterrent but that it is the emphatic denunciation by the community of a crime."

If one grants the theoretic validity of that pronouncement, one may wonder whether in practice the use of the death penalty, however restricted, isn't bound to result in the community's denunciations of particular crimes being either too emphatic or not emphatic enough. Thus it may or may not have been necessary in 1955 to hang Mrs Ruth Ellis as a means of "adequately" reflecting the revulsion felt by the majority of English citizens for her crime, which was to shoot her faithless lover to death. But if it *was* necessary, then clearly the hanging of Adolf Eichmann a few years later was a grossly inadequate way of reflecting the revulsion felt by the majority of citizens throughout the civilized world for the crime of genocide.

In sum, the same moral considerations that turned the death penalty into a penal anachronism undermined the case for retaining it on either deterrent or retributive grounds; and this case has been further weakened by its own proponents who have consistently advocated that the hanging process itself should be as delicately and painlessly conducted as possible, or, in other words, be made as little deterrent and as little retributive as possible. Even Lord Wensleydale wanted an end to public executions, though he believed that Press reporters should be allowed to attend executions carried out within prison walls.[13]

It is possible to imagine a penal system, or more accurately a non-penal preventive system, that would permit the extermination or permanent removal of criminals who are found or considered to be irreformable. In fact, it was just such a system that Bernard Shaw envisaged when, in his preface to the Webbs' book, *English Prisons Under Local Government*,[14] he appeared to advocate the idea of dealing with incorrigibles by euthanasia. This is now regarded as one of the most reprehensible of Shaw's occasional aberrations, but it must be remembered that during the early part of the present century humanitarians were apt to be far more disturbed by the persistent cruelties of imprisonment than by the execution of occasional murderers.

It could be said then, and not infrequently was, without outraging the liberal conscience, that to hang habitual offenders would be a great deal less inhumane than to subject them to repeated periods of penal servitude. Winston Churchill, who was moved to tears by the scene of solitary confinement in Galsworthy's play *Justice*, and is rightly remembered as one of the most liberal of Home Secretaries, spoke words in the House of Commons in 1910 which still serve as a clarion call for penal reformers: "The mood and temper of the public with regard to the treatment of crime and criminals is one of the most unfailing tests of the civilization of any country. A calm, dispassionate recognition of the rights of the accused, and even of the convicted, criminal against the State—a constant heart-searching by all charged with the duty of punishment—a desire and eagerness to rehabilitate in the world of industry those who have paid their due in the coinage of punishment: tireless efforts towards the discovery of curative and regenerative processes: Unfailing faith that there is a treasure, if you can only find it in the heart of every man." Yet Churchill remained an advocate of the death penalty for murder and treason to the end of his life. So, for that matter, did Galsworthy.

Still, as Shaw at least recognized, under a system that permitted the extermination of incorrigibles, deterrent and retributive principles would not only have to be further modified, but in effect wholly renounced, since the question of whether or not a criminal is reformable has no necessary relevance to the gravity or otherwise of the crime he is convicted of. A petty thief may be an intractible social pest, whereas experience has shown that, as a group, murderers are the least likely of all offenders to offend again.

To say the same thing in another way, if preventive extermination were ever to become a recognized alternative to reformative imprisonment as a response to crime, the punitive purpose of both practices would have to be renounced. That was precisely what Shaw wanted. But he was crying for the moon.

As it happened, the replacement of the exterminatory penal system by the prison system did not, of course, represent either the abandonment of a punitive response to crime or the adoption of one. Punishment for its own (or deterrence's) sake was common to both systems; it was only the method of applying it that changed. But this change—from the use of punishment to liquidate criminals to its use for fitting them to live within the community—was founded on moral principles. And, whether those principles were mistaken or not, they logically left no room for exceptions.

In short, one may see that the death penalty was bound to go in the end. Its abolition was an inevitable process. The fact that this process took so long to complete—indeed, that it is still incomplete, since the death penalty for treason remains on the statute books—is due to what may be called the deterrent superstition or the punitive obsession. And this, as we shall see, equally accounts for the slow progress and repeated retrogress of penal reform.

2

THE REFORMATIVE IDEA

PENAL HISTORY MIGHT have taken a different course, if transportation had remained a practical possibility. This was a punishment with a morally much less objectionable look to it than hanging, for it had originated as a measure of executive clemency for capital offenders and even after it had developed into a punishment at the disposal of the criminal courts it was still represented as merciful. Though a sentence to exile and forced labour, which was what transportation meant, might be for life, it was ordinarily for a fixed term of either fourteen or seven years, so that in most cases the punishment was theoretically no more exterminatory than imprisonment. In practice, however, transported criminals very rarely returned home to plague the community anew, and this was so for two very divergent reasons. On the one hand, there was better than an outside chance that they wouldn't live long enough to complete their sentence. On the other hand, if they did survive the horrors of the long voyage in a convict ship and the likely brutalities of their subsequent servitude, they were eventually given every encouragement to stay put as free settlers and none at all to repatriate themselves.

As late as 1831, a House of Commons Select Committee[1] referred to transportation as follows: "Unless there existed some such mode of disposing of criminals whose offences do not merit the penalty of death, but whose morals are so depraved that their reformation can hardly be expected, no alternative would remain to a choice between perpetual imprisonment and the constant infusion into society of malefactors, who, after the term of their punishment had arrived, would again be thrown as outcasts on the world, without friends, without character, and without the means of gaining an honest livelihood."

When that statement was made, transportation was within

thirty years of its final demise, and would already have long ceased to exist but for a supposed need of convict labour in the development of the new Australian colonies. For the potential dilemma, to which the Committee referred, had been an actual one half a century or so earlier, when the loss of the American colonies seemed to mean that there was no suitable place of exile left for criminals in large numbers. This was the immediate cause of Parliament's decision in 1779 to authorize the building of penitentiaries.

But meanwhile a sort of *ersatz* transportation had been hurriedly introduced. Under an Act of 1776, the courts had been empowered, for a limited period, to pass sentences of hard labour, ranging from three to ten years, on male offenders who would previously have been found suitable for penal banishment to America. Convicts undergoing this new punishment were employed by day in chain gangs raising gravel from the Thames at Woolwich, and were confined at nights in one or other of a couple of vessels that had been fitted up as floating gaols. Thus the so-called Hulk system was born. It was intended as merely a stop-gap measure, and was to last for nearly a century.

The Justices of Peace of the Middlesex Quarter Sessions had been made responsible for appointing an administrator of the system, or overseer, as he was officially styled, and their choice had fallen on a certain Mr Duncan Campbell. His qualification for the job was that he had been one of the private contractors engaged in shipping convicts across the Atlantic on the Government's behalf—originally in consideration of a flat payment of £5 a head and latterly in return for a concession to sell the members of his human cargo for what they would fetch from individual employers. On his last voyage, Campbell had found Maryland and Virginia to be the only worthwhile markets. There he had been able to dispose of females for £8, unskilled male labourers for £10, and artisans for between £15 and £25, though even so he had been obliged to *pay* "humane personages" to take the senile and crippled convicts off his hands.

It was in the role of a private contractor that Duncan Campbell operated the Hulk system. He supplied, equipped and staffed the two vessels, and undertook to feed, clothe and discipline the prisoners as well as care for their physical health and see to it that the prescribed punishment was suitably inflicted on them. He received an annual grant from the Treasury for his services—initially, at the rate of £38 for each of the convicts committed to his charge—out of which he was required to meet his overhead expenses. However, he had no stake in the prisoners' labour. The return from this went to the Government, which, through the Home Department, exercised a supervisory power over Campbell's activities and made provision both for remitting sentences in deserving cases and for the payment of gratuities to convicts on their discharge. In short, one might say that as in the case of banishment to America before it, the Hulk system had a mixed economy.

In 1779, three years after it was instituted, Campbell gave an account of his stewardship to a House of Commons Select Committee.[2] He revealed, among other things, that there were at present 510 convicts aboard his two Hulks, including 31 lame men and eight boys under 15. He had, he said, dispensed with hammocks since the prisoners found these difficult to manage because of their irons. Sleeping accommodation now consisted of mats, six feet long and four feet wide, with one mat for every two prisoners and a rug to cover them. He gave details of the diet: porridge for breakfast, porridge for supper, and for dinner half an ox's head to a mess of six men, with the addition twice a week of bread and cheese. There was also a standard weekly beer allowance of four quarts and a daily bonus of one quart for good behaviour.

No fewer than 176 convicts had died aboard the Hulks during the first two years of the operation, or more than a quarter of the total number sentenced during the same period. This was a high figure even by comparison with what the average mortality rate had been in the transport ships, and Campbell attributed it in part to the generally low spirits of the convicts faced with a new and therefore especially dreaded punishment and in part to the fact that many of them, having been sent to him from fever-ridden gaols, had spread infection. At the same time he denied reports that the food he provided was persistently tainted, or the drinking water brackish, and assured the Committee that none of the convicts had died for want of proper care on his part or on that of the captains, officers and guards whom he employed.

This assurance was accepted by the Committee who found that the situation was rapidly improving and called the new system both useful and healthy. Actually, it continued to prove somewhat lethal, but it was only after it had started to discharge more prisoners than it buried that Parliament became aware of its defects.

The 1785 Committee, which, as has been said, bemoaned the failure of public executions to halt a mounting crime rate, also expressed deep regret that rebellious America was no longer willing to receive the Mother Country's unwanted citizens. They believed that urgent consideration should be given to the advantages and disadvantages of remaining British overseas possessions as dumping grounds. They took note of a proposal, that had been seriously mooted, for using convicts to colonize some remote and uninhabited island; but this they rejected on the grounds that criminals would be bound to kill and rob each other, if they were left to their own devices. Indeed, the very idea of using transportation for no higher purpose than the undisguisedly utilitarian one of removing undesirable members of the community, without a care for their eventual fate, evidently shocked the Committee profoundly. "Such an experiment," they said, "had never been made in the history of mankind." On the other hand, they found that Transportation to America, though it might have been insufficiently deterrent, had otherwise "answered every good purpose that could be expected of it"; and they were no less emphatic in denouncing the Hulk system as a thoroughly unsatisfactory substitute.

Manifestly, they recognized that whereas a transported convict was a criminal eliminated at little cost to the nation's conscience or pocket, a convict sent to the Hulks was a criminal only temporarily out of the nation's mind and sight. "After expiration of sentences, convicts return into the mass of the community, not reformed in their principles, but confirmed in every vicious habit. No parish will receive them, and no person set them to work . . . The danger of starving almost irresistibly leads them to a renewal of their former crimes."

That, of course, was to state a problem which the 1831 Committee was to re-state and which to this day remains unsolved: the problem of how society can use a prescribed dose of imprisonment to exact a payment from its offending members without, in the end, impelling them to incur further and worse debts. But though at this time there was supreme confidence in "reform" as the answer, and no less confidence in what methods of "reform" were needed, the 18th century was over before any serious attempt was made to apply that answer on a national scale. Moreover, the resumption of full-scale transportation, which became possible with colonial development in Australia, allowed the penal system to remain largely exterminatory during the first half of the 19th century.

In fact, it was not until 1812 that work was begun on building a penitentiary.[3] The Government had originally intended to delegate this job, too, to private enterprise, and in 1791 had accordingly entered into a tentative agreement with Jeremy Bentham who, unlike Duncan Campbell, was, of course, a man obsessed with convictions about what punitive imprisonment could and should be used to achieve by way of both deterrence and reform.

After the agreement had been drawn up, Bentham was advanced £3,000 from Treasury funds for the purchase of a river-bank site in the Metropolis, where, for a further £31,000, he undertook to build what he called a Panopticon. This was a prison of his own design which, if it had ever come into being, would have looked like a huge cage. He planned to run it out of the profits of convict labour.

The thing that chiefly distinguished Bentham's design for a Panopticon from any prison known to man was an arrangement which made it possible for the inmates, whatever they might be doing, at any time of the day or night, to be watched by a disciplinary staff whom they could not see. In this way, Bentham claimed, "seclusion", which was regarded as the paramount necessity of reformative treatment, would be attained without going to the expense of providing individual cells for every prisoner. He planned to put as many as eight or nine prisoners in the same cell, and yet to make sure that they were as effectively isolated from each other's corruptive influence as they would be if they were locked up separately.

Bentham also proposed to allow representatives of the Press and Public free access to the observation post at the Panopticon. He believed that the more people who underwent the experience of watching men silently toiling, in total isolation from the living world, the better the Panopticon's deterrent purpose would be fulfilled. Further, he relied on "public vigilance" to furnish a guarantee against the maladministration of the institution or the suppression of legitimate inmate grievances. The spectators were to be permitted to speak to the prisoners by means of a system of tubes connected with the cells, and to ask them anything they might wish to ask about their treatment.

Because the Panopticon was a vision of Big Brotherism, which mercifully came to nothing, Bentham is apt to be remembered as a sort of malevolent clown of penal history. Yet in some ways we have not advanced so far beyond his theories of appropriate prison training and treatment as we may suppose. He undertook to provide his captives with a rudimentary general education as well as religious instruction, and he was prepared to give them a financial stake in their labour which, in real terms, would have amounted to more than the gratuities which prisoners receive today for their work. Moreover, one might reasonably suggest that Bentham's security plans, so long neglected, have now finally been adopted nearly two centuries after he proposed them. At least, the following of his suggested measures may seem remarkably similar to some of the recommendations in the Mountbatten Report of 1966, which are at present being enforced:

> 1. Light thrown upon the whole surface of the four surrounding walls
>
> 2. On top of the walls all round, a range of spikes, iron or wooden, of such slightness, that in the attempt to set a ladder against them or throw a rope over them to get up by, they would give way and break, and in either case strike against

a range of wires, by which a number of *bells* would be set *a-ringing*

3. On the outside of each of the surrounding walls a *ditch*, the water of which would, on any attempt to undermine the contiguous wall, inundate the miners, and while it betrayed their operations, render an exit, if not absolutely impracticable, at least impracticable without such noise as would give abundant warning to the Guard-House

4. To each such Guard-House, a dog or *dogs*, of the sort of those which in the night are set a-barking by any the least noise.

One may be sure that if television had existed in his day, Bentham would have been no less alive than Mountbatten was in 1966 to its potential value in prison security. Almost certainly, he would have planned to have spy cameras not only atop the walls of the Panopticon, but in the cells as well. As it was, he meant to depend on "light", and, as he put it, "eyes in considerable number constantly availing themselves of that light."

But Bentham did not for a moment suppose that his emphasis on security would be at the risk of minimizing the effectiveness of his reformative programme. On the contrary, he recognized an essential truth which modern Home Secretaries, in particular the Home Secretary who asked for the Mountbatten report, either don't realize or prefer to forget: namely, that if a prison administrator has failed in his duty to the public whenever a prisoner escapes, he has also failed, and should logically be held no less accountable for his failure, whenever a discharged prisoner reverts to crime. Bentham agreed that crimes committed by graduates of his Panopticon, as well as escapes from the institution, should be treated as breaches of contract, for which he would be liable to pay the Government a fixed sum in compensation.

The sum payable in the former case was to be dependent on the length of time a man had served in the Panopticon or, in other words, on the size of the opportunity Bentham had been given to prove the worth of his reformative measures. Thus he was pledged to pay less for a crime committed by an ex-inmate who had served only one year than for a crime committed by an ex-inmate who had served five years, though five years, he believed, was the maximum sentence that anyone should receive. He also meant to insure himself against loss through finding jobs for his released prisoners and housing those of them who had nowhere else to go, and were willing to take advantage of the opportunity, in a "subsidiary establishment." This particular idea was somewhat similar to what is possibly regarded as the most advanced of present-day practices: the scheme under which a selected number of long-term prisoners are transferred to a hostel during the last six to ten months of their sentences, work in outside employment and spend weekends at home.

Bentham's contract with the Government was never concluded, and the 1812 Committee recommended that it should be torn up. This was not because they lacked confidence in reformative treatment or doubted the need for a penitentiary. "Many offenders," they said without qualification, "may be reclaimed by a system of imprisonment, not confined to the safe custody of the person, but extending to the reformation and improvement of the mind, and operating by seclusion, employment and religious instruction." But the Committee questioned the propriety of entrusting a project of such public importance to a private individual who, they maintained, would inevitably be tempted to exploit the prisoners for his own "pecuniary advantage." In particular, they criticized Bentham's scheme on the grounds that it provided no assurance of "sufficient religious instruction."

The result of their report was that Parliament voted £450,000—£419,000 more than Bentham had required—for the erection of a penitentiary on the site that had been acquired for the Panopticon. Four years later, Millbank penitentiary as it was called, was built or sufficiently built to "receive" prisoners; and the central Government was launched on the first of its experiments in reformative imprisonment.

3
THE MILLBANK EXPERIMENT

The expression "reformative" imprisonment has been used advisedly, because it must not be supposed that imprisonment for the punishment of offenders was unknown prior to the advent of Millbank. As we have remarked, the makeshift Hulks system was already in existence, and more must be said about it later. In addition, there were the locally administered common gaols and houses of correction, with a history centuries old, and although these places had largely come to be used for the safe custody of persons awaiting trial and convicts awaiting execution or transportation, their population included minor offenders serving definite sentences of imprisonment. They, too, will be discussed later.

But in so far as our present penal system has a reformative as well as punitive purpose, its history may be said to have begun with the Millbank experiment. If it proved an inauspicious beginning, and it did, it was also, in both principle and practice, closer to what is happening today than to the developments that followed it. Indeed, in at least one respect we have only very recently caught up with it again. Under the Millbank regime, in its pristine state, the flogging of prisoners for offences against discipline was absolutely prohibited. To judge how advanced this rule was, it should be remembered that in 1816, violent penal methods, such as the stocks and the pillory, were still being widely used as a corrective for petty crime, and even women offenders could be sentenced to a public flogging, though admittedly this practice was to be outlawed two years later.

The prison building itself—and here a lasting precedent was set—long survived its original purpose. It was, to quote the Webbs, a "monument of ugliness"[1] and at the same time perhaps the most extravagant architectural achievement that "the world had seen since the Pyramids of Egypt." One may doubt whether "the Taj at Agra, the Cloth Hall at Ypres or the Cathedral of Chartres" were anything like so costly. It was a sprawling fortress, with dank, labyrinthine passages and subterranean punishment cells; and though it was in no sense a realization of Bentham's Panopticon design, its hideousness was doubtless in some degree owed to his influence, for Bentham believed that the very sight of a penitentiary from the outside should fill all who beheld it with such dread of what might await them inside that they would never dare take the risk of being put there.

Yet, despite its formidably deterrent appearance, Millbank was, in theory, as dedicated to rehabilitation as any prison has been since. Convicts weren't sent there *for* punishment nor even, strictly speaking, *as* punishment, because they weren't sent there by the courts at all. The Government was empowered to use its penitentiary for the benefit of selected offenders who, in its view, deserved a chance of reformation, instead of being hanged or transported, and who were on the face of it likely to respond to such mercifulness. The chosen, as it turned out, were mostly first offenders, some of them of remarkably immature years.[2]

A Committee of Management was appointed under the authority of the Home Secretary to run the establishment. They were responsible for engaging the staff, which consisted of a Governor, a Matron in charge of the female prisoners (who were supposed to be strictly separated from the males), a chaplain, a medical superintendent, a surgeon, a steward (or book-keeper), tutors, task-masters and task-mistresses, and finally male and female turnkeys. Most of today's larger prisons are staffed in the same way, except that there is rarely more than one medical officer employed and women's central prisons are separate from men's.

The Committee was also responsible for seeing that the rules were carried out, and these, based on the three accepted principles of seclusion, employment and religious instruction, were precisely laid down in an Act of Parliament. Seclusion was considered of paramount importance, because it was believed, and one may think very logically believed, that criminals could not be taught to fear God and labour honestly for man so long as they were in a position to lead each other astray. However, Bentham's idea of enforcing seclusion by means of constant supervision was rejected in favour of the more obvious and less economical method of locking up every prisoner in a separate cell. But this didn't amount to quite the same thing as solitary confinement. There were two or three daily half hour exercise periods, when the prisoners were permitted to walk round the courtyards in pairs and converse, if they wished to. Moreover, after they had served half their time—the total varied from ten to five years—they graduated from working in their cells to working in association, when again they were allowed to talk, provided their conversation was suitably circumspect.

Their day began at 5.30, when the "first bell" rang, and they were obliged to do an early morning stint at cranking the pumps before breakfast. But otherwise their employment was not hard labour; it was productive and designedly vocational. The men were engaged in tailoring and weaving; the women in sewing and laundering. The produce of their work was for sale in the open market. Part of the proceeds went to the task-masters and task-mistresses, part to the institution, and three half pence out of every shilling to the prisoners themselves. But the prisoners, whose earnings averaged 2s 3d a week for the men and 1s 5d for the women, weren't actually paid the money until their discharge, when they were also handed a gratuity of £3. They were entitled to a further gratuity in the same amount a year later on proof of good conduct: the germ of an idea for preventing crime by reward, rather than punishment, which, regrettably perhaps, has never been pursued.

Religious instruction largely took the form of compulsory attendance at services in the prison chapel, which were held on weekday mornings as well as Sundays, though the prisoners were also encouraged to read the Bible and other devotional works, and some limited provision was made for classroom study. The punishment for those who displayed overt signs of failure to find their way to repentance was to be locked up for a period of days or weeks in one of the subterranean punishment or dark cells, as they were called, where not a glimmer of light could penetrate.

Millbank received its first batch of guinea pigs—all female—on 26 June 1816, though the building at that time was not yet completed. On the previous afternoon, according to a report in *The Times*, "several noblemen and ladies of distinction went over the different cells which were then ready for the reception of the female convicts." The cells were "very comfortable, lofty with an arch and glazed window, furnished with an iron bedstead, table and stool, and warmed by flues placed in the passage." At 3 o'clock next morning, the forty female convicts "were carried in caravans, chained together, from Newgate to Blackfriars Bridge, there put on a barge prepared to receive them, and conveyed under a strong guard of Police Officers to Millbank, where they were landed and conducted into the Yard prepared for them; they were then classed, and shown to their respective cells, the doors being all numbered along the galleries." Those of them that could not read, the report added, would be "instructed."

There was eventually to be single cell accommodation in Millbank for over 1,200 prisoners, male and female. By the beginning of 1817, this "national establishment", as *The Times* proudly called it, was "getting into full operation" and was, therefore, "exciting considerable attention." On 4 February, the Grand Duke Nicholas of Russia, accompanied by Sir William Congreve and suite, went to view it, and afterwards "expressed himself much gratified at the general demeanour of the prisoners, and the general arrangements and management of the prison." Visits followed from other dignitaries, including the Bishops of London and Salisbury, Mr Justice Bayley and the Hon. H. G. Bennett, who were all deeply impressed by the "progress in religious instruction . . . as well as the industry, cleanliness, good order and discipline of the prison." On 1 March, H.R.H. the Duchess of York was present when several female convicts were "examined in their religious instruction." Later, she was shown round the kitchen, bakehouse, wash-house and laundry, "with the whole of which she was pleased to express her approbation."

But what these distinguished visitors saw, or were encouraged to see, bore little or no relation to reality. Millbank was inherently an unhealthy place, because the site had been badly chosen and the building badly designed. The cells were so appallingly ventilated that an immediate compromise had to be made with seclusion in order to avoid a huge death toll. During working hours, the outer, wooden door of the cells was left open, and only the inner door, an iron grating, closed, with the result that though the prisoners were securely locked in, they could see each other and talk to each other, too, when the turnkeys weren't around.

Still, the situation might have been less deplorable, if the astronomic sum invested in building Millbank had been matched by a comparably generous grant for running it. In fact, the Committee of Management had less money to play with than the first overseer of the Hulks: with a population of over eight hundred an annual £26 per prisoner for the maintenance of the institution. Consequently, the inmates were not only under-fed, but at the mercy of a custodial staff as ill-educated as they were poorly paid, and as brutal, most of them as they were corrupt.[3]

In these circumstances, it is no wonder that from the outset the captives seemed troublingly unresponsive to the reformative efforts being made on their behalf. Some of them (the women in particular) behaved violently and hysterically. There were frequent disturbances; notably, a demonstration in protest against the poor quality of the bread, which was staged in the chapel when, embarrassingly enough, the Chancellor of the Exchequer had accepted an invitation to be present. Deep listlessness was characteristic of other prisoners, while not a few were suicidal or "feigned" madness.

Clearly, things could not be allowed to go on in this way, and eventually the Medical Superintendent, Dr Copland Hutchinson, came up with a suggestion. He attributed all the trouble to over-eating. The established dietary, he said, was "too ample" for the prisoners' own good. With the support of Sir James McGrigor, Head of the Army Medical Board, he recommended that their daily allowance of one pound of potatoes and six ounces of coarse boiled beef should be stopped, so that in future their diet should consist unvaryingly of three quarters of a pound of bread and a pint of gruel for breakfast, one pint of soup (made out of one oxhead for every hundred of them), thickened with pease or barley, for dinner and one pint of unthickened soup for supper.

This extraordinary recommendation—extraordinary since it was seriously represented as therapeutic rather than punitive[4]—was accepted by the Committee of Management (without Parliament's authority) and became operative in July 1822. Not surprisingly, it was shortly followed by an outbreak of scurvy.

Dr Copland Hutchinson stuck to his guns. There was nothing wrong with the new dietary, he said; the unhealthiness of the building was to blame, especially the inadequate ventilation and the foul air. For a while the Committee were content to accept his word for it, but as more and more prisoners became affected, they took fright and called in two outside consultants, Drs Roguet and Latham, who urgently recommended the addition of an orange and four ounces of flesh meat to the daily diet. This advice was either too little or too late. The disease continued to spread, until finally the whole building had to be evacuated and the surviving inmates transferred to the Hulks.

A Select Committee of the House of Commons conducted an investigation, and in 1824 produced a remarkably liberal report. While they decided that the institution could be safely re-populated, they found that Dr Hutchinson's revised dietary had, in fact, been too low. More importantly, they came to the conclusion that the poor physical health of the prisoners had had much to do with their mental depression. They recommended that a "greater degree of relaxation" should be introduced, including "some kinds of organized game or sport" and the provision of "books combining rational amusement with religious and moral instruction."

It is conceivable, that if this last recommendation had been accepted, the Millbank experiment might yet have had a happier and longer history. But it was a proposal far ahead of its time, and invited widespread expressions of ridicule and anger in and out of Parliament. Hence, though the institution was duly re-opened, and the dietary restored to its original state, the repressive discipline remained unchanged. Equally, the disturbances continued. Inmates persistently broke up their cells and took violent reprisals against the more unpopular of the turnkeys, whenever they got the chance.[5] Finally, in 1828, there was a full-scale riot, and the police had to be called in to restore order.

The response was to make the discipline more repressive than ever. A special Act of Parliament was passed, which authorized the governor to order floggings subject to the Committee of Management's approval. In 1831, yet another Select Committee[6] inquired into the whole problem of secondary punishments (i.e., punishments short of hanging) and in regard to Millbank made proposals as reactionary as those of the 1824 Committee had been progressive. Prisoners, they said, should no longer be permitted visits or to write and receive letters. They described the system of gratuities as an extravagance, which ought to be abolished. They recommended that the "most reprobate" of the inmates should be put to hard, unproductive labour, and that there should be an end to associated work for the female prisoners, which they found to be "subversive of all good." They reached this last conclusion in spite of hearing from Elizabeth Fry, famous for her benevolent work among the derelict women of Newgate, that though she favoured the enforcement of silence in a purely custodial institution where the inmates were herded together, she doubted whether separate confinement and strict discipline in a penitentiary provided the right sort of preparation for a "return to social life."

Soon afterwards, associated work was abolished completely—for the men as well as the women; and, as a further move towards the ideal of total seclusion, a stop was put to conversation during the exercise periods, through obliging the prisoners to walk in single file instead of in pairs. However, the Committee of Management recognized that there was a limit to the length of time human beings could be expected to endure such conditions, and that if that limit were overstepped, the discipline might defeat its own reformative end. Length of sentences was, therefore, reduced from a maximum of ten years to five and a minimum of five to three.

At the same time, an increased emphasis was placed on religious instruction with the appointment of a member of the

Committee, the Rev. Whitworth Russell, to the positions of both chaplain and governor. This signified an even greater commitment to "treatment" than previously, and in a sense made Millbank the forerunner of the modern psychiatric prison at Grendon-Underwood, where the offices of governor and medical superintendent are combined. Grendon-Underwood is, one may hope, a very much more enlightened rehabilitative centre than Millbank proved to be. But the fact that it is administered by a doctor is in principle expressive of the same dedication to treatment that the Rev. Whitworth Russell's appointment symbolized.

Nor was the Millbank discipline, toughened though it was under its new religious management, nearly as tough as prison discipline was later to become. Major Arthur Griffiths,[7] an Inspector of Prisons and author of a history of Millbank published in 1875, recalls how, during the Rev. Whitworth Russell's benevolent administration, an inmate had his sentence of 100 lashes with the "cat" for an assault on an officer remitted to 50 lashes. "Were proof required," Griffiths writes, "of the exceeding mildness of the rule under which Millbank was governed we should have it here. But, really, all milk-and-water tenderness is misplaced in the management of criminals."

This later appraisal of Millbank's silly, soft old days echoed a sentiment which the 1831 Select Committee on secondary punishments expressed in general terms: "If it is a principle of our criminal jurisprudence that the guilty should escape rather than the innocent suffer, it appears equally a principle in the infliction of punishment that every regulation connected with it, from the first committal of a prisoner to gaol to the termination of his sentence, should be characterized rather by an anxious care for the health and convenience of the criminal than for anything which might even by implication appear to bear on him with undue severity . . . The criminals know that the worst that can befall them will be a change to a condition often scarcely inferior to that they were in before . . . "

Still the time for "tender-heartedness" was not yet over. In 1837, the Rev. Whitworth Russell was succeeded by the Rev. Daniel Nihil, a fanatic in the cause of "treatment." At the start of his reign, Nihil addressed a sort of order of the day to the turnkeys (or officers, as he called them) in which he said: "I wish them, as members of a religious institution, to cultivate the demeanour of true Christians—not only for the sake of the prisoners under their charge, but for their own . . . To fall into a passion, or to enter into a war of words, only lowers the authority of the officer, and adds to the irritation it is intended to allay."

In a sense that was an extremely far-sighted exhortation, for it implied something which the most progressive-minded of today's prison governors are convinced is true: namely, that rehabilitation ultimately depends on overcoming the natural hostility between captors and captives and hence on persuading the officers to develop what is now called a "treatment relationship" towards the inmates. Unfortunately for the Rev. Daniel Nihil's place in penal history, he failed to realize that a true Christian demeanour was not necessarily proof of a true Christian spirit. It was enough to satisfy him that his officers had transformed themselves into devout missionaries when they took to carrying Bibles around with them, and were to be heard (whenever he was within earshot) loudly declaiming the word of God as they patrolled the galleries, while the prisoners were toiling in their cells. But the prisoners found another name for them. They called them Pantilers—hypocrites or purveyors of cant. They knew how rough-mouthed these missionaries still were when the coast was clear. They also knew that each of them had his price, and, for the few inmates who could contrive to pay it, would smuggle contraband luxuries into the institution, not excluding pornography.

Nor was the Rev. Daniel Nihil himself an altogether merciful type of Christian. Like Dr Copland Hutchinson before him, he believed that the diet was "far too high" and considered the prisoners "saucy", if they complained about it. "Sauciness" was one thing he would not tolerate, and his lasting contribution to penology was to institute an organized report system, whereby any prisoner accused by an officer of a breach of discipline could be brought before him as governor, formally charged, and suitably dealt with. He was not afraid to order floggings, and he was profligate with his sentences to solitary confinement in a subterranean dark cell on a diet of bread and water.

Like his predecessors in office—and this was to become a tradition of the prison system—the Rev. Daniel Nihil was inclined to equate manifestations of mental derangement with deliberate "sauciness" or, rather, to regard all such manifestations as *prima facie* feigned and therefore curable by disciplinary action. However, if a prisoner, after frequent spells in a dark cell, was still too mad to be controllable, the only resource left was to have him committed to an asylum. One such case, that of a young woman transferred from Millbank to Bethlehem Hospital, happened early on under Nihil's regime, and it led to a political uproar.

Somehow, the Chairman of Middlesex Sessions got wind of the case, and learned that the young woman in question had been of perfectly sound mind before she was sent to Millbank. As a result, he conducted an investigation of his own into conditions at the penitentiary, and unearthed some horrific details, which he duly made public in an address at the Middlesex sessions. The most provocative of his disclosures concerned three little girls, two aged ten and the third only seven and a half, who, he alleged, had been subjected to all the rigours of solitary confinement for the past twelve months and were faced with another two years of the same treatment. He told how the youngest of the three had begged in vain for a doll when she was first put to bed in her lonely cell, and how she had since developed a serious impediment in her speech. "If these gentlemen succeed," he said, referring to the Committee of Management, "it is perfectly clear that gaols will be turned into receptacles for lunatics."[8]

Most probably, the Chairman of the Middlesex Sessions had an axe to grind, for the very existence of a government-run penitentiary was resented by the magistracy as a threat to their local autonomy in gaol administration. Moreover, at a time when the direst cruelties were still being inflicted on children in the name of justice—any child over seven was as liable under the criminal law as any adult to be flogged, transported or hanged—there was certainly a strong element of hypocrisy in calling it scandalous—a cause for the nation to weep, as *The Times* put it—that three little girls should be confined at Millbank. When the Government came under strong attack in the House of Lords, Lord Melbourne[9] denied that the girls were suffering solitary confinement, inasmuch as they were "frequently" permitted to see their friends, were visited by "benevolent ladies", had regular exercise, attended chapel on Sundays and on two other days in the week, and spent two hours every week in classroom study.

Though this may have sounded a pretty lame sort of re-assurance, and Lord Melbourne was accused of drawing a distinction without a difference, he nevertheless had a stronger case in the circumstances than the Government's critics. He pointed out that while a special institution for juvenile offenders was being built in the Isle of Wight (this was to be called Park-hurst), none existed at the moment. So what else, he asked, could or should have been done with the children, except to send them to the penitentiary? The youngest of the three, he explained, had been sentenced, along with her mother, to seven years transportation for stealing; and the Home Secretary's decision to save her from this fate had been taken on representations from the trial Judge himself. All three children had to some extent been victims of a corruptive home influence, and could not be considered irredeemably wicked. On the contrary, as a result of their confinement, they had already "greatly advanced in morals and education." Reform, Lord Melbourne said, was the policy of the Government, even though he was aware that in some people's opinion this policy had "gone too far."

However, Lord Melbourne yielded to demands for an official enquiry, and since the result was to find that the three little girls were, after all, so far gone in sin that they needed (and "deserved") to be kept under severe restraint, it dried the nation's tears. On the other hand, it couldn't in the long run stifle an awareness that whether or not the policy of reform had "gone too far", there was something disastrously at fault with it. The facts spoke for themselves. The re-conviction rate among Millbank's graduates showed that over 50% of the selected first offenders, instead of being rehabilitated, were being turned into hardened criminals.

In 1841, the Committee of Management in an effort to reverse this trend, decided on a small step backwards—back to a less repressive discipline—and accordingly authorized "modified intercourse" for inmates who had served three months of their time. But no significant drop in the re-conviction rate followed, and three years later the Government conceded that as a penitentiary Millbank had proved an "entire failure." The Committee of Management was abolished, and the establishment itself, under the administration of an Inspectorate, appointed by the Home Secretary, became a "reception" centre for convicts facing transportation, the hulks, or, if they were young enough, the new training centre at Parkhurst.

In short, less than 30 years after nearly half a million pounds had been spent on building a penitentiary, the place was found to be useless for its purpose. This fact might have proved a warning for the future against too rash and heavy an expenditure on prison construction. But if the history of the central Government's system of punitive imprisonment is one of perennial disappointment and of extravagant decisions taken on the basis of wrong guesses, it is also one of unquenchable optimism and self-assurance. Characteristically, the transformation of Millbank into a reception centre was hailed in an official report as a major advance.[10] ". . . The convict is no longer lured back to crime by being thrown among his old associates and exposed to new temptations . . . nor does his tainted character, closing against him the path to honest employment, almost compel him, as under the former system, to seek for subsistence by renewed depredations. On the other hand, Society is protected from the Return of one of the most mischievous classes of its members, who are almost compelled to live by plunder, and will seek to indemnify themselves for what they consider the harshness of their penal treatment by fresh acts of violence or fraud, committed with greater recklessness or dexterity, instructed as they have been in the ways of their associates in punishment."

Though one may note there an exact re-statement of the problem that a House of Commons Select Committee had stated, 70 years earlier, in its animadversions on the Hulk System, it was now supposed that this difficulty could be overcome, or rather eliminated, if imprisonment were used, not to train convicts to live peaceably at home, but in part to punish them appropriately before they were sent overseas and in part to teach them how to behave themselves when they got there.

The fulfilment of the second of these two objectives had, in fact, become imperative, if transportation to Australia were to continue. For though a few of the convicts went into private service, the majority of them had to be absorbed in Government-run penal settlements, and this was proving not only an immensely costly and wasteful operation in itself, but a severe disincentive to voluntary emigration and hence to profitable colonization. Australia, with its thousands of exiled, unregenerate criminals, governed by the lash and the gallows, was, to quote *The Times*, "a more vulgar thought than the meanest suburb of the city." Hence there was a growing realization that transportation would cease to be an economic proposition, unless the convicts could somehow be reformed *before* they left England, so that they would make willing and useful labourers in servitude and upright members of the colonial population after their "emancipation."

For this specific purpose Parliament had authorized the building of another penal institution under the Government's control. This was Pentonville, the "Model Prison", completed in 1842, the brain-child of, among others, the Rev. Whitworth Russell, who attributed his own failure at Millbank to the impracticability of enforcing perfect "seclusion" in a penitentiary where whole sentences had to be served. Pentonville was designed to make transportation safe for the colonies through subjecting selected convicts to a sort of crash treatment programme, and initially this took the form of eighteen months of complete solitary confinement, or "separate" confinement, as it was euphemistically called.

But the subject of Pentonville, and its consequences, comes later in the story. Something more must be said first of all about the Hulks which, even before the Millbank experiment had started, were pointing in their own slatternly way to a different development in the creation of a national type of imprisonment for convicts.

4
THE PRISON HULKS

THE HULK SYSTEM, instead of being abandoned as soon as it had served its purpose as a stop-gap measure, rapidly grew. Parliament guaranteed its continuance, when the authority of the courts to pass substitute sentences of hard labour ran out, by vesting a new power in the Crown: to remove persons sentenced to transportation to a "place of confinement within England or Wales, either on land, or on board any ship or vessel in any river or port." As a result, Duncan Campbell lost his monopoly. Additional overseers were appointed; more floating prisons appeared; and use for convict labour was found in other places besides Woolwich—for example at Sheerness and Portland.

In 1802, the Government made a move towards improving the system, or silencing the criticism it was provoking, with the appointment of a gentleman named Aaron Graham as "Inspector of Vessels." Shortly afterwards, on Graham's advice, it instituted a plan at Portsmouth for running its own service and this was the start of a complete Home Department take-over. The overseers were no longer engaged as private contractors, but were instead employed as chief administrative and disciplinary officers on the various vessels, which the Government both supplied and manned.

One reason which came to be given for maintaining the system was that transportation to the Australian colonies was not a dreaded enough fate. This was alleged to be especially true of so-named "gentlemen convicts" who, because of their superior educational qualifications, might escape hard labour in their place of exile and be put to work immediately in a responsible position. The Hulks supposedly provided a means of inflicting an appropriate amount of punishment on them before they were banished.

But, from first to last, it was also true that by reason of age, infirmity, or simply because they were supernumeraries, many convicts—including nearly all those who received the minimum transportation sentence of seven years—were sent to the Hulks instead of being sent overseas, and the problem of how to make the system reformative as well as deterrent could not, therefore, be ignored. Again, on Graham's advice, the Government built chapels aboard the vessels, supplied the prisoners with Bibles and prayer books, and engaged chaplains to hold regular services and furnish individual religious instruction. But the best that could be done in the all-important matter of seclusion was to block the means of communication between the decks where the prisoners were locked down at nights; and even this measure was defeated in one instance, because "the convicts rose and tore down the works."

In 1812, a Select Committee[1] found that despite Graham's efforts the position was unsatisfactory in respect of all three of the accepted principles of reformative training. There was not enough work available in the dockyards to keep the convicts fully employed ashore. Some of them spent half their days aboard idling or, worse, manufacturing goods, such as toys made out of bone, which they were able to sell for their own profit. On wet or foggy days none of them was sent ashore for labour.

The Committee further complained that there were no schoolmasters in the service to remedy illiteracy, and more seriously, too few chaplains for the task of religious instruction to be properly discharged; in fact, in one vessel, which didn't receive so much as an occasional visit from a chaplain, prayers were read by a convict. But what disturbed the Committee most of all was the continuing want of seclusion. Even where communication between the decks had been prevented, about 150 prisoners were likely to share the same quarters, and from the time they were locked down in the evenings until the early morning muster no attempt was made to keep them under supervision. "Neither the Captain, nor any other officer, ever visits the parts of the ship in which the prisoners are confined . . . And it seems doubtful whether an officer could go down without risk of personal injury."

Since a light was kept burning all night, and the prisoners were allowed to purchase their own candles, it was possible for them to spend the hours before they fell asleep reading their Bibles and prayer books. But the Committee were told that most of them engaged in less healthful pursuits, notably coining, which was frequently indicated by a noise of hammering. And though the Committee were assured—an assurance which they were happy, if gullible, to accept—that "rumours of a more atrocious vice" were baseless, they warned that so long as "these persons" were permitted to contaminate each other without restraint they "must be expected to return into society with more depraved habits and dispositions than those with which they went into confinement."

Still, the Committee didn't regard the situation as hopeless. They noted that in one vessel a quarterly muster was held at which each prisoner was closely questioned by the chaplain, the overseer or any other of the officers present, and his progress assessed in accordance with his answers as well as with his previously known record. The result was occasionally most encouraging: for example, "Very good, religiously inclined, and attends the Sacrament." In the same vessel, a plan for promoting moral improvement, industriousness and orderly behaviour had been introduced, under which a prisoner could, by passing through various "stages", qualify for a remission of sentence or a pardon. (Usually, four years was the maximum time served.)

Moreover, the Committee decided that the Hulks had two inherent advantages over land-built prisons. They were much cheaper to provide, and they were also mobile; that was to say, they could easily be moved to places where there was the greatest demand for convict labour and the greatest supply to meet it near at hand. The Committee concluded, therefore, that for all its existing shortcomings, the Hulk system ought not to be abandoned, and they made several proposals for bringing about an approximation of seclusion. Among these was "classification"—that magic formula which, in our own time, continues to be represented as a potential guarantee against the obvious harm that might otherwise be assumed to result from locking up criminals together and allowing them to associate with one another. The Committee wanted the boys segregated from the men, the more depraved offenders from the less depraved, the permanent residents from the transients receiving punishment before transportation, and so on. "It would be an important consequence of these arrangements," they said, "that officers and guards belonging to each Hulk, instead of directing their attention and observation to all the convicts on board the vessel generally, might be in some degree attached to particular classes or companies of them, and would in that case become acquainted with their individual characters, and be able to make useful reports of their disposition." And there in essence, incidentally, the Committee advocated a policy which the most advanced of today's prison governors are trying to pursue.

As a result of the Committee's recommendations, a special training hulk for convicts under 17 was provided. Some attempt was also made to divide the prisoners' decks into compartments. But this didn't come near to equalling "seclusion", nor did it allow for better than a crude pretence at "classification." Fourteen years later, in 1828, a Committee on Criminal Commitments and Convictions,[2] observed parenthetically that the Hulk system appeared to be "very defective", and recommended that it should either be abolished or made the subject of a special inquiry. They drew this conclusion from the evidence of Samuel Hoare, Chairman of the Prison Discipline Society, who had told them that while a man might get over being in gaol, the Hulks were "quite fatal." "Everything that degrades a man prepares him for crime hereafter," Hoare said; and what he considered especially degrading about the Hulk system was that it encouraged indolence. "At Portsmouth labour by day is merely an apology for work; one sees the convicts idling about the yard, several of them together drawing a light cart which perhaps a donkey might draw as well."

By now, Aaron Graham had long since been succeeded as Inspector of Vessels by a clerk in the criminal department of the Home Office, named J. H. Capper, who was styled "Superintendent" of the Hulk Establishment. Capper's job was not to make or advise about policy, but simply to see that the rules and regulations laid down by the Home Secretary were being enforced. He carried out occasional visits of inspection, but largely relied on reports from the overseers, and though he was paid an allowance of £131 a year to provide himself with his own office space, in addition to his salary of £400 a year, he found it more convenient (and profitable) to work from his regular desk in Whitehall. At the same time, he seems to have possessed a remarkable degree of autonomy in his role of Hulks administrator. He was able to appoint a nephew, Robert Capper, to be his clerk and assistant. And he kept the gratuities payable to convicts on their discharge in a private Bank account.

In 1831, the inquiry, which the Committee on Criminal Commitments and Convictions had considered imperative three years earlier, fell within the terms of reference of the Committee on Secondary Punishment.[3] They took the opportunity of examining several actual victims of the system—primarily an 18-year-old youth, whom they referred to in their report as "A.B." and who had recently been pardoned after serving time aboard a hulk at Sheerness for stealing a pair of shoes. Contrary to what Samuel Hoare had observed at Portsmouth, A.B. had found the labour at Sheerness to be not only very hard, but dangerous. He was with a gang engaged in house demolition, and there were a lot of accidents, resulting in broken legs and arms or worse. The prisoners had to work—as they also had to sleep—in irons. The penalty for idleness was to be double-ironed, or to be docked a week's earnings.

A.B. had other things to complain of. The food was worse than it was intended to be, because the Captain (or Overseer) underspent the money he was allowed for purchasing it. "You can just break the bread in two and throw a bit against the wall and it will stick like clay." Moreover, although under Home Department regulations prisoners were entitled to a new set of "slops" (clothes) every six months, they were forced to wear the same filthy, thread-bare outfit for three times as long as that. One officer, who wanted to be fair, started handing out replacements for worn out shoes from the ship's stores. But he was promptly dismissed. The captain and the other officers ganged up on him.

Yet on the whole A.B. thought it "rather a jolly life," thanks to what the prisoners were able to do for themselves, licitly or illicitly. He certainly far preferred it to life aboard *The*

Euryalus, the young convict's training hulk, where he had served the first few months of his sentence. For though it was true that the Euryalus boys were "taught a trade" instead of being put to hard labour ashore, they were half starved and persistently lashed by the guards. "Flogging," A.B. told the Committee, "only makes a man courageous and hardens him the more."

There was much less of it aboard the vessel at Sheerness—and much less interference in general with convict pleasures. The prisoners were paid three shillings a week, and out of this they were at liberty to purchase extra food as well as beer, tobacco and newspapers. Their correspondence was unrestricted, and every three months they were excused labour for three days on end to receive visits from their friends. These visits took place on the quarter deck, lasted all day, and were virtually unsupervised. If a prisoner had a lady guest, he could retire with her to the smoking room, where they would be undisturbed. In other words, the "conjugal visit" was allowed, though it wasn't, of course, known as such.

The visits provided an easy way of smuggling money and contraband goods aboard, though there were other means of doing that. The guards were bribable; so were the crews of the boats in which the work parties were rowed ashore. The strong preyed on the weak, the experienced on the inexperienced, and there were men who set themselves up as traders in groceries and tobacco. They charged premium prices. Bread changed hands at six pence a loaf.

A.B. was locked down at nights with a hundred other prisoners. He wasn't the youngest of them. There were several boys of twelve or thirteen, which showed that even in this respect segregation was still incomplete. Though the deck was divided into "compartments" or cells, each with hammocks for twenty men, full association was permitted (or at least not prevented) until 10 o'clock. One Christmas, the prisoners feasted off two pheasants, fourteen different joints of meat and a fowl. They were in possession of two fiddles and a clarinet. Every evening they danced and sang. "We all dismiss at 10," A.B. told the Committee. "We all break up just like a public-house being shut up; we all turn out."

Three other youthful graduates of the system were subsequently examined, and their evidence, though it revealed that conditions varied somewhat from hulk to hulk, particularly in regard to pay and gratuities, broadly confirmed A.B.'s testimony. Manniston Wortz, who had been at Portsmouth, said that pornography was smuggled aboard and "flash" songs sung at night. He complained of the "filthy manner in which the prisoners were kept." While beer and tobacco were allowed (the tobacco helped to "keep off disease") there were no towels provided or water to wash in.

William Brett, who had also been at Portsmouth, though in a different vessel, said that the men were only required to wash themselves once in every five weeks, and that many of them were verminous. He had heard of "indecencies" being committed between them, though he could not testify to this of his own knowledge.

Thomas Knight, who had been at Woolwich, said that vermin used to drop on him from the prisoner sleeping in the hammock above. He also said that the prisoners spent their time on Sundays as well as at nights, chatting, smoking, gambling and playing games, such as "pricking the garter."

While A.B. had been freed, these other three witnesses had been transferred to Millbank, and it was there, in their separate cells, that they were questioned. They had had no forewarning of the examination, and in any case it would have been impossible for them to get together in advance with a view to cooking up a common story. Hence the Committee found it proved that "flash songs, dancing, fighting and gaming" were taking place in the Hulks; that the "older offenders were in the habit of robbing the newcomers"; that "newspapers and improper books were being clandestinely introduced"; that the convicts "frequently kept up a communication with their old associates on shore"; and—the final horror—that "occasionally spirits were being introduced on board." All of which led the Committee to report that "the most assiduous attention on the part of ministers of religion would be insufficient to stem the torrent of corruption flowing from these various and abundant sources."

But it was not only or even chiefly on the grounds of its

reformative deficiencies that this Committee condemned the system. They were more appalled by what they regarded as its blatant shortcomings as a deterrent, and they found these most graphically illustrated by A.B.'s reference to a "rather jolly life." It did not occur to them that A.B. might have been speaking ironically. He very probably was, because in another part of his evidence he explained that the overseer of his vessel was able to get away with defalcations because the prisoners, when the time came for their release, would "sign anything" to get off the ship without trouble or delay, including receipts for money and clothes they never received. Still, this was one of A.B.'s statements that the Committee preferred to ignore, just as they discounted his complaints about the hardness and dangerousness of the labour. They accepted the evidence of various non-convict witnesses that the labour was, in fact, much too light.

All in all, the Committee decided that the system was irremediable. They believed that stricter discipline would make it less harmful, and urgently recommended that a stop should be put to prisoners' earnings and visits. But they were convinced that the vessels were basically unsuited for their purpose, and ought to be replaced by public works prisons on land, where the convicts could be confined in separate cells during the hours that they were not engaged in hard labour out of doors. They suggested that Dartmoor might be an appropriate site for one of these prisons, especially since an encampment, that had once been used for French prisoners-of-war, already existed there.

If their report may be said to have sounded the death knell of the Hulks, the knell went on tolling for a remarkably long time afterwards. It cost nothing to provide Mr Capper with a new set of rules and regulations to superintend, and this was promptly done. Tobacco was banned, and though earnings weren't entirely stopped, the convicts were forbidden possession of money. In future they were not to be paid for their labour until after they had served two years of their sentence, when part of their earnings were to be used to purchase them a weekly ration of white bread (as opposed to the coarse brown bread of the regular diet) and the rest was to be withheld until their discharge. Visits, though again not absolutely prohibited, were now only allowed from wives, parents or siblings, and under close supervision.

It was reasonably inexpensive to have a survey of Dartmoor made, and this job, too, was undertaken with despatch. But another seventeen years were to pass before the first of the public works prisons—Portland, as it happened, not Dartmoor— was built, and over a quarter of a century before the last of the Hulks went out of commission. These were two periods characteristic of the prison system's history—a period of action postponed followed by a period of action slowly and tardily taken.

Nevertheless, the Hulks were a thorn in the social conscience, and at one point it seemed as though the thorn could be removed painlessly—without charge to the Exchequer. For in 1842—in the same year that Millbank became a "reception centre"—the Government was persuaded of the eventual practicability of transporting every convict without exception. Hence it announced that the Hulk establishments were to be abolished rather than replaced, and that meanwhile recruitment of new personnel and expenditure on "improvements" to the various vessels in use had been halted.

This "suppression of the Hulk system", as it was hyperbolically and prematurely called in an official report,[4] was also described as a "most important improvement in the penal system of the country", because, "lightness of the convicts' labour, good clothing, ample diet, general comfort . . . suggested to beholders an unfavourable comparison between the condition of the convict and that of the honest labourer." And in the same report, it was stated: "Experience has proved that the practice of commuting sentences of transportation to periods of imprisonment in England is unsound in principle and injurious in practice."

This last admission referred to the Millbank experiment as well as the Hulks, and was doubtless as true as it was honest. But it was also made in a spirit of misplaced optimism, and soon had to be tacitly withdrawn—too soon to allow time for the promised "suppression" of the Hulk system to be effected. In fact, transportation was already a visibly contracting business, for New South Wales could find no more room for the mother country's unwanted citizens, and the penal settlement in Norfolk Island, which had formerly been reserved for the worst of them, was soon to be closed down, on account of the "atrocities" committed there.[5]

Nevertheless, the Government assumed that if convicts could be reformed before they were shipped to the Antipodes, the less developed colonies, Tasmania in particular, would gratefully accept, and readily absorb, an unlimited number of them. Moreover, with the building of Pentonville, the model prison, where the separate system was in operation, the means of reforming convicts supposedly existed. For the most responsive of the Pentonville graduates there was to be a ticket of leave as soon as they reached their place of exile; and all other convicts were to be granted a ticket of leave after they had served a probationary period at associated labour, which was ordinarily not to last longer than half their sentence[6] (less, in cases where it applied, the eighteen months of separate confinement at home). A ticket of leave left convicts free to earn their own living, under certain specified conditions, though not to return home.

That was the plan. But it turned out to be a costly failure, because, among other things, there wasn't a sufficiency of public work to keep the captive convicts usefully occupied, while opportunities for the freed convicts hardly existed at all, so that they had to be supported in idleness out of Treasury funds. In 1846, the Government decided to order an entire suspension for two years of transportation to Tasmania, and to accept the inevitability of continuing to deal with a considerable proportion of the convict population in England. By this time, as we shall see, the locally owned common gaols had come under increasing Parliamentary scrutiny. A number of area inspectors had been appointed to report to the Home Office on their administration, and Colonel Joshua Jebb, the man who had designed Pentonville and may properly be regarded as the Founding Father of the prison system, held the post of Surveyor-General of Prisons. The Home Secretary now entrusted Jebb with the job of drawing up plans for developing and re-arranging the convict Hulks establishment as well as for building a public works prison at Portland.

As it turned out, Jebb considered the Hulks unsalvageable, but, before he was ready with his report, they came under yet another public onslaught, and on this occasion the familiar charge that life aboard the vessels was disastrously anti-reformative was not complemented by any suggestion that it was too little punitive or too "jolly". Thomas Duncombe asserted in the House of Commons[7] that the "cruelty exercised was so excessive . . . " that it was "utterly disgraceful to a civilized and Christian country." He produced detailed evidence in support of this allegation. For instance, he described the case of an elderly man who was given 36 lashes of the "cat" for being five minutes late at the early morning muster: a chastisement that was not actually administered until three months after it had been awarded, because the overseer happened to forget about it in the meanwhile.

Most of Duncombe's information came from convicts who had been aboard the hospital vessel at Woolwich, and their complaints were chiefly directed against the surgeon, Peter Bossy, whom they accused of grossly taunting and neglecting his patients. There was the case of a man named George Monk or Taylor, who had eventually been transferred to Bethlehem hospital, where he died. "He was admitted on board with a broken leg; he was allowed to lie in his own water and filth until such time as a large piece, putrified with his urine, fell from the bottom of his backbone. He was sometimes handcuffed to each side of the bed which he lay on, at other times with a straight jacket on."

There was another somewhat similar case of an epileptic named Brandish: "The first time Mr Bossy saw him he began to laugh at him and told him, those fits would not do there. Brandish had a fit after this, which deprived him of the power of opening his jaws. Bossy placed his thumb on his cheek and pressed against his teeth; he then opened his mouth. Bossy began to laugh, and said, 'It's all gammon, Mr Brandish. I will have you well flogged if you don't alter your course of conduct.' After the doctor went away I [Duncombe's informant] examined his mouth and I found that his cheek was cut opposite where he pressed it with his thumb. They frequently handcuffed his hands to each side of the bed, and kept him lying in this position in his dirt and water until a large piece mortified out of the bottom of his back. He became completely childish. The doctor frequently threatened to have him flogged. He allowed him wine before he died, a part of which he took off [immediately] before his death, with his usual threat of having him flogged."

Duncombe had offered to keep his information to himself, if the Home Secretary would agree to investigate it. This the Home Secretary declined to do, and in the House he attempted to evade the issue. While he admitted that conditions in the Hulks might have been allowed to deteriorate as a result of the decision to do away with the system, he suggested that the survey which Jebb was now conducting offered sufficient assurance that things were going to be put right. He spoke hopefully of a new policy under which it was proposed to grant some convicts tickets of leave before they were shipped to Australia and after they had served their time in public works at Bermuda or Gibraltar, where penal settlements had been established. He re-affirmed the Government's faith in separate confinement as a guarantee of rehabilitation in advance of exile, and referred in particular to the graduates of Pentonville. Their conduct, he said, "had been most regular and excellent, and despatches had been received both from Port Philip and Western Australia, expressing the great desire of the colonists to receive them."

But Duncombe's charges were not to be dismissed so easily. On the contrary, they created such an uproar (particularly in *The Times*) that in the end the Home Secretary found it impolitic to rest content with a refutation of them which Capper, the old Superintendent, hastily furnished after his nephew had bullied some of the witnesses into changing their evidence. Belatedly, the Home Secretary discovered that it was his "inescapable duty" to order a full and impartial inquiry. This was conducted with remarkable thoroughness by a Captain Williams, one of the Government's inspectors of the common gaols.

The result was a blacker report than the Home Secretary may well have supposed imaginable. Although Captain Williams rejected Duncombe's detailed charges on the grounds of insufficient evidence, he found that in general the situation was even more disgraceful than Duncombe had represented it to be. Capper, after 32 years in office, was now too old and infirm to carry out his duties as Superintendent, and had entrusted the job to his nephew and assistant. The latter either connived in, or failed to prevent, flagrant violations of the Home Secretary's rules for the conduct of the service.

For example, there was a rule about hygiene: "Every prisoner is to wash himself clean from labour, and is expected at all times to be perfectly clean in his person, clothing, bedding and cell." In fact, the great majority of the prisoners were infested with vermin. No towels or combs were provided; no regular change of "body linen"; no water to flush the lavatory pans, which were encrusted with excrement. One apartment (or cell), 20 × 16 ft., with an uncovered privy in the middle of the room, was shared by 25 men, and the stench was "insupportable."

Practice fell just as far below declared intentions in regard to the disciplinary treatment of the convicts. Here a general directive by the Home Secretary had a remarkably liberal sound—even more liberal, incidentally, than the equivalent assurance in today's Prison Rules: "Every person belonging to the convict Hulk establishment is on all occasions to treat the convicts with humanity, and lend a willing ear to their complaints and grievances, whether real or imaginary." Under the regulations, flogging was forbidden, except by permission of the Superintendent and even then was limited to 24 "stripes." And the punishment of confinement in a dark cell on a diet of bread and water, though it might be awarded on the authority of the overseer, was never to exceed seven days at a time.

In practice, the former of these two rules was evaded on the pretext that it was only meant to apply to the scourge; and hence birch rod beatings—84 strokes in one recorded instance—were regularly administered without reference to the Superintendent. The other rule was simply ignored. In the hospital ship a sort of cage, with hardly enough room inside it for a man to stand upright, served as the dark cell. A supposedly convalescent patient was kept there in double irons for two months on end. He died soon afterwards.

Overseers and officers persistently disobeyed a rule that forbade them to employ the convicts in their own service. This detracted from the potential usefulness of the prescribed labour—at Woolwich landing and discharging coal. Moreover, since there was a shortage of guards, free labourers were hired to supervise some of the gangs, and these men could often be suborned by the convicts, who used them to pass messages to their friends or to obtain contraband. Clandestine meetings took place in the dockyard privies.

If the surgeon, Peter Bossy, was innocent of deliberate cruelty, he was none the less extremely negligent. He permitted men to be kept aboard whom he knew to be insane and who ought, therefore, to have been transferred to an asylum; on one occasion he even allowed a lunatic to be flogged. Equally, though he was aware that many prisoners were afflicted with symptoms of scurvy, and that this was due to the diet, which was wholly lacking in vegetables, he failed to protest. Nor did it perturb him that so little respect should be shown the dead. If a patient died at night he was left where he was until next morning, when his body was taken out on deck and washed in full view of the prisoners. A post-mortem examination was then conducted ashore, and convicts were employed in cleaning the dead-house. "On one occasion at least, a portion of the interior of the human body was left in a pail."

The immediate consequence of Captain Williams's report was a drastic re-organization of the Hulk establishment; Capper was dismissed, and was replaced by another of the common gaol inspectors, Herbert P. Voules, who was given the title of manager and wider responsibilities than his inactive predecessor. Bossy was pensioned off. New chaplains and schoolmasters were recruited; provisions were made for compulsory classroom study aboard after the convicts returned from their daily labour. The diet was improved with the introduction of a regular allowance of white bread, potatoes and cocoa.

But this re-organization was not intended to prolong the life of the Hulks, or if it was it was self-defeating, for the service's new administrators were its most determined antagonists. "The Hulks", said Voules in his first report to the Home Secretary,[8] "are altogether so ill adapted for the purpose of reform that I do not anticipate it will be possible to establish any satisfactory system of discipline so long as the prisoners are associated as at present in classes of 12 or 16 each." Voules had experienced a most unfortunate first year in office. There had been an outbreak of cholera at Woolwich, and the overseers of one of the vessels had absconded with £855.11.3¼. There had been a mutiny at Portsmouth. "Eight or ten convicts obtained such a system of terrorism on board that many prisoners, who had been previously well conducted, joined them . . . They openly scorned threats of punishment . . . Fifty-three were removed to Millbank."

Though the newly appointed chaplains had been doing their best, they, too, regarded their task as fundamentally hopeless. One of them urged the Home Office to supply his vessel with a library. "The men have vacant moments of frequent occasional occurrence. If not occupied with good, they are sure to be filled up with plotting or exercising mischief." An overseer complained that the ban on smoking also contributed to plotting and mischief-making, since the men were so hungry for tobacco that they would risk the severest punishments in order to obtain it.

Voules' first annual report was his last as "Manager" of the Hulks. In the following year, the establishment was placed under a directorate, of which Jebb was chairman and Voules one of the two other members. At the same time, the overseers (or captains) were re-named governors, the first mates deputy governors, and so on. This change, which coincided with the opening of Portland prison, nominally did away with the Hulk system as such, in the sense that it ended its separate or nautical identity. But nearly another decade went by before enough public works prisons had been built (Portland was followed in 1850 by Dartmoor) for the whole male convict establishment to be placed on dry land, and that time would possibly have been further delayed but for the attacks that continued to be made on the Hulk service, as often as the opportunity occurred, by its own officers. "The Hulks have not even the advantage of economy," the directors urged in their report for 1849.[9] 'On the contrary, experience enables us to say that they are expensive as well as unsuitable places for the confinement of convicts. The *Defence* Hulk, recently fitted at Portsmouth for the accommodation of 400 invalid convicts, cost £8,960.9.5d. before she was fit to be occupied by prisoners; and the further annual cost of maintaining and keeping a Hulk in repair, with other expenses, such as moorings, boats etc. contingent on the use of the vessels for this purpose, is much greater than in ordinary buildings."

In the same report, a chaplain spoke of prisoners who themselves understood that his task was impossible: "Their simple reasoning and plain language will, perhaps, carry conviction where a formal statement may fail to do so: if the Government is so anxious for our improvement, why, in punishing us for being bad, put us where we are sure to become worse?"

But that, it must be noted, was not a question which ceased to be asked after the Hulks were no more. Nor, indeed, is it a question which has ceased to be asked today. Just as it was once imagined that in principle there was nothing at fault with the Hulk system but the Hulks themselves, so it is now contended that there is nothing wrong with the Prison system except the 19th century buildings with which it remains encumbered. And one of these buildings is Pentonville.

5

THE PENTONVILLE EXPERIMENT

THOUGH ITS DEMOLITION was promised over 30 years ago,[1] Pentonville still stands as an apparently irremovable, if badly run down, monument to the disastrous experiment in reformative penal discipline known as "separate confinement." Certain practices, which were part of that discipline, survive; for example, the regulation bath that prisoners take on reception and, indeed, much of the traditional reception procedure. But its central purpose has long since been betrayed, particularly at Pentonville itself, which is at present largely used for the irrelevant containment of petty recidivists, serving short-term sentences, and which is so grossly over-crowded that many of the inmates have to sleep three to a cell. Nor can Pentonville in its "model" pristine state be blamed for what is commonly regarded as the least attractive and most backward feature of contemporary prison life, namely, "slopping out."

For when Pentonville was first built, and until latter-day "improvements" were made to it, every one of its cells was equipped with both a water closet and a wash-basin. This "convenience", extravagant though it was, was believed to be part of the price that had to be paid for the separate system.

The Pentonville experiment, as has been said, began as an attempt to fit convicts for freedom in the colonies, just as the Millbank experiment had started as an attempt to fit them for freedom at home. It owed something to American inspiration, for the decision to embark on it was taken after William Crawford, a Home Office delegate, had visited the recently built Eastern Penitentiary in Philadelphia and on his return to London had reported most favourably, if a little prematurely, on the "results of the discipline" there.[2] This was the discipline of total, uncompromising solitude, which was to shock Dickens so profoundly, though he was no disbeliever in the virtues of punishment: "Now I solemnly declare that with no rewards or honours could I walk a happy man beneath the open sky or lie me down at night with the consciousness that one human being lay suffering this unknown punishment in his lonely cell, and I the cause or consenting to it in the least degree." At the Eastern Penitentiary, newly arrived prisoners were led blindfolded to their allotted cells, where they were locked in for the duration of their sentences, with nothing to occupy their time, not even toil, except (so it was confidently assumed) repentance.

As a matter of fact, Parliament would never have consented to an exact duplication of this system, and though William Crawford was one of the Commissioners appointed to administer Pentonville—the others included the Rev. Whitworth Russell, the crusading ex-chaplain of Millbank, and the inevitable Joshua Jebb—the discipline established there was said to be something quite distinct from solitary confinement. This was true in the sense that no radical departure was made from the original Millbank formula, and nominally "employment" and "religious instruction" continued to be regarded as no less important aids to reform than "seclusion." On the other hand, since the failure of the Millbank experiment was attributed to the fact that it had been found impractical to enforce a sufficient degree of seclusion on convicts who served the whole of their sentences in a penitentiary, the main objective, if not the whole *raison d'être*, of the Pentonville experiment was to make seclusion absolute for convicts during a probationary period of eighteen months before they were transported.

Thus the Pentonville prisoners were supposed to be so "rigidly kept apart" that it would be impossible for them so much as to recognize each other by sight when they left the institution. Each of them took his daily exercise alone in one or other of the small, bricked-off "airing yards" provided. In the chapel, which was used for schoolroom classes as well as services, each of them was placed in a separate stall, so that he could neither see nor speak to his neighbours. And if he was let out of his cell for any other reason—he might be one of a party detailed to work the water pumps in the early mornings—he was required to mask his face by pulling down the peak of his cap over it.

But though separate confinement was dedicated to reform,

its most convinced advocates realized that it was extremely punitive, or at least that it was too painful a form of "treatment" to be easily borne. For this reason the candidates for Pentonville—there was room for about 500 of them in all—were at first very carefully selected from among convicts who were held in the common gaols while they awaited transportation or transfer to the Hulks. None of them was older than 35 or younger than 18. All of them were judged to be of exceptionally high physical, mental and moral stamina, and hence unlikely either to break down under the discipline or to rebel against it.

Even so, considerable reliance had to be placed on punishments, such as the dark cell, in order to command the submission of these ordinarily submissive offenders, and from the beginning there was a disturbingly high incidence of suicides and cases of mental derangement among them. Moreover, the first batch to be embarked for Australia made a remarkably poor advertisement to the rehabilitative effects of the experience they had endured, for though they may have been cured of criminality, they also appeared to be deprived of initiative. "They were", according to one contemporary account,[3] "literally unable to take care of themselves on the voyage. A day or two after the dead weight of silence and isolation was taken off, a great number of them became half idiotic, that is, light-headed, low-spirited, silly, and a few (the worst) subject to sudden faintings."

Though these facts were undenied—the Commissioners made no bones about calling the faintings convulsions—official confidence in the experiment remained unshaken. It was not surprising, considering how carefully chosen they were, that some convicts did survive the treatment to make good use of their freedom in Australia, and this provided grounds for sweeping claims to success. "The result of our entire experience", the Commissioners wrote in their fifth (1847) report, "is the conclusion that separation of one prisoner from another is the only basis on which a reformatory discipline can be established with any hope of success." Nor did they admit to the slightest doubt that this hope was being realized. "We feel warranted in expressing our firm conviction that the moral results of the discipline have been most encouraging and attended with a success which we believe is without parallel in the history of prison discipline."

But by the time this jubilant report appeared transportation to Tasmania had been suspended and the Government had decided that since there was little or no point left in training specially selected convicts to be colonizers, every convict without distinction might as well have a taste of separate confinement before being placed in associated labour overseas or sent to the Hulks to serve the balance of his sentence. So large an undertaking called for more single cells than were available at Pentonville and Millbank, the two Government-owned prisons, and Joshua Jebb was, therefore, authorized to rent suitable additional accommodation in the common gaols from local justices.

This decision was not taken without an awareness that the result might cause convicts more mental and physical suffering than public opinion would be prepared to tolerate, and accordingly the period to be served in separate confinement was reduced from eighteen months to a year. Simultaneously, the Pentonville Commissioners took certain steps which they described euphemistically as a "salutary safeguard" of their "system", but which in fact compromised the principle of absolute seclusion. Prisoners were permitted to associate freely during their last week or so in the institution, or to work in association before then if they showed signs of losing their senses, but were otherwise sufficiently docile to be trusted. A possibly somewhat hyperbolic account of what these modifications of the discipline amounted to is given in a book by Hepworth Dickson, a writer on penal affairs, who though no advocate of treating criminals softly, was a passionate opponent of separate confinement. ". . . in one place, you may see eight or ten men in the garden working; if you ask the meaning of this departure from the rule of the cell, you will learn that this gardening list is a new regulation, by which the tedium and silence of the cell are diminished, in cases where the inmate could bear them no longer safely. . . . Again, in another part of the grounds, you come upon a large tent, from which proceeds a strange sound of revelry. Well, what can this saturnalia, for such a place, mean? Here are fifty of the prisoners, laughing, shouting, talking, without let or hindrance, very jolly, and in high spirits. But, what is it about? You may wonder, and think it a ludicrous farce; but the cause of it is serious enough for the muse of tragedy to deal with."

But, despite the modifications, the hazards of separate confinement became increasingly apparent. In their report for 1848, the Pentonville commissioners had evidently awoken to a perhaps obvious fact: that it could serve no better than a negative purpose to isolate criminals from destructive influences, i.e., each other, unless they were simultaneously exposed to constructive influences. "In carrying out any system of separate confinement we are of the opinion that it is quite indispensable to secure a constant and vigilant medical superintendence, and those mitigations of absolute solitude, which we believe to have operated so beneficially for the bodily and mental health of the prisoners at Pentonville; we mean, chiefly, a regular and frequent visitation by the superior officers; moral and religious instruction judiciously imparted; employment that will interest the mind as well as occupy the time of the prisoners, and regular exercise."

If these things had been adequately provided, in particular if there had been officers with sufficient time to spend an appreciable part of every day talking to the prisoners and with sufficient qualities of mind and heart to make a go of the job of counselling, the advent of Pentonville might possibly be remembered today as a genuine penal advance. For cruel and abortive though separate confinement turned out to be in practice, it does not follow from this that seclusion was in itself a mistaken theory; still less, that association is a better one. On the contrary, it may be unalterably true, at least in the case of professional or dedicated criminals, that "separation of one prisoner from another is the only basis on which a reformatory discipline can be established with any hope of success." Whether imprisonment was ever the best or the only means of trying to isolate criminals from each other is another matter; deterrent theory excluded, and would presumably still exclude, consideration of an alternative choice. But, granted the suitability of a punitive basis for "reformatory discipline", the separate system may have been as sound a one as has ever been thought of. Unfortunately, governmental parsimony prevented anything worthwhile from being built on it. For if, as the Commissioners said in another of their reports, the Pentonville system "allowed a prisoner as much intercourse with instructors and officers as was compatible with judicious economy," the proviso therein meant that for all the individual attention a prisoner actually received he would have been hardly less lonely under the frankly solitary system at the Eastern Penitentiary in Philadelphia.

Strictly speaking, the history of Pentonville as the "Model Prison" ended in 1850, for in that year it lost its independent status and along with Millbank, the Hulks and the public works prisons, became part of the Government's consolidated convict establishment under the management of Joshua Jebb and his two fellow directors. However, it continued to be used for separate confinement and now that selectivity had been dispensed with, any and every type of male convict might be sent there, including on occasion boys of thirteen or younger. Since this had resulted in a serious exacerbation of the problem of suicide and mental derangement, Jebb felt obliged to make further compromises, or, as a House of Commons Committee put it, to "encourage self-respect, self-reliance and hopefulness for the future" without impairing the discipline's "penal and deterring character, essential to any system of imprisonment."[4]

The small separate airing yards were replaced by a general exercise yard for the prisoners to walk round in single file and concentric circles. The partitions in the chapel were removed. The prisoners were no longer required to mask their faces when they were out of their cells. They could earn a badge for good conduct after serving six months, and if they behaved exceptionally well (and were also, presumably, near breaking point) they might be employed as the institution's cooks and bakers. Finally, they were rewarded with a gratuity for their work (8d a week for those of them who had earned a badge, and 4d a week for the others), and could look forward to being paid the accumulated sum when they were eventually released from captivity either at home or in the colonies.

But these concessions, such as they were, did little or nothing to make the discipline more bearable for its victims, and in 1854 humane considerations forced a second reduction in the period to be served: from a year to nine months.

One may wonder why, at this point, the discipline wasn't simply abolished. Apart from its manifest practical dangers and shortcomings, its purpose was bound to be defeated in principle so long as convicts were placed in associated labour after they had been subjected to separate confinement. For this meant that they were immediately re-exposed to the very influences from which such painful care had been taken to isolate them, or, in other words, they were unfitted for freedom as soon as they had supposedly been fitted for it. As contemporary critics frequently observed, the system's own logic required separate confinement to follow associated labour, not to precede it.[5]

But this was in reality an irrelevance, because from the moment separate confinement was made applicable to all convicts, instead of a selected number of them, it came to be regarded less as an experiment in reform than as an essential part of deterrent penal practice. The point is well illustrated in the annual report for 1851 of the Chaplain at Pentonville[6] who, though he was presumably meant to concern himself exclusively with his efforts at imparting "religious instruction," dilated at some length on the peak of deterrent perfection that transportation had reached under the new system. "The adventurous young criminal, and all who have no friends at home, make very light of being sent out of the country; to many, indeed, of this class transportation has been an object of desire . . . But the thought in such a one of being shut up by himself for six, twelve or eighteen months first, having only religious and respectable people to speak to . . . fills him with dismay. The educated and well brought up . . . can bear the thought of seclusion for awhile, and of an exile to follow in a country where he is not known; but his heart sinks within him when he hears that after the ordeal of separate confinement he is to be worked at penal labour in a convict's dress, and in some measure exposed to public view . . . Others, perhaps most, dread exile above all . . . The diversity, therefore, in the character of the punishment in the several parts of the scheme of probation is not its least valuable part."

As a matter of fact, the Pentonville chaplain betrayed a

certain *naïvete* in that appraisal, since regardless of how acutely Britain's criminals dreaded being sent to the colonies, the colonies were becoming less and less willing to receive them. Consequently, in 1853, Parliament required the courts to substitute a new-styled punishment, called penal servitude, for every sentence of less than fourteen years transportation. In the case of male convicts—the position of female convicts will be described later—this meant that the initial period of separate confinement was followed by a period of associated labour at home, though the whole sentence was commuted in advance, so to speak, to rather less than half of what the transportation sentence would have been.

This development was in reality a reversion to the expedient that had been adopted when the courts were temporarily authorized to pass sentences of hard labour on convicts after transportation to America became impossible. The only essential difference between the Hulk system that had originated then and the penal servitude system that now came into being was the difference between the makeshift floating prisons and the prisons solidly built on land, with individual cells provided for confinement, instead of communal deck space. But in both cases the aim was to make a virtue of necessity through exploiting convict labour to the best possible national advantage. At Portland the prisoners were already employed in quarrying cement and building a breakwater, and at Chatham, where another of the public works prisons was to be erected in due course, they would build the fortifications.

Five years after penal servitude started, it virtually replaced transportation, though for a while longer a number of convicts continued to be shipped to Western Australia. Under an Act of 1857, proportionately shorter penal servitude sentences were to be substituted for all transportation sentences regardless of their length and at the same time a remission scheme was introduced into the system. Convicts were to be given a ticket-of-leave (release on licence) for good behaviour after serving two thirds of their sentences. Thus a man who would previously have been exiled for, say, 20 years might now be returned to the community within six years.

This last provision provoked a widespread reaction of alarm, which was understandable if it indicated a want of faith in the preliminary period of separate confinement as a guaranteed means of rendering criminals innocuous. But it was otherwise quite irrational, since there were no grounds for believing that a convict would be less of a danger to the community after receiving the whole of his measured dose of punishment in associated labour than he would be after receiving two thirds of it. A quarter of a century earlier, it may be recalled, a House of Commons Committee had foreseen a "constant infusion of malefactors into society", if transportation ever ended, and this was now an immutable fact. But it was not a fact that anybody connected with law enforcement could henceforth afford to acknowledge, or one that the public wished to face.

Legislature, executive and judiciary were now finally committed to the proposition that punitive imprisonment, while it was an indispensable means of deterring honest citizens from becoming criminals, possessed the power of transforming criminals into honest citizens. The only question left over for debate was *how* punitive did imprisonment need to be if it was to deter and how punitive could it be if it was to reform.

The simplest (and cheapest) answer to that question was to say that imprisonment should be made as punitive as was compatible with "humanity", since (so the argument went) it thus attained its maximum deterrent *and* reformative effectiveness. However, this answer, though always much favoured by the judiciary, was not immediately acceptable to either the legislature or the executive. On the contrary, Joshua Jebb specifically rejected it, when he began administering penal servitude in his capacity as chairman of the directors of the convict prisons. "Coercive discipline", he wrote,[7] "persevered in for years, would only harden and brutalize a man and render him wholly unfit for liberty and dangerous for the rest of his life—a result which would not be satisfactory either at home or in a colony, and which would be unworthy of the Government of this country."

It was due to Jebb's influence that Parliament was persuaded to introduce the ticket-of-leave scheme, for Jebb believed that good order and discipline ultimately depended on rewards and incentives, in particular the hope of an early release. In fact, conditions in the public works prisons were to begin with remarkably liberal by comparison with what they were later to become. There was no rule that prohibited the convicts from communicating with one another when they were out of their cells. The gratuities they earned, though ordinarily not payable to them until their discharge or release on licence, were higher in real terms than the best paid of prisoners receive today, and for overtime or exceptional industriousness a prisoner was entitled to a bonus, part of which might be applied to the purchase of beer, tobacco or extra food. It was also possible for the very best behaved inmates to obtain a ticket of leave *in* prison, and they were then trusted to perform so-called "special services" without being supervised by the warders. At Dartmoor, which was classified as an "invalids prison", because it was reserved for convicts considered physically unfit for heavy labour, most of the ticket-of-leave men worked as farm hands. There were "honour parties" at Dartmoor then as there are now.

"It must be admitted", Jebb wrote,[8] "that a prisoner in a modern prison enjoys many comforts, but it must not be forgotten that with all his comforts he wants the priceless treasure of freedom." Whether the average convict would himself have agreed that he "enjoyed many comforts in a modern prison" is, to say the least, doubtful, but one may note a remarkable similarity between those words of Jebb's and words used by a reforming Home Secretary (R. A. Butler) one hundred and two years later: "The deterrent effect of imprisonment must finally lie in the loss of personal liberty and all that this involves under any kind of prison regime, and that effect is not reinforced if the period of loss of liberty is used in a merely repressive and punitive way."[9]

Similarly, Jebb eulogized the ticket-of-leave scheme on much the same grounds that it was to be eulogized by its 1968 sponsors when they re-introduced it, in a more refined and sophisticated form, under the name of parole: "Next to the religious teaching and training, the great merit of the plan lies in the habits of industry, obedience and self-reliance kept in ceaseless operation, whether the convict desires it or not, for months and years together, and in the practical lesson of the advantage of all of these, which results from making the hope of early liberation depend upon them; and, finally, there is the certainty that if known to fall into crime, or even to frequent the haunts of criminals, his pardon must be forfeited . . . This much must be conceded even by its opponents, that it fairly takes away the reproach so often directed against our old criminal law, that though we punished we did nothing to reform, that a man necessarily came out of prison worse than he entered in, made so in spite of himself."[10]

Still, Jebb didn't question the desirability of retaining the preliminary period of separate confinement, although he was well aware that most convicts considered it a torture added to the punishment of "losing the priceless treasure of freedom." If this was inconsistent of him, his assurance about the reformative potentialities of associated out-door labour evidently contradicted his emphatically declared view that "the separation of one prisoner from another provided the only basis upon which a reformatory discipline could be established with any hope of success." But Jebb, like some of his successors, was adept at reconciling the apparently irreconcilable. After transportation had come to an end, and there was no longer any point in training men for freedom in the colonies, he found a new rationale for the separate system: it served the essential purpose, he said, of conditioning convicts to appreciate and respond to the rehabilitative opportunities offered them by penal servitude. Indeed, he obtained the Home Secretary's authority to return convicts to Pentonville or Millbank for a further period of preparation in solitude, if they persistently idled or misbehaved themselves and thereby showed themselves unready for the "comforts" of a public works prison.

In any case, an unambivalent penological attitude was hardly to be expected from an official whose responsibilities were so manifold and varied. As one of the original Pentonville Commissioners, Jebb was closely identified with the attempt to safeguard transportation; as chairman of the directors of convict prisons, he was the chief administrator of the national system of imprisonment, which ultimately replaced transportation and was called penal servitude; finally, as Surveyor-General of prisons, he exercised a considerable direct influence over the systematization of what he himself called "ordinary imprisonment"—imprisonment in the locally administered common gaols and houses of correction.

Since this last development was to some extent entangled with the creation of penal servitude, it has usually been regarded as part and parcel of the same historical process. This has led to such over-simplifications as Lord Mountbatten was guilty of when he assured an alarmed public in 1966 that during the 19th century imprisonment was "in effect solitary confinement," that "all security was dependent" on that fact and that the principal reason why surviving 19th century prisons "are not secure today is that solitary confinement for long periods of years is no longer tolerable to the public conscience."[11]

But enough has been said to show that solitary confinement "for long periods of years" never was "tolerable to the public conscience", and was only a preliminary part of the discipline associated with penal servitude, to which the spies, the train robbers and the others, whose escapes provoked the Mountbatten inquiry, would have been sentenced. Nor was security ever dependent on solitary confinement in the public works prisons. It was dependent on chains and armed guards.

It *is* true, however, that with a few exceptions (Dartmoor, Parkhurst and Pentonville are among them) most of the 19th century prisons still in use were built at a time when discipline in local gaols had at last been systematized; an achievement that made ordinary imprisonment and solitary confinement one and the same thing. How and why this happened must be treated as a story in itself.

6

THE COMMON GAOLS UNDER LOCAL GOVERNMENT

In 1774, coincidentally with the end of transportation to America, and the advent of the Hulks system, John Howard published the first of his massively documented and horrifying reports on the state of the prisons in England and Wales. It has frequently been said that imprisonment at this period bore no relation to what we understand by imprisonment today in the sense that it wasn't used as an instrument of punishment. This, however, is somewhat misleading, and it would be more accurate to say that imprisonment was *no longer* being used as an instrument of *reformation*. For while it is true that the bridewells or houses of correction, which had originated as training centres for the shiftless, were by now virtually indistinguishable from the common gaols, which traditionally existed for the safe custody of debtors, people awaiting trial and convicts awaiting transportation or execution, the courts could none the less pass sentences of imprisonment with or without hard labour on some felons as well as on vagrants and other minor offenders. And for them imprisonment came close to physical and mental suffocation. Without regard to their sex, age, character or record, they were manacled and herded together like cattle in airless wards and dungeons. If they were penniless they often had to rely on charity for bread; and though their collective wealth was sufficient to encourage drunkenness, gambling and pilfering, many of them died of starvation and exposure or of the gaol fever, which was a concomitant of the appallingly insanitary conditions under which they were held.

Although the prisons were, with a few exceptions, publicly owned by local government authorities—by city corporations as well as by magistrates—most of them were actually administered by private contractors, who were in the business of gaol-keeping for what they could get out of it. This meant that the treatment a person received in prison depended not only on why he was there, or on his degree of culpability, but on the extent of his financial resources. In many gaols nothing was provided free, except fetters—no clothing, heat, bedding, medical care, not even food; and the heaviest and tightest-fitting irons were reserved for those who could raise no money at all to purchase lenience. By contrast, luxuries, such as tobacco, alcohol and opportunities for sexual intercourse,[1] were on sale and a private room or suite of rooms (with service) in the gaoler's own apartment could be had at a price. In fact, for the rich imprisonment was as pleasant an experience as it could possibly be made. But the great majority of prisoners were not rich, of course: they were extremely poor.

John Howard and his followers believed that reform was dependent on two things above all: first, the replacement of the independent gaol-keepers by salaried employees; secondly, the prevention of unrestricted association, which was assumed to result in the contamination of the innocent by the guilty and of the less by the more depraved. While the reformers regarded the profit motive as the root cause of all the barbarities practised, they also regarded unrestricted association as the root evil—the thing that made a gaol a "seminary of vice", a "university of crime", and hence a festering danger to society instead of a safeguard. But a question they never faced and which, for that matter, has not been faced since, is whether this evil can be eradicated short of turning gaols into even more socially destructive institutions than they are otherwise bound to be.

When Bernard Shaw wrote[2] that the "neglect, oppression, and physical torture of the old common gaol" became "the pretext for transforming it into that diabolic den of torment, mischief and damnation, the modern model prison", he was referring to those 19th century buildings, such as Wandsworth, Wormwood Scrubs, Wakefield and Reading, to name only a few of them, which were originally designed for separate confinement and with which we are still burdened. They are, of course, no longer considered "modern", since the separate system has, in theory at least, been wholly renounced. Nor can Howard himself be held to blame for them. He was an advocate not of rigorous separation, but of classification. While he insisted that prisoners should be accommodated in single "sleeping compartments", he believed that they should also be provided with day rooms and work rooms for association in selected groups; the women being kept apart from the men, the children from the adults, the untried from the convicted, minor offenders from hardened criminals, and so on. If it was simple-minded of him to suppose that contamination could be avoided in this way, it should be noted that we are in our own time no less simple-minded, or we are a great deal more hypocritical. At any rate, we have finally settled for classification out of an awareness that the alternatives proved intolerable.

Had Howard's campaign to arouse the conscience of the nation happened sooner, it might have provoked the suspicion, or by now have led to it, that the root evil of imprisonment is imprisonment itself. But by an unfortunate accident of history, Howard spoke out against the scandalous conditions in the common gaols at the very time when Parliament was first concerned with discovering a substitute for transportation. Consequently, his relatively simple and comparatively humane proposals for looking after the physical and moral welfare of ordinary prisoners (the majority of whom were probably innocent of any crime) became confused with more "sophisticated" notions about using imprisonment to punish and reform convicts. The 1779 Act, which authorized the building of government-run penitentiaries, and laid down detailed rules for their administration, was followed in 1791 by an Act requiring local authorities to adopt these same rules in existing common gaols and houses of correction throughout the country. Yet the rules provided for a very much tougher regime than the central Government was to establish at Millbank over a generation later. They required seclusion to be as nearly as practical absolute, with the prisoners not only denied social intercourse with one another, but isolated from their friends and relations in the outside world. Moreover, they specified that labour should be of "the hardest and most servile kind . . . little liable to be spoilt by ignorance, neglect or obstinacy."

Since the 1791 Act set up no machinery for the enforcement of Parliament's wishes, it was more of a request than a command,

and there was in fact no immediate response to it from the majority of local authorities who, for economy's sake, preferred to stick to their bad old ways. On the other hand, a scattered few of them were already dedicated to reform. Notably, the Gloucestershire justices, under the zealous leadership of Sir George Paul, had in 1775 obtained a Treasury grant of £50,000 to help them re-organize their entire prison system. In both the county gaol and the half dozen houses of correction, they had got rid of profiteering gaolers, done away with the "tap" (drinks for sale), engaged chaplains and medical officers as well as a full complement of custodial staff, eliminated chains and fetters, outlawed violent punishments, and made supervision the basis of security. Indeed, one may say that many of the features which today seem to be accepted as inextricably a part of imprisonment, such as the compulsory reception bath, the monastic segregation of the sexes, the fixed dietary tables, the exercise yard, and even the cell itself, are all owed to local initiative during the last quarter of the 18th century, and in turn to Howard.

But these same pioneering ventures were also the earliest essays in separate confinement, and as such gave practical expression not to Howard's ideas, but to those of Sir William Blackstone and Sir William Eden, who had jointly fathered the Penitentiary Act of 1779. The old county gaol in Gloucester, a "dark pen" as Paul called it, was converted into something close to a prototype for "model" Pentonville. There, and elsewhere, the price in suffering which even untried prisoners had to pay for protection from starvation, filth, disease and physical torture was even higher than that which convicts were to be forced to pay in return for being fitted for transportation. The Webbs[3] record that in 1783 an inmate of the new "separate" gaol at Salisbury, though he was serving only a year's sentence, found the discipline so unbearable that he petitioned to be hanged: an event which one may doubt if our contemporary apologists of the death penalty have heard of, or they might consider it disillusioning.

Still, if the 18th century sponsors of the separate system knew it to be painful, and never intended it to be painless, they were none the less intent on making imprisonment reformative as well as deterrent. This is more than can rightly be said for their 19th century followers who eventually succeeded, where they had failed, in establishing a uniform prison discipline based on "strict separation combined with hard labour, hard fare and hard bed." For though it is true that Pentonville provided the structural model for the local gaols that were built after a final commitment to separation had been made, and true, too, that Pentonville itself was designed as a reformative institution, there is a clear distinction to be drawn between the two developments. Jebb pointed it out when he gave evidence before a House of Commons Select Committee in 1850:[4] "Pentonville must be regarded as a penitentiary connected with the convict management of this country, and the objects in reference to that convict management are entirely different from those in reference to ordinary prisons. In the former case you are training the man to be disposed of with advantage to himself and the colony when his period of probation is over; and that is very different from any object in view in connection with a common gaol or house of correction."

It would not have been considered "very different" in 1791 when Parliament made its initial attempt to establish a uniform prison discipline. But since then, and particularly in more recent years, the incidence, or at least the detection, of petty crime had steadily mounted, and consequently the use made of imprisonment as a punishment had vastly increased.[5] At the same time, the great majority of sentences were, as they always had been and for that matter still are, short sentences. For example, of the 3,999 "receptions" of offenders under sentence at Wakefield gaol in 1847, 3,609 were for less than three months and only 104 were for more than nine months, that is to say for more than half the minimum period which was then deemed necessary to teach convicts to behave themselves in the colonies. Hence it was palpably ridiculous to maintain that separate confinement in common gaols and houses of correction had a reformative "object in view", especially when it was accompanied by "hard labour and hard fare", which was supposed to be precisely not true of the Pentonville training.

Yet, ironically, the uniform prison discipline that was eventually established by the 19th century sponsors of the separate system differed hardly at all from the kind of discipline which, at the end of the 18th century, had been considered appropriate to the aim of "moral improvement." Still more ironically, it was only after that aim had been officially abandoned—which didn't happen until 1865—that the standardization of prison conditions proved a practical possibility.

As has been said, there was only a limited response on the part of local authorities to the requirements of the 1791 Act, and although some 46 new gaols had been built on the cellular plan by 1800, a House of Commons Select Committee[6] reported in 1814 that by and large the state of the prisons was hardly less deplorable than it had been in Howard's day. At Newgate, for instance, as many as 30 debtors might be required to share a room 23 feet long by 15 feet wide; and untried prisoners, unless they could afford to pay for better accommodation, were allowed only one and a half feet of sleeping space. Worse, though the gaoler himself was a salaried employee, he hadn't nearly a large enough staff to run the prison without the help of so-called wardsmen, who were prisoners themselves and ruthlessly abused the power they exercised over their fellows to line their own pockets.

In 1823, after a lengthy period of inaction, Parliament passed another comprehensive Gaol Act, again with the declared aim of turning imprisonment into an instrument of "moral improvement." In a sense, this was a weaker attempt at intervention than before. It obliged the Justices to submit quarterly reports to the Home Department, which would show whether or not conditions in their gaols were up to standard, but it still left the central Government without any powers of inspection or enforcement. Moreover, it was not even nominally binding on over a hundred private franchise and, except in London, city gaols, which were notoriously the least savoury in the country.

On the other hand, the Act laid down new rules, which were more easily observed than the old, for while they required provision to be made for the "regular employment" of prisoners and for their physical and spiritual welfare, they in effect renounced seclusion in favour of classification. In fact, they introduced a discipline which was, on paper at least, remarkably similar to the discipline that has been gradually fashioned (or re-fashioned) during the present reforming century, though the provisions for "classification" were considerably more "sophisticated" than those nominally in force today. For example, it was not enough for untried prisoners to be separated from convicted prisoners. The untried prisoners accused of felony had in turn to be separated from the untried prisoners charged with misdemeanour, and so on.

But although the Act came closer than the Act of 1791 to embodying Howard's original proposals for the humane treatment of prisoners, it permitted a notable betrayal of Howard's principles by making it legal for three or more inmates of any given gaol in any given category (but no fewer than three) to sleep in the same cell, if there were insufficient accommodation available to give each of them a single cell. While this concession to practicality may have been made with reluctance, it was presumably found unavoidable—no less unavoidable than is the fact that, for want of enough space, or, rather, of the willingness to spend enough money on providing it, thousands of prisoners[7] today sleep three to a cell, in spite of repeated Home Office plaints that this is as inimical to "training and treatment" as it is palpably degrading and insanitary.

But one may suspect that the Act itself was fundamentally a compromise with economic necessity. Why else should seclusion have been abandoned at the very same time that it was considered so desirable in the national penitentiary at Millbank? Admittedly, there were reformers, in and out of Parliament, who stoutly objected to it on humane grounds, and for that reason championed classification. But it is also true that classification, though manifestly a less certain means of preventing contamination, was far cheaper both to institute and to operate. And while nobody disputed the necessity of isolating prisoners from corruptive influences if they were to be morally improved, the cost of constructing purpose-made gaols and employing large custodial staffs, which seclusion entailed, was, as Parliament doubtless recognized, higher than most local authorities were willing or could be forced to invest in a reformative policy; the more so since the mounting number of commitments meant that the original "separate" prisons were already too small for their purpose. Even Gloucester gladly went over to classification.[8]

On the other hand, local authorities, without direction or encouragement from Parliament, adopted a sort of poor man's substitute for seclusion. This was the so-called silent system under which prisoners worked, ate, exercised and slept in association, but were forbidden to communicate with one another by word or sign from the beginning to the end of their sentences. Though the system was not necessarily as cheap to operate as classification, it obviated the need for major structural alterations. The London prison at Coldbath Fields was an example. It had originally been designed for a total of 250 inmates, but by 1830 the population averaged over a 1000 and was still climbing. Hence, although an additional ward for 200 vagrants had been built and an additional ward for 300 females was in process of being built, there could obviously be no seclusion nor even compliance with Parliament's classification requirements, apart from segregating the sexes and using single cells for three (or more) prisoners. However, a "reforming" governor, named George Laval Chesterton, relied on the silent system to protect the "hopeful", as he called them, from being corrupted by the hopeless. This necessitated a constant day and night watch, and in fact some 270 supervisors or "monitors" were employed, though only 54 of them were paid officers. The rest were prisoners themselves, like the wardsmen at Newgate and other old-style gaols, and were doubtless as corrupt as they were unpopular. At any rate, the difficulty, not to say the utter impossibility, of enforcing the silence rule may be judged from the fact that in one year alone 11,624 punishments were inflicted at Coldbath Fields for talking or swearing. Not that Chesterton believed this to be a reason for criticizing the discipline or doubting its efficacy. On the contrary, he implied that the more punishment it provoked the better, since punishment, flogging included, was in his view a "great benefit." "It softens men", he said.[9]

"Softened" or not, about two thirds of his graduates offended again, and in 1830 a ten-year-old boy was serving his ninth consecutive sentence at Coldbath Fields. Even if the Silent System was a satisfactory method of preventing contamination, there could be no pretence by Chesterton or anyone else that imprisonment was preventing crime. For the number of prison commitments continued to mount. During the seven years' period 1810 to 1817 it stood at 56,208; during the next seven years' period it rose to 92,848 and during the one after that to 121,518. In Howard's day the annual figure had been under 2,000.

These facts invited two conclusions: first, that imprisonment was a fundamentally unsuitable means to a reformative end; secondly, that it had become too weak a deterrent. In 1828, a House of Commons Committee[10] reported that whereas a prison had formerly been "dreaded on account of the filth and disease which were said to be its constant companions", it now held no terrors for the criminal, since it meant "a good roof over his head", "good, wholesome food", and less demanding work than would be required of him as a free labourer. Though the Committee believed that it would be "unwise as well as inhuman" to revert to the practices of the 18th century, when people literally "rotted in gaol", they none the less recommended that discipline should have a purely deterrent purpose. It would be more sensible, they said, to set up a criminal "in a small shop" or find him a "place in domestic service", if the object were to reform rather than punish him. "As places of reform gaols have failed and ought not to be considered."

But that pronouncement didn't result in any immediate change of policy. On the contrary, in 1835 Parliament appeared to rededicate itself to the task of making gaols "places of reform" with an Act empowering the Home Secretary to lay down rules for their administration and to appoint district inspectors. The very first reports of the inspectors[11] (there were five inspectors at the start, though later their number was reduced to two) revealed once again how far conditions in many gaols still fell short of the law's minimum requirements. At Newgate, six prisoners were found sharing the same ward, two of them untried and four convicted. There was a 38-year-old man serving a year's sentence for attempted buggery in the latter group; there were also a couple of teen-age youths.

While the Home Secretary remained powerless to do more than take note of such abuses, the inspectors were none the less in a position to influence local prison administration, if only through the weapon of publicity. In effect, they set themselves up as policy-makers, and the keystone of their policy was separate confinement. They emphatically rejected both classification and the silent system on the grounds that neither offered better than an illusory safeguard against contamination. Equally, they extolled the separate system as a reformative panacea, and in 1838 they urged the Government to demonstrate this by building a prison of its own.[12] In the following year—three years before Pentonville was built—Parliament passed an Act which permitted the separate system to be instituted in gaols where the appropriate cellular accommodation was available. This cleared the way for Pentonville to serve the "model" purpose that the inspectors hoped that it would and believed that it should. In fact, between 1842 and 1862 the number of "separate" local gaols increased from two to 79 and the number of cells "certified" by the inspectors as suitable for separate confinement from 200 to 14,959.

Yet by the end of that period a considerably greater number of gaols still remained unsatisfactory from the Home Office's point of view. Cost, as always, was the basic problem. This was especially true of the boroughs, where magistrates needed authority from town councils to spend money on prison improvements and where town councils were in turn reluctant to impose such a potentially unpopular burden on rate-payers. In one borough gaol an inspector found that there weren't enough towels to go round—only one for every six prisoners. But the magistrates declined to buy more on the grounds that if they did, the town council would require them to foot the bill.

Moreover, as has been said, and as Jebb understood, "convict management" and ordinary imprisonment were two entirely different things. In the one case, both the purpose and methods of the separate system were clearly defined. In the other they were not, so that there was still no uniformity of discipline even in gaols where the system was nominally established. The policy of "hard labour, hard fare and a hard bed" which Jebb first enunciated in 1850[13] had not at that time been endorsed by Parliament, and the emphasis on a punitive as opposed to a reformative aim was far greater in some separate gaols than in others, particularly in respect of employment.

What "hard labour" meant for a prisoner who was sentenced to it all depended on which gaol he found himself in. It might be strictly unproductive—something calculated to break his spirit as well as weary his body. The treadwheel, or the "everlasting staircase", as it was more graphically called, was one of the instruments used for this purpose. Another was the crank, which in 1850 had recently been invented by a Pentonville warder.

At the other extreme, hard labour in Reading gaol—the very first of the local gaols to be built in Pentonville's image—meant as little labour as possible. "An extraordinary crotchet" Edmund Du Cane was to call this when, writing[14] years later as the first supremo of a centralized prison service, he recalled the bad old days of local gaol administration. "The inmates learned lessons all day, except when exercising, attending chapel, and cleaning cells, etc. As a privilege they might, 'when tired of reading', 'pick a little oakum', but this was quite optional, and hard, heavy labour was absolutely forbidden in order that the whole attention might be devoted to literature—the establishment was a criminal university, and acquired the name of the 'Read-read-reading Gaol.' As a final climax of burlesque absurdity the Bible was made the principal lesson book . . . and a reformatory influence was supposed to be achieved by requiring the criminals to commit large portions of the Testament to memory. This result was figured by one irreverent critic to be so effectively achieved that a felon was said to have been so distressed, when the end of his sentence interrupted his studies, and he had only 'got as far as Ephesians,' that he came back (under sentence for sheep-stealing) to learn the rest of the Testament."

That, as a matter of fact, is a somewhat exaggerated account, for the inmates were required to spend an hour or two a day in their solitary cells grinding flour with single-handed mills. More importantly, it ignores the rationale of the discipline, which was, of course, reformative. The Visiting Justices at Reading grew disillusioned with conventional hard labour when they realized, in the word of their Chairman, William

Merry, that "the same man came back to the same treadmill [a misnomer for treadwheel] a dozen times or more."[15] They were, therefore, easily persuaded by the chaplain, a zealot named Field, that labour of any kind was a "mistake", since the prisoners found it a "relief from separate confinement" and his own task of enforcing repentance and religious enlightenment upon them was thereby impeded. The argument went that if a man were given nothing to do, he'd be bound to accept an invitation to read the Bible, or to be taught to read it, if only to save himself from going mad. A government convict, according to Merry, learned the whole of the New Testament by heart during a year's stay in the gaol.

In between these two extremes of penal labour and anti-labour, there was productive work, intended partly as punishment, inasmuch as the prisoners were kept at it for long hours and were usually, though not invariably, unpaid, and partly for "training". Though the idea of productive work for training has, of course, been restored to favour during the present century, it is worth noting that work in some of the local gaols of the 1850's was very much more productive than work in any penal institution is today. There were, in fact, full-fledged Factory Prisons, of which the Webbs give some examples. Wakefield Gaol earned a gross annual revenue of £40,000 from mat-making. It employed its own trade-managers, its own commercial travellers, and even its own foreign agents. The warders as well as the governor were given a cut of the profits, and the prisoners, too, received gratuities, in the form of money or special meals, for exceptional industry. Moreover, the gaol ran an establishment for discharged prisoners who wished to continue their employment in mat-making. Other gaols went in for the manufacture of clothes, brushes, boots and shoes, and again marketed their goods both at home and abroad. Steam power was used, and in one or two instances the prisoners were paid on a piece work basis. At Preston gaol, which was a cotton-weaving factory, 50% of the profits went to the prisoners on their discharge, 40% to the county, and 10% to the task-masters.

If all this sounds most advanced by the standards of our own time, one must add that there was no gaol in the country where the discipline was what we could now accept as sufficiently humane. At Wakefield, a prisoner was required to produce six mats a day, or face a spell in a dark cell on a diet of bread-and-water; for persistent failure he was flogged. At Preston, where, for want of a sufficient number of cells, the separate system could be only partially enforced, the inmates employed on cotton-picking were assembled in one large room. "The order preserved in this room is admirable," a visitor recorded,[16] "in fact, too admirable. The prisoners' eyes never wander from their occupation. To a certain extent this is desirable; but the discipline may be pushed to a ridiculous extent; and when Mr Clay [the chaplain] boasts that they would not raise their eyes even if ladies and strangers entered the room, we confess our inability to see the virtue and the merit of the abstinence."

Doubtless, there were prison administrators who genuinely believed in productive work as a training for freedom. W. L. Clay, the Preston chaplain, was one of them, and apparently he persuaded neighbourhood employers to share his faith. A discharged prisoner was said to be assured of a job, if Clay gave him a letter of recommendation. Fundamentally, however, one may again suspect that the resistance among local authorities to the concept of useless labour was economic. After all, a gaol, where the prisoners were painfully employed in grinding air, cost money to run: money that had to be got from the rate-payers. But a gaol, where the prisoners served as a slave labour force for the production of mats or some other marketable commodity, might be better than self-supporting.

At the same time, rate-payers were presumably more agreeably parted with their money for the pleasurable end of punishing criminals than for what they were being increasingly encouraged to believe was the highly uncertain end of reforming them. By 1847, even one of the Home Office inspectors—the same inspector (Captain Williams) who investigated the Woolwich hulks scandal—had come to recognize that "moral improvement" was a nonsensical aim to pursue in a prison, considering the brevity of time ordinarily allowed to attain it. "I have no question," he told a House of Lords Select Committee,[17] "that a considerable proportion of prisoners might be reclaimed if you went to the expense of so doing, and if you placed the prisoner in a very much better situation in life than he was in before he committed his crime; but I think a great mistake has been made in prisons by attempting two things—reformation and punishment. The objects cannot be carried out together. For all short sentences the deterring agency should be resorted to."

It did not occur to Captain Williams, or to any of his listeners, that it might be more sensible to go to the expense of reclaiming prisoners in the ways he suggested than to persevere with what was now admitted to be the largely self-defeating business of punishing them. One says this was admitted, because no one concerned with prison administration believed that the "repressive part of the discipline" was or (within civilized bounds) could be made repressive enough to dissuade individual offenders from offending again. Chesterton described his system at Coldbath Fields as being "far too soft" for that purpose.[18] Jebb endorsed the opinion of "most governors and chaplains" that "short imprisonments, under any system of discipline, were calculated to remove the terror of gaol."[19] Merry of Reading did not believe that men would ever be "deterred by anything in the shape of punishment."[20]

J. G. Perry, perhaps the most liberal of the Home Office inspectors, underlined the same view with a story of a prisoner he once met who was serving his seventh sentence for poaching. The man had been on "numerous treadwheels" and had been flogged several times. But he could still say to Perry, "Well, sir, if I can't get a gamekeeper's place after my discharge, I shall be in again."[21]

Yet none of these experts was ready to advocate an end to the punishment of petty offenders. Nor, though they were still inclined to differ about ways and means, did they doubt the need for a uniformly tough and (by the standards of today) an appallingly cruel prison discipline. To illustrate the impossibility of deterring by terror, Merry recalled that in the Wall Street Prison, New York, 80 men had been incarcerated for ten months in "living graves"—cells only seven feet long and hardly high enough to stand up in. Five of the men, Merry said, had died, two or three had gone mad—and yet no fewer than fourteen had been re-convicted within a few weeks of their release.

But Merry didn't make this point with any intention of stamping himself a "softie"; still less of implying disapproval of the separate system, which he knew very well was extraordinarily punitive, whatever its reformative justification. "A man would jump mast high to get upon the treadwheel," he said, "rather than be confined in a solitary cell." Though he hadn't much use for dark cells, he had great faith in dietary punishment. The "animal" in every criminal, he said, "fails him when his food is reduced"; and he had known the "roughest" of prisoners go down on their knees "begging to be let off a second week of bread and water." Incidentally, Visiting Justices, under the 1823 Act, were empowered to order dietary punishment to last for a month on end.

The reason for such apparent illogicality and reckless cruelty—or at least the pretext for it—was the old, undying, and unkillable attachment to the theory of general deterrence; the conviction that punishment was an indispensable means of "deterring society." Inspector Perry was, as we shall see, one man who was inclined to reject this theory. But for the great body of opinion, in and out of Parliament, it was axiomatic that if crime was unsuppressed in spite of punishment, the punishment had become too little feared. Hence the growing disillusionment with imprisonment as a sensible response to individual offenders, instead of prompting a search for a more hopeful alternative, only produced a determination to increase its effectiveness in enforcing respect for the law on the general population.

The question was how. As has been said, faith in deterrent theory remains unshaken to this day. But though the faith may be mere superstition, and to an extent is certainly a rationalization of the urge to punish, the courage of deterrent theory has progressively dwindled. This has resulted in a curious dichotomy of social attitude, for while there is no surer way of courting popular favour than to lambast the "coddling" of prisoners, a politician or editorial writer can assure himself of an almost equally satisfactory response with an exposure of prison "brutalities". Moreover, History suggests that what may safely be derided as "coddling" today can with no less safety be called "brutal" tomorrow.

"Consider the victim" is a slogan to command as much applause at this moment in time as it ever did. But any suggestion that prisoners should be treated as they were in the mid-19th century would undoubtedly be greeted with horror, even though the discipline then was thought to be provenly too lenient to keep crime in check. Similarly, the 1828 committee, which spoke of the deterrent excellence of prison conditions in Howard's time, implicitly denied that that was a good enough reason for restoring them.

In 1850, this same disavowal was made by Charles Pearson, the man who initiated the investigation carried out that year by a House of Commons Committee.[22] "The prison discipline that existed in his [Howard's] time was torturing prisoners, starving prisoners by cold and hunger," he said. ". . . If I have at all given the impression that I consider the increased number of commitments, which I believe to be the consequence of the increased comforts of gaols, as a test of a good system, I do not. I do not desire to see a return to the sanguinary system that prevailed in the days of Howard . . . But if the object of prison discipline is to repress the commission of offences, I think then that the present system is not an improved system."

Pearson had a radical plan of his own, which will be mentioned later, for using imprisonment to better effect as a "deterring agency." Though it was not one that the rest of the Committee endorsed, they agreed that the object of imprisonment *was* "to repress the commission of offences" and that this object was being defeated by an over-emphasis on reform and consequently too much lenience. What, then, could be done to rectify the situation without outraging the public's conscience?

To judge how extraordinarily untender the public's conscience still was by comparison with the public's conscience today, one has only to consider the sanctions that were cheerfully tolerated for the maintenance of discipline within prisons. "It is not easy", Hepworth Dickson wrote[23] in the very same year that Pearson's committee reported, "to get punishments which are at the same time humane and deterring. Discipline must be maintained at any price. Order must first be taken care of. And it is believed, from long experience, that, with many of these abandoned wretches, the fear of punishment is the only incentive to good behaviour. Nor is a light and ordinary severity sufficient. The fellows are hardened, physically as well as morally. A course of prisons, and the rigours incidental to a life of crime, have taught them to deride the dark cell, and to laugh at the stoppage of a dinner. Some minds are so low they can only be reached by the cat—and this is especially the case with hardened street-bred juvenile offenders."

Hepworth Dickson witnessed a punishment of "light and ordinary severity" when he visited Millbank: "The dark cells . . . are fearful places, and sometimes melancholy mistakes are made in committing persons to them. You descend about twenty steps from the ground-floor into a very dark passage leading into a corridor, on one side of which the cells—small, dark, ill-ventilated, and doubly barred—are ranged. No glimpse of day ever comes into this fearful place. The offender is locked up for three days, and fed on bread and water. There is only a board to sleep on; and the only furniture of the cell is a water-closet . . . I was told there was a person in one of these cells. 'He is touched, poor fellow!' said the warder, 'in his intellects' . . . Poor wretch! He was frightened with his solitude, and howled fearfully. I shall never forget his wail as we passed the door of his horrid dungeon. The tones were quite unearthly, and caused an involuntary shudder. On hearing footsteps, he evidently thought they were coming to release him. While we were in the corridor, he did not cease to shout and implore most lamentably for freedom: when he heard us retreating, his voice rose into a yell; and when the heavy bolts told him that we were gone, he gave a shriek of horror, agony, and despair, which rang through the pentagon, and can never be forgotten. God grant that I may never hear such sounds again!"[24]

Still, the public did *have* a conscience, and, as that last passage implies, it could be wounded when a punishment of even "light and ordinary severity" was mistakenly inflicted on a madman, especially since madness had to be very mad, indeed, before it was distinguished from wickedness. The fact that 6,959 floggings took place in the country's gaols during 1822 caused no dismay, but ten years earlier, Sir F. Burdett had provoked an outcry in Parliament with his revelations about the ill-treatment of a lunatic, named John Rawlings.[25]

This man, convicted of murder but found insane, had been confined for three years at Lancaster Castle Gaol, when he hanged himself with a stocking in an underground cell, after receiving a merciless thrashing from a turnkey. His whole body was found to be a "mass of congealed blood."

Suicides in prison were frequent occurrences (for that matter they are still far from uncommon).[26] Ordinarily, they passed unnoticed; indeed, if they had been a cause of general concern, the separate system would have had to be abandoned almost as soon as it was introduced. But in 1853—three years after Pearson's committee reported—there was a suicide at the Birmingham gaol, which resulted in a possibly greater disturbance of the public's conscience than any that has been produced since by a prison event.

The story, which is immortalized in Charles Reade's *It is Never Too Late to Mend*, began when a 16-year-old youth, named Andrews, was sentenced to three months' hard labour for stealing a piece of meat. Hard labour at the Birmingham gaol meant the crank, though the prisoners were put to this useless task in a yard, and not in their separate cells, despite the fact that the great advantage of the crank was supposed to be the opportunity it allowed for hard labour in solitude. All the prisoners, no matter how young, old, physically frail or feeble-minded they might be, were required to clock up 10,000 revolutions a day—2,000 before breakfast, 4,000 before the midday meal and the rest before bedtime. In Andrews' case, this proved to be a sheer impossibility, for though the crank he was assigned to had a nominal resistance of 5 lb, its actual resistance, as a result of a misadjustment, deliberate or accidental, was about 20 lb. But the governor, a certain Lt. Austin, would accept no excuses, and as often as Andrews failed to complete his quota, his food was withheld. After this persistent starvation had made him even more "idle", Lt. Austin decided that the punishment of "restraint" was called for. The boy was strapped to the wall of his cell, his arms were bound across his chest, a high, stiff leather collar was buckled tightly round his neck so that he couldn't move his head, and he was left in that position for four hours, when a bucket of water was thrown over him and he was returned to the crank yard. Next morning at

7.30, the dose was repeated for another two and a half hours. That evening Andrews hanged himself.

Now before his appointment as governor, Lt. Austin had served as deputy governor under Captain Alexander Maconochie. The two of them had fallen out when Maconochie protested against Austin's excessive use of punishments. Austin offered to resign, but the Birmingham Justices decided that he was better qualified than his superior to preserve good order and discipline, and asked for Maconochie's resignation instead. This was a palace revolution that attracted some attention, because Maconochie was nationally known for his previous pioneering work as governor of the dreaded Norfolk Island penal settlement, where he had substituted a reformative system of his own invention for the traditional methods of brute terrorization. The Birmingham Justices had given him an opportunity to institute a modified version of the same system for the juvenile offenders committed to their new gaol. He called it the "mark" system, and it meant, broadly speaking, that the treatment a prisoner received, particularly in regard to diet, depended on the number of marks he earned for industriousness and did not forfeit for bad conduct. Maconochie believed that labour should be the coin in which all "debts to society" were paid. He hoped that eventually a prisoner who accumulated more than the minimum number of daily marks required of him would be able to expend the surplus, if he chose, on purchasing a remission of sentence instead of on food. But under the existing law no remission of an ordinary prison sentence was permitted.

One may truthfully say that Maconochie was both ahead of his time and behind it. He was behind it in the sense that he was concerned to make imprisonment reformative when the trend was in the opposite direction—towards, as he himself observed, "employing prisoners as scarecrows." [27] He was ahead of his time inasmuch as his basic idea of "work as a cure for crime" is at present once more in vogue. Thus, apart from repeated Home Office declarations of faith in "training" (which means training in habits of industry, if it means anything at all), Miss Kathleen J. Smith, a former assistant governor of Holloway, has published a widely welcomed proposal for what she calls the "self-determinate sentence",[28] under which prisoners would "pay" for their crimes by their labour. And Miss Pamela Hansford Johnson has suggested in her treatise on the Moors Murders case (1957)[29] that Alexander Maconochie was a penal reformer of unrivalled stature. "I am quite sure", she concludes after a glowing account of his achievements on Norfolk Island, "that our greatest hope for regenerating the criminal is to provide him with work of an intrinsically valuable and socially productive kind."

It may be that if penal settlements still existed, we should have a great deal to learn from Maconochie. (His reforms were considered so dangerously liberal by the powerful proponents of deterrent theory that he was eventually recalled and conditions on Norfolk Island were temporarily restored to normal.) Just the same, one may question whether his system ever offered much hope of making better sense of ordinary imprisonment. For the idea that work equals rehabilitation, and is therefore to be encouraged by reward, presumably pre-supposes that all prisoners are equally capable of it. This, as even the official statistics allow, is quite untrue today. It was far less true in Maconochie's time when, apart from the lunatics, morons, epileptics and mental defectives, who constituted, as they still do, a high percentage of the captive population, sickly, undernourished children were indiscriminately sent to prison for the pettiest of offences.

In other words, Maconochie's system—and the same objection would apply to any similar system that might be tried today—could not have worked equitably in a gaol, since some of the inmates were bound to be better fitted, bodily and mentally, to earn more marks than others, while quite a few of them might be fundamentally unfit to earn any marks at all. As a matter of fact, it seems unlikely that the sturdiest among the juvenile inmates (under 16) of the Birmingham gaol could have afforded to expend marks on a reduction of sentence, except at the cost of malnutrition, since the food available for "purchase" was never better than the best which the miserable prison diet allowed. (Maconochie spoke of encouraging "self-denial" and also described the objective of his system as "reform through suffering.")[30] In practice, moreover, the discipline in the gaol met with resistance from some prisoners, adult as well as juvenile, who would not (or could not) get through the minimum amount of labour demanded of them. The response to this resistance was punishment, and despite Maconochie's eventual breach with Austin, he permitted the same methods to be used, on a smaller scale, that were subsequently to kill Andrews.

Ironically enough, Maconochie's marks system had a lot in common with Charles Pearson's radical plan, to which reference has been made above, for an "improved" deterrent prison discipline that would exclude a reversion to the "sanguinary" practices of the previous century. Though Pearson didn't actually speak of a "self-determinate sentence," that was what he wanted: a sentence to a fixed amount of labour for the benefit of the community, instead of a fixed term of imprisonment, so that convicted offenders would either have to learn to be industrious or stay indefinitely in gaol. But while Pearson argued that the punishment would almost inevitably have a reformative effect on the individual, that for him was only an incidental point in its favour. Since his main objective was general deterrence, the scaring-off of all the potential offenders in society's midst, he proposed that prisoners, while they were forced to toil for their liberty, should be deprived of "comforts"—be obliged to sleep on wooden planks in unwarmed cells and be fed on a diet only just sufficient to keep them alive.

Still, the fact remains that Maconochie, unlike Pearson, had a reputation both as a practising reformer and a humanitarian. Accordingly, the disgraceful story of Andrews' suicide, which came out by chance at the inquest, could be interpreted as a direct consequence of Maconochie's dismissal and the appointment of his rebellious deputy in his place. The result was very probably to exacerbate the revulsion felt by the Birmingham citizenry at what had been going on in their name, and to make their cries of anger and indignation louder than they would otherwise have been.

They were loud enough to promote a national scandal. A parliamentary commission,[31] which was set up to investigate the facts, reported that Austin had persistently ordered punishments to be carried out, or failed to prevent his subordinates from carrying them out, which were both grossly cruel and, worse, illegal. These included, besides the torture of starvation and restraint used in Andrews' case, a system of rotatory beatings, whereby a prisoner might be subjected to so many strokes of the 'cat' or the birch rod daily until he was pronounced suitably contrite. The Commission's report refuelled public fury. Lt. Austin was charged with malpractices and put on trial. He was convicted and sentenced to three months imprisonment, though "characteristically" (to quote the Webbs) as a first class misdemeanant, which meant that he was privileged to maintain himself and was spared most of the hardships and indignities that he had inflicted on others.

What the whole incident had proved, or proved again, was that there were limits beyond which a repressive discipline could not be pushed—at any rate officially. Moreover, since the shock came at a time when the crime rate, though still far higher than in Howard's day, at last seemed to be levelling off, the effect was temporarily to halt the movement from reformative aspirations to all-out deterrent practices and to an extent even to reverse it. Prison governors took heed of Austin's fate. They feared the danger of laying themselves open to similar charges of cruelty, and for that reason the crank was banished from most of the gaols where it had previously been used.

But this reaction proved remarkably short-lived. In 1861, there was an outbreak of violent robberies in London which aroused quite unjustifiable suspicions that crime in general was again on the increase. In 1862 the so-called "Garotters Act", which made garotting punishable by flogging, was rushed through Parliament. In 1863, a Royal Commission was set up to investigate the conditions of penal servitude. And in the same year a powerful House of Lords Select Committee, under the chairmanship of the Earl of Caernarvon, made recommendations for an uncompromisingly ferocious prison discipline, which Parliament was in due course to accept virtually without reservations.

7

LOCAL PRISONS UNDER CENTRAL GOVERNMENT

Lord Caernarvon and his colleagues were men with a pre-determined mission, and acted in defiance of the evidence of the two remaining prison inspectors, Perry and Voules, both of whom, particularly the former, remained loyal to reform. Perry displayed great courage in saying things that their lordships were plainly averse to hearing. He stated, without equivocation, that "reformation" was the most important objective of imprisonment, since the "effect of deterrent punishment on the public mind" was "very small." "If that [reformation] could be brought about without punishment", he said, "I should be very glad to see such a change, but I do not see at present how we can produce reformation of the individual without some admixture of punishment."

The "admixture" which their lordships demanded was far in excess of what either of the inspectors considered sufficient. Perry favoured the abolition of flogging; the committee thought flogging should be encouraged. "The most experienced of our witnesses," they reported, "are unanimous as to the wholesome influence of corporal punishment." Both inspectors disliked the treadwheel on the grounds that while it did permanent physical damage to some prisoners, others, who were experienced and able-bodied, suffered very little from it. Perry thought that the use of the crank put too much power in the hands of warders, who by tightening the spring could make it an intolerably painful form of labour. In principle, moreover, he was opposed to unproductive work of any kind. "[It] stirs up all the bad feelings of a man against the authorities," he said, "and therefore produces deterioration of his moral character." Again, the committee disagreed. There might, they suggested, be a place for industrial training under a system of "gradations", which in turn would be desirable since "the majority of prisoners are within certain limits, open to the influences of encouragement and reward." But their lordships found industrial occupation to be "wholly unfit for those offenders who are undergoing short sentences, or are working out the earlier stages of their imprisonment." In the latter cases, they declared, hard labour should invariably be made to mean what it said; and they had no doubt that what it said was the treadwheel or the crank or something similarly useless and tormenting.

Similarly, they asked for "hard fare" and a "hard bed" to be clearly defined and strictly enforced. They proposed that prisoners should be required to sleep on wooden planks, instead of in hammocks, during the first three months of their sentences, and they deplored the fact that in a number of gaols the inmates were allowed to sleep for ten or eleven hours out of every twenty four; eight hours, they said, should be the limit.

They noted with keen disapproval that there was still no uniformity of diet in gaols, in spite of the fact that the Home Office had issued standard dietary tables for adoption twenty years ago, when Sir James Graham was Home Secretary. In fact, the weekly allowance of meat varied from zero to 25 ounces and the total allowance of solid foods from 100 to 340 ounces. The Committee wanted something nearer the bottom than the top, and though they refrained from being specific, they said very clearly why they wanted a minimal diet: "The low animal natures of too many of the criminal class, and the admitted efficiency of reduction of food in cases of prison offences, render plain the value of diet as one form of penal correction."

That statement appeared to be diametrically opposed to a principle which Sir James Graham had laid down when the Home Office dietary tables were first issued: namely, that while a prison diet should be no more than sufficient to "sustain health and strength", it ought on no account to be made an "instrument of punishment." However, Sir James Graham had immediately compromised his own principle by providing for higher and lower dietaries according to the length of time served. Thus the highest diet, which included meat, was not allowed until after three months, while during the first seven days, which might in some cases be the whole sentence, a prisoner was fed on bread and oatmeal gruel weighing 10 lbs in all.

Though the Caernarvon Committee had no quarrel with this system as such, since it had a manifestly penal effect and was in line with their own ideas of "gradation", they decided that each of the Home Office's four dietary scales was "excessive".

Finally, and above all, their lordships declared that separate confinement "must now be considered the foundation of prison discipline", and they asked for it to be as rigorously enforced in local gaols as it had originally been enforced at Pentonville, with the use of masks, individual "airing yards", and so on. Both inspectors, and several other witnesses besides, vainly tried to convince the Committee that separation in Chapel simply provoked "infractions of discipline", and hence undermined the spirit and purpose of public worship, whereas prisoners seated next to each other in ordinary pews could easily be kept under constant supervision and were the more likely to concentrate on the service and open their hearts to the word of God. Voules remarked that at Preston, where the prisoners associated in chapel, tears could often be seen streaming down their faces during Mr Clay's sermons; and though Voules conceded that in some instances this might be a manifestation less of true repentance than of a cunning desire to "curry favour", it made his point. But the Committee brushed all such arguments aside. "Separateness", they maintained, should not be compromised, and they reproduced a plan of the chapel at Bristol prison, where a monstrous-looking complex of cages, rising from floor to ceiling, had been installed for the use of the congregation.

They were equally opposed, of course, to associated labour, and received a doubtless very welcome assurance from the Surveyor-General that this did not rule out the treadwheel. "I know of one prison", Jebb told them, "where a most effective discipline is kept up by the Governor, with very inadequate means as regards construction; he has small cells, which are only fit for sleeping in, and cannot be certified for separate confinement; but by dividing his treadwheel into close compartments, and letting out the prisoners from their cells at certain distances from each other, and shutting them up in the compartments of the treadwheel, and marching them back again to their cells in the same way, no two prisoners can ever see each other, and you really obtain the advantages of separate confinement without the expense which is entailed by the construction of a prison."

The "advantages" of separate confinement, Jebb was honest enough to recognize, were exclusively deterrent. According to the committee, they were deterrent and "reformatory". But though their lordships paid considerable lip service to the second of these two objectives, it is clear that they had little or no real interest in it. Under questioning from Caernarvon, Perry revealed that during 1861 there had been 24,763 recommittals of males to prison and 96,763 committals. Though these Home Office figures were, as Perry pointed out, incomplete and unreliable, since there was usually no telling whether an offender had been in prison before unless he happened to be returned to the same gaol, Caernarvon solemnly deduced that the ratio between "reformed" criminals and "new" criminals must be three to one: a deduction which, to his mind presumably, *proved* the need for draconian measures to "deter society."

Indeed, if the Committee had been capable of a greater degree of intellectual honesty, they might logically have recommended that features of the discipline associated with "moral improvement" should be entirely dispensed with—that no useful purpose was served by daily chapel services or a "schooling", which under Home Office regulations was supposed to occupy two hours out of every prisoner's day.

As it was, they went as far as they could in that direction, short of laying themselves open to a charge of ungodliness. They took a hefty side-swipe at Field, the Chaplain of Reading Gaol. "We regard as extremely unsatisfactory", they said, "a prison discipline in which instruction by the schoolmaster or 'self-instruction' is made the substance of prison discipline." They also implied a certain distrust of all chaplains, for, after noting that the Governor of the West Sussex County gaol had once seen a novel in a prisoner's cell, they suggested that the responsibility of choosing books for issue to prisoners should no longer be the chaplain's alone, but should preferably be shared with the Visiting Justices and that in any case the supply ought to be more limited than it was. Moreover, they called it "essential" that the "means employed for the reformation of offenders (chapel service apart) should always be accompanied by "due and effective punishment." Better no schooling at all, they intimated, than schooling in association, though they disclaimed any intention of restricting "the cellular . . . religious instruction which the chaplain may think fit to administer to any prisoners."

Possibly, their lordships were aware, when they made that last concession, that "cellular religious instruction"—the visits that chaplains found the time or inclination to pay the individual members of their flock—was ordinarily already so restricted that it posed no serious threat to the deterrent "influence" of solitude. Possibly, they were aware, too, that compulsory attendance at daily chapel services, however morally imperative, was not without its own deterrent usefulness. At any rate, they produced a charter for giving prisoners hell, which, having regard to the civilized sensibilities of the age, went as far as any such charter could possibly have gone. And, with some slight modifications and refinements, it was soon to be enforced.

At this point, it should be remembered that imprisonment was, broadly speaking, only a defence against minor crime. The defence against major crime was penal servitude, and the distinction between these two separate parts of the penal system, though it was soon to become increasingly blurred, was still drawn. Now that it no longer exists we can the more easily evade a discomfiting truth: that even though it may be theoretically possible to rehabilitate criminals in prison, training and treatment methods are useless without time enough to make them work, and hence in the great majority of cases are bound to fail.[1] The House of Lords Committee of 1863 had logic on their side in deciding that unless "short imprisonment", which, as they knew, was what ordinary imprisonment mostly meant, served a strongly deterrent purpose, there was no sense to it at all. But the consequence of their decision was also logical: the creation of a calculatedly punitive system which, irrationally, was at its most punitive in dealing with the pettiest of offenders.

This did not happen immediately, for although an Act of 1865, which laid down minutely detailed new rules for prison discipline, represented a total commitment on Parliament's part to the "hard labour etc." policy, the economic resistance among some local authorities both to unremunerative labour and separate confinement could not be entirely overcome. Thirteen years later, however, in 1877, a Conservative government, which was pledged to lighten the burden on ratepayers, used this as a pretext for a take-over of the common gaols. Under the relevant legislation, Visiting Committees of Justices, elected by the magistracy, retained some supervisory powers, notably the power of awarding punishments; and every magistrate had the right—a right which still exists but nowadays seems to be rarely exercised—of entering any prison within his jurisdiction without notice for the purpose of inspection. Otherwise local authorities were stripped of their last vestiges of autonomy. The ultimate responsibility for prison administration was vested in the Home Secretary, and delegated to a central Commission, whose first chairman and virtual dictator was Edmund Du Cane.

Thus the way was at last cleared for the establishment of a centrally controlled, streamlined prison system with the clearly defined objective of "deterring society" through inflicting an equal and exactly measured amount of suffering on almost every offender committed to its charge, without regard to sex, age, culpability or mental responsibility. It must not be supposed, however, that this was ever admitted to be a wholly oppressive system—on the contrary, Du Cane called it 'reformatory'—and the extent to which it differed, both in principle and practice, from our existing prison system, can easily be over-estimated. "Prison governors are now expected to treat the prisoners in their charge with humanity," Lord Mountbatten wrote in his 1966 security report, as though to suggest that under the Du Cane regime they weren't. But it is only the definition of "humanity" that has changed; there is nothing new in the assurance that it is being practised. Nor is there any substantially greater guarantee than there ever was that the assurance is being honoured.

The present prison rules provide that "discipline and order shall be maintained with firmness, but with no more restriction than is required for safe custody and well ordered community life." As we have already seen, the corresponding Home Office rule regarding the maintenance of discipline aboard the Hulks promised an even more permissive approach. So, equally, did the prison rule, which was promulgated after the passage of the 1877 Prison Act.[2] "It is the duty of all officers to treat the prisoners with kindness and humanity, to listen patiently to and report their complaints and grievances." Yet "groundless complaining" was one of the numerous offences against discipline for which a prisoner could be and, for that matter, can still be, punished; and in effect complaints were invariably "groundless", if the officer, to whom they were made, chose to call them so, for a prisoner charged with an offence before the governor was guilty virtually by definition. He was not permitted to cross-examine his accuser, or to call witnesses, though these were rights that had been allowed in one or two of the locally administered gaols. And though he could, of course, deny the charge, it was impossible for the governor, whatever he might really believe, to accept a prisoner's word against an officer's, except at the risk of undermining authority: a risk which he was rarely, if ever, prepared to run.

This feature of the prison system under the Du Cane regime has remained unchanged, and manifestly it leaves room for conditions to be considerably less "humane" than they are officially said to be, especially since a governor's powers of inflicting punishment have not been reduced. For example, a governor can still order what is euphemistically known as "restricted diet No. 1." (bread and water) for a period of three days without authority from a visiting committee. (Incidentally, the reforming legislation of 1823 prohibited gaolers from imposing dietary punishment for longer than 24 hours.) And while some, perhaps the majority of prison governors today consider dietary punishment an undesirable and largely unnecessary sanction, there are evidently a few who continue to place more than a modicum of reliance on it. Thus during 1967 no fewer than 110 instances of "restricted diet" were recorded at Eastchurch, an open prison. Yet at Hull, a maximum security institution for confirmed or dangerous types of criminal, there were only nine.[3]

One must also be wary of the official claim that uniformity of discipline has been renounced in favour of individualization of treatment—that imprisonment is now used as a punishment to fit the criminal instead of the crime. To begin with, this confuses developments outside the system with developments inside it. Du Cane said of the legislation which brought his regime into existence that it had "completely succeeded in its object of promoting . . . the repression of crime." Du Cane and his associates possessed an unquestioning faith, typical of the Victorian era, in both the end they were required to pursue and the means they were given for pursuing it. Yet, to be fair to them, they never believed that their uniform discipline, guaranteed though it might be to offer society a near perfect protection against crime, was an equitable or even sensible way of treating every individual subjected to it. In a book published in 1896,[4] the Rev. J. W. Horsley, who had been chaplain at Clerkenwell prison from the beginning of the Du Cane regime, gave short shrift to criticisms of prison food and conditions generally. Many prisoners, he suggested, were better treated than they deserved to be, and he referred in particular to Oscar Wilde. But he made two major exceptions. "Obviously", he wrote, quoting from one of his early reports to the Commissioners, "nothing can be said in favour of a boy of six years being remanded here and kept in silent and solitary confinement on a charge of vagrancy, nor for a girl of seven being sent here for running an errand for her mother with a bad fourpenny bit; both of which instances have occurred lately." And, again, "You the prison Commissioners speak in your eighth report of the 'manifest injustice of sending to prison people whose mental condition is doubtful.' "

So they had. Du Cane himself wrote: "A large number of prisoners are persons who are absolutely unable, or find it extremely difficult, through mental or physical incapacity, to earn their livelihood, even under favourable circumstances." And he clearly implied that some means other than imprisonment should be found for dealing with them: "There are a great number of prisoners who are below par mentally, all over the kingdom, and I think the thing to do with them, if their weakmindedness leads them to become criminal, is to put them under control permanently. That, perhaps, is more than public opinion would warrant, but that still is my idea of the right thing to do."[5]

But any such idea was beyond the power of Du Cane and his fellow Commissioners to implement. As servants of the Executive, it was their duty, as they saw it, to carry out the will of Parliament, however misdirected the result might be in the case of certain individuals or classes of individual. As a matter of fact, it is inaccurate to describe Du Cane's methods as "punishment to fit the crime." The judiciary supposedly used imprisonment for that purpose, through deciding on the length of sentence a particular offence merited (two years was the maximum). But, apart from the fact that women and children were spared hard labour, and subject to statutory exceptions or exceptions ordered by the courts, the executive used imprisonment as a punishment to fit every misdemeanant without distinction. Though the "gradation" principle, or the system of progressive stages as it was officially called, meant that a prisoner could earn some amelioration of the punishment in return for good behaviour—a mattress to sleep on, for example, instead of a plank—he did not qualify for any such privileges until after he had served three months. Otherwise, one prisoner was in neither a better nor worse position than another. No consideration whatever was given to varying treatment needs or, for that matter, varying deserts. The discipline was inflexible, and one may judge how strictly uniform from the regulation in regard to hard labour on the treadwheel: "Eight thousand six hundred and forty feet at thirty-two feet per minute during a period of six hours, divided into two equal portions, in which the prisoners work by spells of fifteen minutes labour and five minutes resting."

Today penal practice generally is, of course, very much more flexible and diversified than it was in Du Cane's time. But this is chiefly owed to developments that have taken place outside the prison system. "So far as can be seen at present, the most practical and the most hopeful of 'prison reforms' is to keep people out of prison altogether!"[6] That conclusion, which the Webbs reached in 1922, appears to be no less valid half a century later. With some exceptions, juvenile delinquents *are* kept out of prison. The same would be true of mentally handicapped offenders, if Parliament were to match its declared policy with a willingness to spend the money needed to implement it. It is only because of the failure to provide sufficient hospital accommodation and other means of care that thousands of certifiable offenders continue to be abortively dealt with by imprisonment.

It would be inaccurate to describe the "training and treatment" they get as a rigidly standardized thing, if only because it is admitted to be sub-standard in the closed institutions, where short-term sentences are served. But while an individual's chances of receiving a specialized form of "training and treatment" to accord with an assessment of his particular needs are better than nil, they are, as we shall see, still very slim: slimmer certainly than Home Office claims would seem to promise or the judiciary to comprehend. Moreover, the principle of a standardized discipline remains enshrined in the statutory rules which, though they may be much more strictly enforced in some prisons than in others, apply to every prisoner under sentence without distinction. To this extent, there is an even greater attachment to uniformity than there was under the Du Cane regime, and one must conclude that variations in the conditions of imprisonment to suit different categories of prisoner according to degrees of culpability are, and always have been, alien to the very concept of a centrally administered system.

This can best be illustrated by considering the few actual variations that were originally provided for. First and foremost, Parliament recognized that inasmuch as remand prisoners were innocent in law, and might be innocent in fact as well, it would be inequitable to subject them to the same discipline as convicted prisoners or, indeed, to a punitive discipline of any kind. Hence the Home Secretary was required to lay down special rules "regulating their confinement in such manner as to make it as little oppressive as possible, due regard only being had to their safe custody, to the necessity of preserving order and good government in the place where they are confined, and to the physical and moral well being of the prisoners themselves."

But it would have cost a great deal more in both money and administrative convenience to observe the spirit of this instruction than there was readiness to expend, and the "special" rules that were duly promulgated provided no substantial guarantee against the punishment of the innocent. Untried prisoners were given only two absolute rights that convicted prisoners did not possess: the right to refuse to work and the right of access to legal advice for the purpose of preparing their defence. In addition, they could claim certain privileges, but the governor was empowered to withhold these if he saw fit or to withdrawn them for any alleged breach of discipline including, for example, "groundless" complaining, talking to a fellow-prisoner or failure to show the custodial staff sufficient respect. Moreover, the privileges that would spare an untried prisoner hard fare and a hard bed as well as hard labour all cost money to exercise. He might be "allowed" to rent an unusually commodious cell, to furnish it with his own furniture and utensils, to pay someone to relieve him of the "duty" of cleaning it, to purchase books and newspapers, and to order in food and drink from outside. This was to perpetuate one of the traditions of the 18th century common gaol, where comforts could be bought. It also meant that the vast majority of untried prisoners, however "privileged" they might be, suffered all the ordinary rigours of separate confinement, save for a daily visit (Sundays excepted) from friends, which lasted a quarter of an hour and was held under the most humiliating conditions of supervision.

Since our sense of social justice has supposedly become increasingly acute during the present century, one might imagine that the rules governing the treatment of untried prisoners had been radically revised. In fact, they are virtually unaltered, except for the abolition of a major privilege. Under the original (1877) rules, an untried prisoner was allowed, where practical, to "continue working at his own trade or profession." Under the existing rules, this practice is so strictly *dis*allowed that when the late Stephen Ward was on remand at Brixton in 1963 he was refused permission to identify pictures, which were to be used in an exhibition of his work.

No doubt, there are a considerably greater number of untried prisoners than there used to be who can afford to purchase their own food and so on. But the privilege of renting an extra-large and comfortably furnished cell is one that could not possibly be granted to more than a tiny fraction of those who are nominally entitled to it. On the contrary, some untried prisoners are obliged to sleep three to an ordinary cell, and it is broadly speaking true that as conditions for convicted prisoners have improved, so conditions for untried prisoners have, by comparison, worsened. Notably, remand imprisonment, unlike imprisonment under sentence, includes no privilege of association, so that it still amounts to solitary confinement—in a good many cases to being locked up for 23 hours out of every 24. Granted that safe custody has to be guaranteed, and that in certain instances this necessitates tight disciplinary control, one may none the less question whether the central prison administration has any real respect for the presumption of innocence. If it had, one would expect the remand prisons that have been built since the end of the Second World War to be places especially designed for making confinement as "little oppressive as possible"—without cost to those subjected to it. Actually, however, they are places where the fare and accommodation are no better than in an ordinary prison, and where the disciplinary rules are enforced with exceptional severity.[7]

Yet the plight of the untried prisoner arouses a great deal less concern in both Parliament and the Press than it did in Du Cane's time. Presumably, this is because the public has been persuaded that inequitable though it may be in principle to make so small a distinction between punishment of the legally guilty and confinement of the legally innocent, in practice imprisonment has become so beneficent that nobody undergoing it can reasonably complain of anything worse than deprivation of liberty. That would certainly seem to explain why the Government's decision in 1968 to do away with the last vestige of non-uniformity in the treatment of *convicted* prisoners provoked not a murmur of protest.

The Act of 1865 empowered the courts to sentence misdemeanants to imprisonment in the First or Second Division instead of to hard labour. The difference between second division imprisonment and hard labour turned out to be very slight under Du Cane's regime. For women it meant nothing at all; and for men only the advantage of picking oakum or something of the sort in place of crank or treadwheel labour during the first three months of their sentence. But the First Division could be considerably more comfortable than remand imprisonment, if the offender was well enough off to pay for its privileges.

This may be judged from the following account written by W. T. Stead,[8] editor of *The Pall Mall Gazette* who, in 1885, spent two months in the First Division at Holloway: "I had papers, books, letters, flowers, everything that heart could wish. I had my own little kettle, and made my own tea; fresh eggs were sent by some unknown benefactor in Ireland, and everything in the shape of food was ordered from outside. I was allowed my own hearth-rug, and easy chairs as well as a writing desk and cosy little tea-table. I could take exercise when I pleased for as long as I pleased in daytime. I worked at my own trade throughout my term. I got the newspapers every morning at 7.15 and at 10.0 the messenger got his copy. From the Governor, Colonel Millman, to the poor fellow who scrubbed out my room, everyone was as kind as could be. Twice a week my wife brought the sunlight of her presence into the pretty little room, all hung round with Christmas greetings from absent friends. On the day after Christmas the whole family came, and what high jinks we had in the old gaol with all the bairns! The room was rather small for blind man's buff, but we managed it somehow, and never was there a merrier little party than that which met in cell number two on the ground floor of the E Wing of Holloway Gaol."

The 1877 Act, while re-affirming the discretionary powers of the courts in dealing with misdemeanants, made First Division treatment mandatory for two classes of prisoner: those sentenced for contempt of court and those convicted of sedition, seditious libel or seditious conspiracy. The former category largely consisted, as it still does, of debtors (imprisonment for debt had been nominally abolished in 1869); the latter category was included as a result of an amendment proposed by Parnell and his associates, who tried and failed to obtain similar protection for treason-felony offenders.

Du Cane himself never approved of excepting debtors from the ordinary rigours of imprisonment, since he regarded them as "morally nothing less than criminals", and in 1899, after his retirement, Parliament evidently reached approximately the same conclusion. Since then both debtors and others sent to prison for contempt have been distinguished from criminals in name only. Though they are called "civil prisoners", they are entitled to no special comforts, other than being allowed to wear their own clothing, if this is found to be "sufficient and suitable."

In 1910, during his brief tenure of the Home Office, Winston Churchill introduced a rule that authorized (without compelling) the prison commissioners to treat any prisoner as a first class misdemeanant whose offence did not involve "dishonesty, cruelty, indecency or serious violence." Churchill's intervention was inspired by a desire to spare political offenders (notably the campaigners for women's suffrage) the indignities and hardships of routine imprisonment. There would have been no point to the Churchill Rule, as it came to be called, if the courts could have been relied on to use their discretionary powers in favour of non-criminal offenders. But judicial practice in this respect had always been capricious, and while non-criminal offenders were far from invariably sentenced to the First Division, criminal offenders on occasion were. For example, when Colonel Valentine Baker was convicted of indecent assault in 1875, the Judge ordered that his sentence of twelve months should be served in the First Division on the grounds that conditions of ordinary imprisonment, which might be bearable for a man of humbler background, would be "torture" for an officer and gentleman; and though this lenience provoked widespread protest, Baker was evidently as well treated in gaol as Stead was a decade later. By contrast, Stead himself, whose offence was to stage a merely technical abduction of a young girl in order to supply himself with evidence for his campaign against child prostitution, received no such dispensation from the trial Judge, and was only transferred to the First Division after the Home Secretary had invoked the Royal Prerogative of mercy.

The Churchill rule itself was never paid much heed by the Prison Commission, and was forgotten as soon as the suffragette activities ceased. Nevertheless, the principle behind it had the support of socialists during the between-war years, particularly those of them who were former conscientious objectors or had had a taste of imprisonment for some other reason connected with their beliefs and ideals. On 30 June 1932, Mr Rhys Davies told the House of Commons: "We . . . as a Labour Party, would like to see a distinction drawn in this country between those who are generally termed political prisoners and ordinary criminals . . . After all, there is a vast difference between stealing and saying things that are unpopular for the time being. That, in fact, is what most of these 'politicals' are sent to prison for—saying violent things."

But by the time the Labour Party came to power in 1945, it had evidently recovered from its aspiration to draw a distinction between common criminals and "politicals." The Criminal Justice Act of 1948, by abolishing sentences to hard labour and to the First or Second Division, wholly deprived the courts of their power to vary the conditions under which a sentence should be served in accordance with degrees of culpability (or non-culpability). That left no bar to the achievement of total uniformity (and administrative convenience), except the statutory requirement for the special treatment of prisoners convicted of sedition, seditious libel and seditious conspiracy. This was to be quietly got rid of twenty years later, with another Labour Government in power, under a new Criminal Justice Act. It can be argued that the effect of dispensing with it is in itself negligible since many years have passed since anyone convicted of the offences in question has actually been "received" in prison. At the same time, it represents the final death blow to a principle, which one may think should in equity have been given much wider application instead of being destroyed. But one may also note, parenthetically, that Mr Roy Jenkins, the Home Secretary who steered the 1967 Criminal Justice Act through Parliament, regards the Race Relations Act (1965), which precisely threatens people with imprisonment for "saying violent things", as one of the Labour Government's most progressive achievements.

In short, demonstrators guiltless of serious violence and other non-criminal offenders under the Churchill rule now have no chance of escaping routine indignities and discomforts if they are sent to prison. Though the chance they would once have had was to a great extent dependent on money and social influence, at least it existed; and no prisoner, today, tried or untried, could hope to be as considerately treated in gaol as Stead was. Yet one can hardly doubt that this was a considerateness that Stead was entitled to, assuming the necessity of imprisoning him at all. Assuming the same necessity, one may feel equally sure that it is a considerateness to which a campaigner for nuclear disarmament, say, a prisoner of conscience like Miss Pat Arrowsmith, is entitled to —but doesn't get.

To this admittedly small extent, then, imprisonment is now more calculatedly punitive than it was in Du Cane's time. In other ways, it is, of course, much less so, and its primary objective is once again said to be rehabilitation rather than deterrence. But one must none the less question whether this objective is best pursued under a system which was, after all, created to serve the opposite purpose. Indeed, granted the desirability and practicability of a reformative policy, there are, perhaps, reasons to regret that the country's gaols were ever brought under the control of the central government. A year after the transfer took place, a magistrate, John Lloyd, wrote to *The Times*: "Our ancestors deterred offenders from repeating their offences by a summary process, and the State Commissioners may, if permitted, adopt equally efficacious though different means to attain the same end. Hard labour, scanty food, plank beds, and solitary confinement will soon either kill or cure . . . But the Justices treated their prisoners humanely, and this character the State has yet to gain."

Though that last claim was too sweeping to be entirely tenable, another *Times* correspondent[9] quoted figures which suggest that it was not without substance. He said that the cost of maintaining prisoners in the locally administered gaols had varied from £15 11s 1d. a year per head to the "almost inconceivable sum of £150 4s 2d." Under the State Commission, which was as much concerned to run the prisons economically as it was to establish a uniformly deterrent discipline inside them, maintenance costs were tidily fixed at £18 per head. This sum may in turn seem "almost inconceivable" in the light of the current figure, which is over £700, and rising. Yet, even so, the practice of economizing at the expense of rehabilitation (as opposed to security) cannot be said to have been abandoned.

It undoubtedly accounts for the perpetuation of one of the most detested, degrading and notorious features of modern imprisonment—"slopping out." "Of all the criticisms I have received from educated and non-criminal prisoners of their first experience of an English prison, I have been most impressed by those who complained of our sanitary arrangements, particularly during the night and early morning hours." Those words were written by the late Sir Alexander Paterson,[10] a former Prison Commissioner, whose ideas and aspirations were so influential during the between-war years that he is still honoured as a sort of Patron Saint by the Prison Department of the Home Office. Yet nothing has been done to remedy what Paterson admitted to be a continuing defect in what he also claimed was the "best prison system in the world."

"In existing prisons", wrote Lord Mountbatten in his 1966 report on security, "there are no water closets in the cells, and chamber pots are provided. This is unpleasant in any circumstances, but when there are three men in a cell locked up for twelve hours at a time, the lack of proper hygiene is intolerable. I was not surprised to find these arrangements in the 19th century prisons, but I was very disappointed to find the same system had been installed in the new prisons."

Lord Mountbatten might have been even more disappointed, if less surprised, had he realized, which evidently he didn't, that in the best 19th century prisons the cells *were* originally provided with water closets. This was the case at Pentonville, as we have seen, and Pentonville was meant to serve as the structural model for locally built gaols. In a good many instances it did. Indeed, at the time of the Caernarvon committee's inquiry in 1863, the inspectors would not certify a cell as fit for separate confinement unless it was up to the Pentonville standard in point both of size (13′ by 7′) and furnishings. Perry spoke to the committee of "old-fashioned" cells, where pails were used instead of water closets: an arrangement which he called "very offensive, indeed."

But the Committee, and in due course Parliament, wanted separate confinement on the cheap. Jebb, the Surveyor-General, believed that this could be had without doing violence to humane principles in the case of prisoners serving six months or under, especially if they were taken out of their cells during the day for labour in closed compartments of the treadwheel. For them, he said, a cell needed to be no larger than 9′ by 6′, and a water closet, which added £8 to the cost of construction, though a "convenience", was not an absolute necessity.

These recommendations were in effect incorporated in the Act of 1865. In that same year Jebb died. Four years later, Edmund Du Cane, who was already one of the Directors of Convict Prisons, became chairman in succession to Colonel E. G. W. Henderson. Du Cane had an opportunity to demonstrate his capacity for economical prison administration before the Government's take-over of the common gaols, when it was found necessary to add a storey to Pentonville. This work, completed in 1870, was carried out at a total cost of £35 8s 4d. per cell, whereas the original cells had each cost £78 8s 6d. Du Cane attributed the whole saving, which he estimated at "fully £10,000",[11] to his idea of using convict instead of free labour, an idea, incidentally, which he used repeatedly—Wormwood Scrubs was built by convict labour—though the Home Office has recently dusted it off and labelled it first-hand. However, something was also saved through the omission of water closets from the new cells; and this was done without compromising uniformity, because at the same time most of the water closets in the original cells were removed.

It is to Du Cane, presumably, that the disappearance of the cell water-closet, and the introduction of slopping-out as a routine part of prison life, are owed. He supported the claim that water closets in the cells were insanitary, because the prisoners deliberately threw rubbish in them in order to block the drainage. This argument has passed into Home Office lore, and is still relied on as a reason for retaining the arrangements in modern prisons which Lord Mountbatten found so disappointing. But one must doubt whether it is, or ever was, better than a superstition serving as a pretext for penny-pinching. There is certainly no evidence to suggest that inmates of American Federal and State penitentiaries, where water closets in the cells are a standard fixture, make a habit of blocking them up. Moreover, the existence of any such hazard was implicitly denied by Jebb in his evidence before the Caernarvon committee, as the following exchange shows:

> Question: Have you ever contemplated any scheme by which you could dispense with the use of water closets in separate cells?
>
> Answer: There is no doubt that a water closet is the greatest convenience you can have, but it is rather an *expensive one*. [Author's italics]
>
> Question: Is it not sometimes prejudicial to health?
>
> Answer: I think not; if the water closet is properly constructed, and the cell properly ventilated, no inconvenience is experienced . . . We have now had the experience of 20 years at Pentonville *without the slightest inconvenience*. [Author's italics]

To be fair to Du Cane, good sanitation was no less an obsession with him than good order; and it was not for nothing that his critics accused him of turning prisons into "white sepulchres." Since every separate cell was equipped with a bell or method of signal, which the rules required warders to answer promptly, Du Cane may honestly have believed that prisoners were assured of being conducted to a recess at any time of the day or night if they asked to be, and therefore never had to sleep or work with the stink of their own excrement in their nostrils. But unless the accumulated testimony of ex-prisoners is to be discounted, the presence of a bell in a cell is a wholly inadequate compensation for the absence of a water closet as a safeguard against intolerable want of proper hygiene. For, rule or no rule, prison officers are constitutionally averse to being summoned by their captives. They consider it, perhaps understandably, an affront to their dignity and authority. To quote from a comparatively recent report (1963) compiled by a group of nuclear disarmers: "Michael Randle was . . . put on report in Wormwood Scrubs for insisting on calling an officer to let out a fellow-prisoner suffering from diarrhoea who was in great pain."

Du Cane may honestly have believed in the efficacy of all his paper guarantees against gaols being more torturesome places than he intended or declared them to be. Though he realized that the treatment prisoners received could eventually be no better than the treatment they were given by those placed in immediate authority over them, he assumed that the attitude and behaviour of warders could be as strictly regularized as the discipline they were employed to enforce. " . . . It is above all things necessary," he wrote,[12] "that the prisoners should feel that the rules are carried out justly and fairly, that the officers are simply administering the law, and that in case of any abuse of power on the part of an officer, he will be held answerable for it." This objective was achieved, he said, through allowing prisoners the right to lodge complaints either by means of appeal to the governor, the visiting committee, the commissioners or by petition to the Home Secretary.

But it was one thing for a prisoner to have the right to accuse a warder of misbehaviour, and quite another for him to feel free to exercise it. As has been said, governors were virtually bound to side with their officers. The prisoner knew this very well. He also knew that to make a charge which he failed to substantiate would render him liable both to legal punishment for groundless complaining and (conceivably) illegal vengeance for putting a warder's career in jeopardy.

The fact is that under a centralized system the control is too remote, too impersonal and essentially too detached to prevent irregularities. If Du Cane was honestly persuaded that the treatment of every prisoner was invariably as "humane" as the directives issued from his headquarters insisted that it must be, it was none the less impossible for him to know what actually went on in all the prisons for which he was responsible

—or, indeed, in any of them. Perhaps, he suspected this himself, for he was remarkably unwilling to put his official assurances to the test of unofficial investigation. What he didn't know himself, he took very good care that nobody else should find out. The prison system was an obsessively secretive system during his regime, and though it is less so today, it is still more so than one can readily believe is justified on the grounds of security alone. Journalists and other independent observers are no longer barred from prisons, as they were by Du Cane. But such access as they are allowed doesn't amount to anything approaching freedom of inspection. Since visits have to be authorized by the Home Office, and are invariably prearranged, whatever may be thought unwise to reveal can very easily be concealed. Moreover, the Official Secrets Act can be (and has been) invoked against talkative staff members.[13]

By contrast, secretiveness was wholly uncharacteristic of the way in which some of the Justices used to run their gaols. "The House of Correction at Preston has acquired a reputation among prisons", Hepworth Dickson wrote[14] in 1850. "Foreigners of distinction visit it from all parts of the continent. Englishmen of all ranks think it worth an inspection. It is open to all comers. In the pages of its visitor's book may be seen the superscription of the Russian or German prince and the Yorkshire artisan, the French marquis and the Preston hand-loom weaver, the minister of state, the journalist, the magistrate and the peasant. This is as it should be in all prisons. Every penal institution should be open to the public. There ought to be no secrets in such places. The treatment should be severe, but open to the control of general manners and opinion."

Du Cane's policy of closing the prisons to Press and Public inevitably provoked suspicions, at least among the more liberally-minded members of society, that the treatment was in fact severer than "general manners and opinion" would consider tolerable. But it may be observed that the contrary policy served a positive purpose as well as the negative one of allaying such suspicions. Clearly, the Preston gaol was regarded by its administrators as a local achievement to be shown off with pride, like a church or a library. Nor was this attitude unjustified by the standards of the time. For the Preston gaol, it will be recalled, was a factory prison; and so much confidence had been built up in the effectiveness of the training it provided (moral and industrial) that many of its inmates, unlike the inmates of most other gaols who faced permanent social ostracism, could be certain of finding employment on their release.

This local pride in the accomplishments of a particular prison regime, where it existed, was bound to disappear under the centralized system, and has not, so far as one can tell, been replaced by a comparable national pride in the prison system or any part of it. Who, after all, is there to enlist such interest? Who is in a position to influence public opinion as the Justices, progressive or reactionary, were in a position to influence community opinion? Home Secretaries come and go—often at very rapid intervals. Few of them are committed to any views on penal matters before they take office and most of them seem to spend their time *in* office absorbing the doctrines of their faceless civil servants. Under these circumstances, policy, though it may be persistently forward-looking, can command little or no popular support or understanding, and for that reason is as persistently ahead of practice. If the public were persuaded to share official faith in the possibility of rehabilitating prisoners, one may feel sure there would soon be an end to those 19th century buildings which Whitehall repeatedly complains are so unsuited to "modern" training methods. But, as it is, the average citizen doesn't seem to care what prison buildings are in use, or how they are run, provided the inmates aren't allowed to escape from them; and while he has heard of places like Pentonville and Wormwood Scrubs, one may doubt if he could name any of the supposedly superior institutions built during the past decade or single out one which he considers especially admirable.

There might, it is true, be many appallingly backward gaols, if prison administration had remained under local government control. But the record implies that there might also be at least a few remarkably advanced ones. At the time of writing (October, 1969) a new prison (Codingley), geared to full industrial employment, where a select number of prisoners can earn the glittering sum of £2 a week, has recently been opened. The venture is described by the Home Secretary as "not just a step forward, but a leap into the future."[15] Remembering the factory prisons of the mid-19th century, such as Preston and Wakefield, it might more accurately be described as half a leap back into the past.

Here, however, one must once again be careful to avoid confusion. The Government's new factory prison is presumably intended as a training centre for men serving comparatively long sentences; for men, that is to say, who prior to 1948, when the prison system was formally made one and indivisible, would have been sentenced to penal servitude. The old locally administered factory prisons, on the other hand, like the rest of the common gaols, were largely used for people serving short sentences; and, to repeat a point, the Caernarvon committee's view that "short imprisonments" must be made primarily deterrent, if they were to be worth retaining at all, was undoubtedly logical.

All that Du Cane relied on to justify his claim of a "reformative" discipline in ordinary prisons (apart from the "admonishments" that the chaplains were employed to deliver to every inmate on reception and at irregular intervals thereafter) was the system of progressive stages—a system designed, as he put it, to appeal "to a prisoner's better nature by setting before him the advantages of good conduct and industry." "Commencing with severe penal labour—hard fare and a hard bed—he can gradually advance to more interesting employment, somewhat more material comfort, full use of library books, privilege of communication by letter and word with his friends, finally, the advantage of a moderate sum of money to start again on his discharge, so that he may not have the temptations or the excuse that want of means might afford for falling again into crime."[16]

Even assuming that such a system possessed any potential reformative influence, it was in practice fraudulent for the simple reason, as the Webbs have pointed out, that the great majority of prisoners, however industrious and well behaved they might be, were in prison for too brief a time to advance from the lowest stage. Nor, as a matter of fact, were the advantages of being in the highest stage overwhelming. For example, the privilege of "communication by letter and word", meant, at its best, a letter and visit once every three months.

In short, for all the verbal camouflage, the discipline under the Du Cane regime was purely terroristic. It was a planned attempt to make deterrent sense of short-term imprisonment at a moment when Parliament realized that no other sort of sense could possibly be made of it. Yet, ironically, this process was not completed, until deterrence had also been adopted as the overriding, if not the whole aim of penal servitude, with results that made nonsense of long-term imprisonment or at any rate defeated its historical raison d'être.

8

PENAL SERVITUDE

IN THE SAME year (1863) that the Caernarvon Committee had produced their blueprint for giving ordinary prisoners more hell, a Royal Commission[1] decided that convicts were not being given hell enough. Penal servitude, they reported, whether it entailed transportation to Western Australia (as it still could) or was served at home, was not "sufficiently dreaded."

There were no apparent grounds for this conclusion, other than the sudden plague of robberies with violence in the Metropolis to which reference has already been made. In general, the crime rate had declined during the decade since penal servitude had been introduced. Only 1,056 of the 16,964 licences granted under the ticket-of-leave scheme had been revoked, and unless these figures gave a misleading impression, which they may have done, they were more satisfactory than anyone had a right to expect.[2] For a ticket-of-leave was automatically granted to a convict after he had served a fixed portion of his sentence, provided he had earned the requisite number of marks that were awarded for good conduct and industry. His ability or willingness to earn an honest living in freedom was irrelevant.

This contravened one of the principles upon which our present parole plan is supposedly based, and even at the time was considered objectionable by some prison governors. "As a rule", one of them told the Commissioners, "the prisoners who are the most dangerous are the best conducted while in prison. This makes all marks for mere good conduct in the observance of rules etc., and all professions of amendment, perfectly fallacious as indicating their real state."

Equally, the scheme included no provision for what is now known as after-care—or less than none. Today, a prisoner released on licence is placed under the tutelage of a probation officer, and theoretically, therefore, has a better chance of making good than if he were to be discharged after serving his sentence in full, when very much more likely than not he has nobody but himself to depend on. By contrast, the ticket-of-leave man was placed under police supervision, with results that made it difficult if not impossible for him to conceal his identity, and hence to obtain or keep a job. The point was not to help him go straight, but to make sure of his prompt apprehension and return to prison if he stayed crooked.

While the Commission, with one dissentient, were strongly in favour of retaining the ticket-of-leave scheme, they were critical of the way in which it was being operated. Licences, they held, were granted too easily and too soon, and at the same time were not readily enough revoked, with results that undermined the deterrent effectiveness of the punishment. The remedy, they believed, would be to increase the minimum sentence permissible from three years to seven years, to make licences more difficult to obtain, and to tighten the controls over licence-holders.

The dissenting member of the Commission was Lord Chief Justice Cockburn, who, loyal to his calling, wanted less not more interference with the judicial power of assessing the measure of punishment called for in each individual case. He was plainly resentful, too, of the implication that Judges had failed to pass stiff enough sentences. The lenience of sentence, he wrote, "has arisen out of the more humane and merciful disposition of men's minds in modern times, whereby punishments inflicted without scruple in former days would now be deemed cruel and inhuman. Neither does it appear reasonable to seek in this increased leniency a cause of the sudden increase in crime, seeing that under the law thus administered crime had materially decreased, while population was steadily increasing."

The last part of that argument was clearly valid. But Cockburn was not content to rest his case on it. Instead, he went on to contradict it with a declaration that penal servitude was, in fact, too little dreaded as a result of a mistakenly indulgent discipline, and he objected in particular to the ticket-of-leave scheme as an example of this misplaced lenience. "The reformation of the offender is in the highest degree speculative and uncertain", he wrote, "and its permanency, in the face of renewed temptation, exceedingly precarious. On the other hand, the impression produced by suffering, inflicted as the punishment for crime, and the fear of its repetition, are far more likely to be lasting, and much more calculated to counteract the tendency to renewal of criminal habits. It is on the assumption that punishment will have the effect of deterring from crime that its infliction can alone be justified, its proper and legitimate objective being not to avenge crime but to prevent it."

One may note there, incidentally, a total repudiation of retributive theory. But Cockburn's main concern was to attack the reformative theory in which, whether he realized it or not, penal servitude or long-term imprisonment was rooted. "It may well be doubted whether, in recent times, the humane and praiseworthy desire to reform and restore the fallen criminal may not have produced too great a tendency to forget that the protection of society should be the first consideration of the lawgiver . . . Moderate labour, ample diet, substantial gratuities, with the remission of a fixed part of the sentence, are hardly calculated to produce on the mind of the criminal that salutory dread of the recurrence of the punishment that may be the means of deterring him . . . It need no longer surprise us that instances have occurred of persons in destitute circumstances actually committing offences for the purpose of being condemned to penal servitude with a view of thereby improving their condition."

Reactionary though Cockburn's arguments may seem, the result in the end would have been less reactionary, and certainly more humane, if Parliament had preferred his dissent to the majority report and simply abolished remission of sentence. For his fellow-Commissioners were as deterrent-minded as he was himself, and their only proposal in regard to the ticket-of-leave scheme that had a reformative aim was the only one which Parliament rejected. This, however, was remarkably ahead of its time. The Commissioners recommended that the supervisory powers should be transferred from the police to a special body of men trained and appointed by the Directors of Convict Prisons. For they had been most favourably impressed by the evidence of a dedicated social worker, named Philip Organ, who was acting under the auspices of the separately administered Irish system, as a kind of forerunner of the modern probation and parole officer.

In Ireland, selected convicts served the last year of their sentences in so-called "intermediate prisons." These may be described as crude prototypes of our existing open prisons, though in one respect they were more advanced, for both prisoners and prison officers wore plain clothes. There were no cells. The convicts slept together in wooden huts, and by day worked as farm-hands. They received a gratuity of 2/– a week, out of which they were allowed to spend 6d on the purchase of luxuries, such as tobacco and extra food for themselves, while the rest was held until their discharge. Organ was attached to the intermediate prison at Lusk, near Dublin. His official title was "lecturer", but his job only began with giving the prisoners regular evening lectures. He helped to find them employment when they were released on licence, continued to serve as their counsellor, and had an impressive record of success in keeping them out of trouble, though he cooperated fully with the police in bringing them to book if they relapsed. The thing that may have made the strongest appeal to the Commissioners about Organ's work was his policy of persuading his charges to emigrate as soon as they were free to do so, since this amounted to transportation on the cheap. Nevertheless, if their proposal for adopting a similar plan in England had been accepted, it might have changed the course of penal history.

It was turned down on the grounds that Organ's achievements were entirely owed to his own unique personal qualities. Parliament showed itself to be in no mood for trifling with deterrent principles, and the ticket-of-leave scheme was retained at the price, as an ex-convict was later to observe, of turning it into a mere cruelty. (Today, incidentally, a similar charge is being levelled against the parole plan by a good many prisoners.)[3] An Act of 1864 raised the minimum sentence from three to five years for offenders who had not previously suffered penal servitude and to seven years for those who had. The same Act provided for tighter police control of convicts released on licence, and made the conditions under which licences were held far more stringent; a man could be returned to prison if he had no visible means of support or was so much as suspected by the police of leading an "idle or dishonest life." Plainly, Parliament had lost all faith in penal servitude as a training for freedom. Seven years later, this was to become plainer still when, under the Prevention of Crimes Act, all ex-convicts, who had served more than one term of penal servitude, were required to report regularly to the police for seven years after the completion of their sentence in full, on pain of a year's imprisonment with hard labour. So much, it may be remarked parenthetically, for the fraudulent pretence that a prison sentence is, or ever has been, a finite debt which society exacts from the criminal.

Meanwhile, new administrative rules were introduced to restrict the issue of tickets-of-leave. The maximum remission obtainable was cut from one third to one quarter of the longest sentences. Marks ceased to be automatically awarded for good conduct. Though they might be forfeited for bad conduct, they could only be earned for industriousness. This meant that unless a man was assigned to heavy or skilled labour, it was impossible for him, however willing, to earn a sufficient number of marks to qualify for full remission, and if he was physically or mentally handicapped he would unlikely be able to qualify for any remission at all. Moreover, the minimum period before a man serving a life sentence could expect a review of his case by the Home Secretary, and a release on licence through the exercise of the Royal Prerogative of Mercy, was extended from 12 to 20 years.

It may be wondered why Parliament didn't do as Cockburn wished, and abolish remission of sentence, rather than make such a mockery of its original purpose. The answer is that the prison administrators were convinced of its necessity as an "incentive to industry" or, less euphemistically, as a security device. And no doubt they were right, for the implementation of the Commission's subsidiary proposals for making penal servitude sufficiently dreaded might otherwise have led to mass riots in the convict prisons.

These subsidiary proposals, to which Cockburn subscribed,

were concerned with toughening the discipline. Among the more savage of them was one that called for a heavier type of cat to be used in the infliction of corporal punishment and for the permissible number of strokes, which were still limited to two dozen under the extant Home Office rules for the Hulks, to be increased to four dozen. The proposal was evidently inspired by I. W. Gambier, one of the directors of Convict Prisons, who had formerly been governor of Millbank. "You think," Gambier was asked in the course of his evidence, "that corporal punishment has very small deterring effects?"

"None at all," he replied.

"You think it ought to be inflicted with more severity?"

"Undoubtedly."

"You think there should be the power of inflicting fifty lashes with a naval cat?"

"I do—if you flog at all."

Assuming Gambier was right—and he spoke from experience—here is yet another instance of how the courage of deterrent theory dwindles, as civilization marches on. Flogging, says a former prison chaplain, the Rev. B. P. H. Ball, in a book published not so long ago (1959),[4] "can and does act as a deterrent, and is therefore not incompatible with a Christian point of view." But one may feel sure that the most passionately convinced of our contemporary proponents of corporal punishment would hesitate to call fifty lashes with a naval cat compatible with a Christian point of view, even if they were to be persuaded that nothing less torturous would serve a deterrent purpose.

On the other hand, the restoration of flogging in some form, unlike that of the stocks, say, is at present still conceivable. Indeed, the demand for it might become irresistible in the event of widespread outbreaks of violence against prison officers; and that in turn is a possibility which has been encouraged by the current judicial fashion of passing excessively long sentences[5] and the emphasis on security which these are thought to demand. History seems to show that advances towards a more liberal penal system are invariably followed by retreats, although the distance backwards is limited by what in the meanwhile have come to be accepted as impassable "humane" or "civilized" boundaries.

The retreat signalled by the Royal Commission of 1863 was as headlong as public opinion would allow it to be, and, like the retreat which Mountbatten was to signal just over a century later, it was irrationally inspired. Yet the arguments in favour of it were not implausible, for to say that penal servitude owed its existence to the idea that criminals were reformable is not to say that as an instrument of reform it was ever reliable. On the contrary, it was manifestly self-defeating, for, as has already been pointed out, if it were true that men could be fitted for freedom during a preliminary period of separate confinement, they were bound to be unfitted for it again during the much longer period of associated labour. Jebb managed to deceive himself over this. But the Rev. Ambrose Sherwin, one of the Pentonville chaplains, never did. As late as 1870,[6] by which time the original point of the separate system had all but been forgotten, he wrote nostalgically in his report to the Directors of Convict Prisons: "I would beg leave to hazard an opinion that reformation is never promoted in the slightest degree by the association of criminals at any stage of their imprisonment. Seventy five per cent of those sentenced to penal servitude from five to twenty-five years might be so disposed of in strictly separate confinement of no longer than two years that they would be restored to society in a condition vastly more favourable for the community than can be expected by a sojourn of years in regions of congregated crime."

Given the fact, then, that penal servitude was, at best, an unreliable instrument of reform, there was sense in arguing that it ought to be made at least as deterrent as ordinary imprisonment, considering that it existed to prevent more serious types of crime. This was what Cockburn had in mind when he spoke of "ample diet" and so on, for it was true that penal servitude, length of sentence apart, was a less dreadful punishment than imprisonment with hard labour—at least nominally. The convict was spared the crank and the treadwheel; and though he was given less to eat during his preliminary nine months in separate confinement than he was after he had graduated to a public works prison, he was not, like the ordinary prisoner, systematically starved at the outset of his sentence. At Chatham, the basic diet consisted of 12 ounces of bread and a pint of gruel for breakfast; six ounces of bread, a pound and a fifth of potatoes, and six ounces of boneless meat and three pints of soup, for dinner; nine ounces of bread and a pint of oatmeal gruel for supper. Under the system of progressive stages, which was already in operation at Chatham and the other public works prisons, a convict who had served two years with a clean enough record was entitled to a mug of tea and two ounces of cheese for his supper instead of gruel, and also to half a pint of beer on Sundays; after three years he was entitled to a dumpling with his Thursday dinner.

If one excepts the beer allowance, which is unheard of in prisons today, it may seem extraordinary that anybody in his right mind could have called such a diet "ample." But "ample" it no doubt was by comparison not only with the approved diet for the common gaols, but, more importantly, with the diet which the mass of the country's paupers and under-paid labourers had to subsist on. The case for keeping the dietary in prisons as close as possible to the starvation level was that otherwise criminals would be better fed than the honest poor, and obviously there was a moral as well as a deterrent point to the argument. Merry of Reading in his evidence before the Caernarvon Committee had protested against giving prisoners beef when free labourers could only afford bacon; and in a reference to the Pentonville diet, he described ¾ of an ounce of molasses to sweeten cocoa as "wicked" and a "little milk" in gruel as "monstrous."

Cockburn and his fellow Commissioners didn't get quite everything they had asked for in the way of toughening the discipline—the naval cat was excluded and the permissible number of lashes raised to only three dozen, not four—but in time they got a great deal. Within ten years the Rule of Silence had been introduced into all the public works prisons as the next best thing to perpetual separate confinement; convicts were forbidden to talk to one another at labour and at exercise were required to walk in single file instead of, as previously, in groups of two or three. Dietary privileges were immediately abolished[7]—a lowered standard diet was established for convicts in all stages—and the purchase of tobacco or any other luxury was outlawed. Gratuities were drastically reduced, so that whereas it had formerly been possible for a long-term convict to accumulate £15 or more before his discharge,[8] the most he could now expect to be paid was £3 (or £6 if he was admitted to a "Special Class" during the last year of his sentence and agreed to place himself under the care of the Prisoners Aid Society).

In short, there was an end put to the "many comforts" of penal servitude, which Jebb had believed necessary, if men were not to be "brutalized" and "rendered dangerous" for the rest of their lives, but which in Du Cane's words had "led to a comparison favourable to a dishonest instead of an honest career." "Public opinion", Du Cane was to write,[9] "therefore demanded that prisoners should have only the barest necessaries in the way of food, and just sufficient money on discharge to enable them to maintain themselves while seeking employment, purchasing tools, etc. . . . and . . . this sound principle . . . adopted by a Royal Commission . . . in 1863 . . . has been carried out."

It is true that Du Cane and his associates none the less continued to credit penal servitude with a "reformatory" objective and maintained that the discipline was designed to achieve it. Yet the one constructive proposal which the Commission had made to that end was ignored. This was a proposal for categorizing prisoners, for separating the lesser from the greater criminals, and in particular for holding the most dangerous among them in a purpose-built prison under conditions of exceptional severity. Presumably, the idea was found to be too expensive and administratively inconvenient for adoption. Nominally, the Silence Rule was relied on to prevent contamination, even though it was known to be an ineffective safeguard. There was no attempt at classifying prisoners, apart from a "disposal" system which was used to distinguish, not between the more and the less corrupted, but between the stronger and the weaker.

A large number of convicts were, in fact, regarded as "invalids"; for example, in 1867, no fewer than 443 out of the 1,237 prisoners who had served their probationary period of separate confinement at Millbank, were "disposed of" in one or other of the so-called invalid prisons at Dartmoor and Woking, where the labour was "light." Among this invalid population were the lunatics and the imbeciles (psychotics and mental defectives in modern parlance), who might be excused labour altogether, if they were found to be manifestly incapable of performing the simplest task. But while the outright lunatics were given "paints" or some other child's pastime to keep them quiet and were theoretically immune from punishment, no "half wit" was considered too half witted to be disciplined by the standard means.

"When guilty of violence," the Medical Officer at Woking stated in his annual report for 1869,[10] "they may talk rationally and appear perfectly conscious that they have done wrong. Still, the power of controlling their vicious dispositions appears to a great extent wanting . . . The punishment of bread and water, as well as reduced diet, has not the usual deterring effect. On the contrary, the depressing measures are not only attended with little permanent benefit in the case of imbeciles guilty of misconduct, but as they impair the bodily health the mind is also likely to become more affected . . . Some of the habitual criminals appear closely allied to the imbecile class, and their insubordinate and destructive propensities are not always to be accounted for; in some instances, the delicate state of their health precludes the possibility of any adequate punishment and they are sufficiently cunning to take advantage of it; but others more robust display the same incorrigible spirit without any apparent motive, and quite regardless of punishment . . . There is generally something in the countenance of these men expressive of their sullen determined dispositions, and their previous convictions tend to prove them incapable of restraining their evil passions when at liberty." One may deduce from that that the madder a prisoner was, and hence the more likely to make a nuisance of himself, the worse he was treated.

If the Directors of Convict Prisons seriously believed in the reformatory purpose of the discipline they were required to enforce, one may doubt whether anybody else concerned with the administration of justice, made better than a pretence of so doing. Certainly, the discipline was no longer regarded as being any more reformative or lenient than the discipline of ordinary imprisonment, and the yawning gap that had developed between the maximum prison sentence of two years (which rarely meant more than 18 months) and the minimum sentence of five years' penal servitude often troubled the judicial conscience, since the difference in gravity between a crime punishable by penal servitude and one punishable by imprisonment might be very slight. Moreover, the object of a number of official investigations, which took place after Parliament had acted on the recommendations of the 1863 Commission, was not to assure the public that the discipline was reformatory, but to still intermittent fears that it had ceased to be "humane."

The first of these inquiries followed published charges in 1867 that certain of the Irish treason-felony offenders, serving sentences at Portland and Woking, had been worse treated than ordinary convicts (though they were supposedly entitled to better treatment); it was conducted by a Surgeon and a Magistrate, acting under the authority of the Home Secretary.[11] They didn't trouble to examine any witnesses, but were content to rely on their personal observations, and they eventually produced a report that positively gleamed with whitewash. Though they admitted that during very heavy storms, the rain might leak through the roof at Portland and wet the occupants of the cells, this was the only cause for complaint they discovered, and they didn't consider it of any real moment. "We were conducted into every hole and corner of the establishment," they wrote, "and we found it far more perfect in all its arrangements than we could have believed it possible that such an institution could be . . . Each cell had its little supply of tin pans, mugs etc., each had its assortment of devotional books as well as others of a lighter character, such as Goldsmith's works." Yet even so—even after painting this halcyon picture—they concluded: "Penal servitude is a terrible punishment. It is intended to be so, and so it is."

How terrible it was on paper may be judged from the unvarying daily routine in a public works prison—week after week, month after month, year after year:

5.30 a.m.	Rise, wash, dress, make bed, clean out cell
5.50	Cells searched
6.10	Breakfast
7.15	Slopping out
7.20	File in for chapel

7.35	Labour parade
11.10	Recall from labour and return to cells
11.30	Dinner
12.55 p.m.	Labour parade
4.15	(5.15 during summer months) Recall from labour
4.35	Supper
5.05	Schooling (During Jebb's regime this had occupied a whole half day in lieu of labour), letter-writing (a prisoner in the third or lowest stage was entitled to write and receive a letter once every six months, in the second stage once every four months, and in the first stage once every three months), search (prisoners were searched naked once a week and sometimes more often) and slops
6.50	Lock-up
7.55	Lights out

There was no labour on Saturday afternoons, which were reserved for haircuts and additional searches. Prisoners spent the whole of Sundays alone in their cells, except for two chapel services and exercise periods. (One half hour period for the least privileged, three half hour periods for the most.)

But terrible though the punishment was intended to be in theory, it was a great deal more terrible in practice, due to the means, both legal and extra-legal, that were used for enforcing it. Since the departmental report of 1867 failed to stifle disquiet about the treatment of Treason-Felony offenders, the Government was obliged, three years later, to appoint a Royal Commission[12] under the chairmanship of Lord Devon to conduct a full scale inquiry, and this afforded the Irish convicts an opportunity not only to voice their particular complaints, but to give evidence about the discipline in general.

"I would state some of the things," one of them (Denis Mulcahy) said, "which are incidental to the conditions of prisoners undergoing penal servitude: broken limbs; loss of the use of limbs; death by accident or design; six months penal class diet and punishment cells, in addition to bread and water; six months leg bolted and loaded with 14 lbs weight of an iron chain fastened to the leg and suspended from the loin, to be worn day and night, in summer and in winter, in the prison or at labour, no matter what the labour may be; to have the hands manacled behind the back for 35 consecutive days; to be flogged to death with the cat o'nine tails as in the case of convict Wilkinson at Portland; to be compelled to labour until your clothes were wet through on your back; to continue to work in them until they dried again, and to have to sleep in them when you left off labour . . . To be confined in a cell, through the roof of which the water poured down on your bed when you slept in it at night; to suffer from ascarides, which I believe is owing to the quality of the food; to ignore disease until fully developed; to neglect it when active; to be sent to the bleak, cold, humid climate of Dartmoor in consumption; to be taken out of bed in the last stage of consumption, discharged to the prison, punished with penal class diet in penal cells, and die within two months or nine weeks after the infliction of such punishment. To be driven mad by the punishment of the prison director—to be driven to attempt suicide, to commit suicide."

Testimony of this sort could be, and in fact was, rejected as unjustifiable generalization, but its particulars were none the less true. Undeniably, for instance, one of the Treason-Felony prisoners had been kept in handcuffs for 35 days on end, with his hands locked behind his back, except at meal-times. This, as the Devon Commission felt bound to note, was done in violation of the Rules, which specified that handcuffs and other methods of restraint, such as cross irons, were never to be used for purposes of punishment, but only if and when they were found to be necessary *as* restraint.[13] The excuse given in this case was that while the offence—throwing the contents of a chamber pot at the governor—would normally have been punished by flogging, there was a prohibition against the flogging of political offenders.

These Irish patriots were no doubt natural rebels against the discipline—men, who, as one member of the Commission (Dr Lyons) put it, "considered that their sufferings ennobled their acts." Quite possibly, they set out to provoke the warders into hitting out with their staffs (or truncheons), which were supposedly carried for self-defence only. But the warders were evidently too easily provoked, especially by the *involuntary* rebels against discipline, the men who had little or no control over their own conduct. "I am of the opinion," Dr Lyons wrote, "that more frequent and strict supervision of warders in charge of refractory or imbecile prisoners is required to prevent the possibility of unnecessary force or violence being employed whenever resistance is offered by a convict in authority over him."

But Dr Lyons spoke for himself alone. The rest of the Commission, in defiance of the evidence to the contrary, were willing to accept official assurances that if a warder used unnecessary violence—something which rarely, if ever, happened—he faced instant dismissal. "Neither in the prison system itself", they concluded, "nor in its ordinary operation, due regard being had to the fact that convict prisons are intended to be places of penal discipline, did we observe anything to justify charges of unnecessary severity or harshness. . . ."

Still, the Commission's report as a whole was not quite so white a white-wash as that conclusion would suggest. For instance, though they had "tasted the soup in several prisons and found it good", they apparently entertained a suspicion that it might not be above criticism on occasions when they weren't there to taste it. "With a view to preclude all possible grounds of complaint on the score of bad quality, we recommend that a more frequent and direct supervision of the meat and other articles of diet should form part of the duties of Medical Officers."

They also expressed some doubt about the sanitary arrangements. "The plan of having a water-closet in each cell is open to much objection," they said, which indeed it was, considering how minute the cells were in the public works prisons—at Portland only 7′ by 4′—and how poorly ventilated. "But", they continued, "it is obvious that in the absence of this convenience, facilities of access to closets in the wards should be freely granted; and this we fear is not always secured by the actual management of convict prisons." In fact, it was a punishable offence for a prisoner to use his pail or chamber pot to defecate, unless he could satisfy the Medical Officer that he was suffering from diarrhoea or some kindred complaint.

Supposedly, he was able to call a warder if he needed to visit the water-closet by pushing his broom through the aperture at the bottom of his cell door. But, as has previously been said, warders disliked responding to summonses of this kind, and were apt to keep a prisoner waiting until his discomfort became unbearable, and he was forced to commit the punishable offence of defecating in his pail.

Finally, the Commission found that in a number of specific instances treason-felony convicts had been unjustly punished as a result of false charges brought against them, and they deplored "the habitual exclusion of one prisoner's testimony in corroboration of a statement made by another, whether on the occasion of a complaint made by a prisoner against an officer, or a report made by an officer against a prisoner."

But none of these objections was or could be met—least of all the last of them. Eight years later, the governor of the convict prison at Chatham, Major J. C. Farquarson, stated unblushingly: "I hear what the complainant has to say, but I shut out corroborative evidence. I should never take a prisoner's word against a warder's. You could never carry on discipline if you did so. I always show I take the warder's part, but if I'm at all doubtful I only admonish him."

Major Farquarson was giving evidence before another Royal Commission[14]—this one appointed, under the chairmanship of the Earl of Kimberley, to inquire into the "working of the Penal Servitude Acts." No doubt he spoke more honestly than his directors wished him to, for to admit to the impossibility of conducting a fair hearing of an issue between a prisoner and a prison officer, and to the inevitability of injustices, was to expose an official hypocrisy. Still, the new Commissioners were assured that since governors (Major Farquarson included) invariably caused "inquiries" to be made of prisoners who wished to give evidence in support of another prisoner, it need not worry them that corroborative testimony might be formally excluded; and in fact they decided not to worry.

In 1879, they reported that penal servitude was now "sufficiently dreaded" as a result of "longer sentences, sparer diet, and a generally more strict enforcement of work and discipline." They also found the punishment to be "free of serious abuses", though, like their predecessors, they had a few reservations. "The Commissioners of 1870," they wrote, "expressed a fear that facilities to the closets in the wards were not always secured to the convicts. We were assured by the officers that ample facilities are given, but from personal inquiries which we made of some of the prisoners at Pentonville we are not quite satisfied that there is no ground for complaint in that respect; and we therefore again draw attention to the subject." They drew attention to some new matters as well. For example, they had learned that at Millbank the prisoners in solitary confinement were searched naked twice a week, and it "occurred" to them that this was carrying security requirements a bit far; a once weekly search, they suggested, would be enough.

But in general they were not inclined to regard any part of the punishment that the rules permitted as being in itself over-punitive. Thus they heard of the case of four Dartmoor convicts who had been punished, on the authority of the directors, with three dozen lashes, twenty-eight days bread-and-water, and six months in cross irons. The men had been members of an outside working party, and according to their own story their only offence had been to cry "shame" when an officer hit an 18-year-old youth, named Murphy, on the head with the butt end of his rifle and felled him to the ground. According to the official version, the men had been engaged in a conspiracy. They had persuaded Murphy to attack the officer, and when the officer closed with the youth, they had "threatened him with their rakes." Since the Commissioners accepted this official explanation, they found nothing excessive in the punishment that followed.

At the same time, they heard a great deal of evidence which, had they chosen to accept it, would have obliged them to conclude that the rules were being breached. This evidence came largely, though not exclusively, from seven ex-convicts. One of them was Michael Davitt, the Irish leader (later a Member of Parliament); the others had served sentences for ordinary crimes, and with the exception of a certain Henry Harcourt, appeared anonymously under the initials A.B., C.D., E.F., G.H. and I.K.

Harcourt was the only one of these witnesses who appeared

to speak out of mere embitterment; he was possibly a paranoiac. Davitt could have had a political motive for telling falsehoods, though he was to repeat the same evidence 16 years later when his sole concern was to advocate penal reform. The others, remarkably, had no apparent bias against the deterrent principles of the system. On the contrary, two of them, G.H. and I.K., believed that it was a mistake to make the discipline progressively less tough during a man's sentence, because this meant that by the time a criminal was released, and returned to his former companions, he was likely to have forgotten the salutary lesson that had been taught him in the beginning. "The people whose imagination he should impress with the terrors of punishment", said G.H., "are exactly the people whose minds are very differently impressed now." By the same token, both these witnesses suggested that when corporal punishment was ordered by the courts in addition to a term of penal servitude, the prisoner should be flogged not only at the beginning of his sentence, but at regular intervals throughout it, or at any rate near the end.

This went further than even one of the judicial witnesses, Lord Justice Bramwell, was prepared to go. "I doubt very much whether the public would permit of it", he said. "And I doubt very much whether I do not sympathize with the objection, because although it might possibly be the best thing for society if one could bring oneself to do it, yet when we think that the man every day of his life must remember that he has at a certain definite time to undergo the same misery he has undergone before, it would be a cruel punishment."

On balance, then, the testimony of the ex-convicts could not reasonably be dismissed as special pleading. While they did not all of them make the same complaints, in combination their charges against the system were the *kind* of charges that had been made before and have been repeatedly made since by ex-prisoners. They may be enumerated as follows:

1. Insanitary conditions: On his arrival at Dartmoor, Davitt had been placed in a penal cell, not as a punishment, but allegedly for his own protection. However, he was obliged to use the bedclothes of the previous occupant, which were soiled with excrement. Later, after he had complained of his inability

to sleep due to the persistent bangings and screamings of the imbeciles undergoing punishment in the penal block, he was put in a cell next door to two ward closets, which were continually left uncovered and piled high with human dung.

Davitt and another witness alleged that while convicts had a bath once a fortnight, a detail of seven or eight men were each required to use the same bathwater, because the warders would not trouble to change it.

2. Diet: Five of the witnesses complained of the paucity of the diet, even allowing for its deliberately penal character. "At Chattenden," C.D. said, "it was so deficient in fat that nearly all the prisoners ate as much of their candles as they could. I knew several prisoners who also drank the oil allowed for oiling their boots." The witnesses alleged that the regulation food, the meat in particular, was frequently putrid and unfit for human consumption; furthermore, that much of it was spirited away in the kitchens, so that prisoners were habitually served with less than their due allowance.

3. Illicit humiliations: Three of the witnesses testified that they had been stripped and searched in front of other prisoners, though this was expressly forbidden by the rules.

4. Illicit violence: Six of the witnesses were agreed that the warders assaulted prisoners without sufficient cause. "Prisoners were frequently beaten underneath me in punishment cells in the night time by the warders", Davitt said. C.D. said he had been struck in the face by a warder at Chattenden. "I think the warders presumed upon the fact of the men being infirm", said A.B., and went on to describe how an old man called Richards had been virtually beaten to death at Parkhurst. "They brought him from the punishment cells when I was in hospital. He wanted to stand because his back was so bad, but they forced him to sit down on the bench. After a long time sitting there, the Principal Officer came in, and ordered him upstairs. The old man could not walk, and he crawled up the steps on his hands and knees. The orderly carried him down in his arms later for a bath. I saw the bruises on his head where he had been struck, and the orderly said he was bruised all over. He was a mere skeleton. He died that night."

5. Injustices: All the witnesses were agreed that it was useless

for a prisoner to complain about his treatment. Thus he was entitled under the rules to demand that his food should be weighed. But if he ever did so, he was likely to be reported for trouble-making or insubordination, and a prisoner put on report had virtually no chance of escaping punishment. Davitt gave an example from his experience at Portsmouth: "An officer charged me with having a paper and pencil in my cell; he opened my cell door, seized me, and brought me out in the hall, and another officer came and caught hold of my hand, and I was taken into the back room and searched, but no paper or pencil was found on me; the officer told the governor I had swallowed both; of course, I did nothing of the sort." But he got two days bread-and-water.

6. Incompetence of Medical Officers: The record showed that Henry Harcourt had been flogged and subjected to an accumulation of some six months bread-and-water punishment —all for the offence of "refusing to work." According to his own testimony, he had been unable to work due to paralysis, and in fact the Medical Officer had eventually pronounced him unfit when he was threatened with a second flogging. In Davitt's opinion, the Medical Officers were generally of a low order; without knowledge or experience enough to tell the difference between genuine illness and malingering, and inclined to call every prisoner, however mentally or physically handicapped he might really be, a malingerer. The standard test was to apply a so-called galvanic battery to a man's back, and see how vigorously he reacted to the shock. Though the witnesses agreed that some convicts did undoubtedly feign illness and went to the length of mutilating themselves in order to evade heavy labour, A.B. testified that the Medical Officer at Parkhurst even permitted lunatics to be flogged.

7. Spiritual starvation: C.D. said that at the conclusion of his separate confinement at Pentonville he had felt he was a "much better man than he had been for many years previous," and he attributed this improvement to the "sympathetic treatment and kindness" that he had personally received from the "Rev. Sherwin." Nevertheless, he thought it "very terrible for a prisoner that he should only be allowed communication with the chaplain once a month at Pentonville." He said that at

Chattenden, an annexe of Chatham, the chaplain did no more than exchange a few formal words with the prisoners when he made his periodic round; and according to Davitt the same thing was true of Dartmoor and Portsmouth. "I think the great lack of the system," C.D. said, "is the almost entire deprivation of, shall I call it, religious communication."

8. Corruption: The witnesses had all known of warders who accepted or solicited bribes. "Any man having friends outside in a respectable position can almost get whatever he requires, especially tobacco, by bribing warders," C.D. said. "There is a regular scale for procuring these articles, i.e., one half to the officer, the other to the prisoner. I could have had tobacco or anything else if I had wished it. It was offered me times innumerable . . . It is sufficient for a man to be a well known thief for him to be remarkably well treated . . . I knew one such in Brixton who could have positively anything he liked. He was never without a Christmas pudding and other dainties." At Portsmouth, according to A.B., tobacco sold at 10/– a pound and was sometimes exchanged for bread. I.K. said the warders at Dartmoor were more dishonest than the prisoners: "When in the office of the clerk of works the stores and other things were placed to a great extent under my charge, and the officers would come there and want to help themselves to such an extent that I had to speak to the clerk, who made an order that no officer should pass into the place."

9. Contamination: Again, all the witnesses were agreed that the silence rule could not and did not prevent the prisoners from communicating with one another. "In our blacksmith's shop," A.B. said, "a robbery was planned, and took place in Birmingham three months later." E.F., who spoke of conditions in the Irish convict prisons, alleged that the younger and more innocent prisoners (some of them were very young) were exposed to the sexual lust as well as the criminal influence of the older men. He gave an example of one such seduction that had been initiated in the chapel and eventually consummated in the hospital!

Of these nine charges, the one the Commissioners took most seriously was the accusation of illicit violence. While they accepted the official denials, and acquitted the warders of "any intentional ill-usage", they none the less conceded that at Parkhurst there might have been some "unnecessary roughness in restraining the outbursts of passion and violence" of the "weak-minded" convicts. "It is with a view to preventing such occurrences," they wrote, "that we have recommended that weak-minded prisoners should be kept apart under officers specially chosen for their intelligence and command of temper."

But their recommendation, which may strike one as being extraordinarily liberal in context, was to go unheeded, and, what is more, remains unheeded to this day.

At present, the Home Office perceives nothing inappropriate or unethical in subjecting the most imbecilic of prisoners to precisely the same form of disciplinary control as the most resourceful.[15] Former Broadmoor patients may be lumped together in the dangerous category with spies, gang leaders and the like, and sent to one of the four prisons (Parkhurst among them, ironically enough) with a special security block.* Very possibly, a weak-minded prisoner, wherever he may be held, is in less danger of being handled with "unnecessary roughness" today than he was a hundred years ago, when the warders (most of them ex-service men) underwent no kind of training for their job and were not encouraged to believe that prisoners existed, except to be punished. But it does not follow from this that the weak-minded are now assured of the care they need or are in no danger at all of maltreatment, if they involuntarily make nuisances of themselves. Prisons are not mental hospitals, nor is the average prison officer a man with any special knowledge or tolerance of mental afflictions. On the contrary, there is probably little less likelihood than there was that he will mistake manifestations of serious mental disturbance for

* Since these words were written, a riot has taken place at Parkhurst. Several of the participants, after a lengthy trial that ended in July, 1970, received additional sentences—among them three men who were manifestly certifiable and had previously been Broadmoor patients. The Home Office thereupon announced plans for reducing "tensions" at Parkhurst, including the establishment of a psychiatric unit for the separate care and custody of the "more disturbed individuals." So it may be said that at last, after a lapse of 92 years, some heed is to be paid the recommendation of the Kimberley Commission. Better late than never, perhaps, though one might have hoped that by this time there would be no question of sending mentally crippled offenders to Parkhurst at all—or to any other punitive institution.

deliberate malingering or cussedness. And indisputably, under the report system, mental defectives and psychotics are still subject to the same punishments as any other prisoner who offends against discipline. To recall an extreme example of this from the comparatively recent past, Frank Mitchell, later to be dubbed the "mad axeman", was flogged at Pentonville on 18 July 1955, though only just over a month later he was certified as mentally defective and transferred to Rampton hospital.[16]

Moreover, one must doubt whether illicit violence, or for that matter any of the other misdeeds with which warders have been so persistently charged by ex-prisoners, can ever be wholly eradicated. A hundred years ago, the warders were miserably paid: from £195 a year for a Chief to about £60 for an assistant.[17] Prison officers are better paid today, but they are still not well enough paid to make the job financially appealing by comparison with less depressing occupations, nor is there any use denying that for some men its attraction is the opportunity it affords for being persecutory. Yet because the system allows the prisoners no rights, or no really effective way of asserting them, it is impossible to prevent officers from abusing their powers, if they are intent on doing so. Indeed, this is a reason for believing that however greatly discipline may be liberalized, the prison system itself remains inherently and irretrievably *anti*-reformative. For in the eyes of the captives, the officers represent society. If one of them transgresses the rules, he demonstrates what most criminals, consciously or unconsciously, dearly want to believe; namely, that society is as criminal as they are themselves, and that therefore society's rule of law is an hypocrisy which they have a moral right to despise and defy. Hence though the great majority of prison officers may be men of impeccable fairness and rectitude, the few who are not are bound to wield a destructive influence out of all proportion to their number. As G.H. told the Kimberley Commission, misbehaviour on the part of any one officer soon became common knowledge among the prisoners, and undermined their faith in the integrity of the entire staff. The same point has been made in an inverse way in a recent, and highly intelligent, book of prison memoirs: "Not all screws are bastards". (See *Life* by Zeno, 1968.)

But if one cannot avoid the conclusion that the allegations of ex-prisoners have been *too* consistent and persistent over the years to be wholly discounted, it is understandable that they should have been as consistently and persistently denied by prison administrators. Still, even the administrators, for all their loyalty to their system's present, have never had much use for its past. Today, the Home Office claims that imprisonment is becoming increasingly reformative as a result of the improved relationship between officers and prisoners. If we are to believe this, we are also left to infer that imprisonment cannot be reformative unless the prisoner/officer relationship is good, and that it has hitherto been bad. Yet Du Cane maintained that the reason why penal servitude was reformatory was precisely because the warders won the respect and confidence of their charges.[18] And the same thing was said by Du Cane's immediate successor, Sir Evelyn Ruggles Brise. "It is in the upright and manly attributes of our warder class, typical of the English National character, that a great reforming influence is to be found," Sir Evelyn wrote in 1922 after his retirement. "Discipline with kindness is the watchword of our prison staff."[19]

The charge of *un*kindness is one to which prison administrators have always been especially sensitive. "It can hardly be necessary to add," Du Cane wrote,[20] "that no officer is allowed to strike or abuse a prisoner. Should he find it necessary to make use of his weapons, he is always called upon to show that he confined himself strictly to the necessities of the occasion." Three quarters of a century later, in 1952, those words were almost exactly echoed by another Chairman of the Prison Commission, Sir Lionel Fox: "Though it cannot be confidently stated that illicit beatings-up never happen, they are very rare and are never condoned."[21]

The Kimberley Commission had to deal with evidence which suggested that illicit beatings-up were not only far from rare, but sometimes condoned. "I frequently saw prisoners knocked down by warders," Michael Davitt said, "when in my judgement no such treatment was at all deserved." This sort of testimony was corroborated to some extent by witnesses whose impartiality was presumably beyond question. Thus a former chaplain, the Rev. J. H. Nowers, stated: "I have seen a man, for instance, dragged down a flight of stone steps, his head coming into contact with the steps." Nowers went on to say that though he himself had reported this incident to the governor (of Portland), the warders responsible had got off with a "wigging." "I think that too much care and discrimination cannot possibly be taken with regard to selecting prison officers," he concluded. "That is one blot on our system or used to be, I think."

So far as the Commissioners were concerned, if that was still a blot on the system, it was, on the one hand, of no relevance and, on the other, was too damning to be recognized. "Whatever regulations are laid down for the government of the convict prisons," they wrote in their report, "it is evident that maintenance, without undue severity, of the rigid discipline which is indispensable must mainly depend on the character and efficiency of the warders." Having said that, the Commissioners could not afford to concede that even a small minority of the warders were guilty of deliberately ill-using the prisoners, unless they were also prepared to admit that the punishment itself was inalienably subject to abuses and affronts to "humanity." Since such an admission would in turn have obliged them to condemn a punishment which they were convinced was "indispensable" for society, one may fairly assume that there was never the smallest chance that they would make it.

At any rate they rejected all the charges of illicit violence or, rather, accepted the official denials of them without reservation. They decided that the warders were, on the whole, a "deserving body of men", and they turned down a suggestion from Sir William Crofton, former head of the Irish convict service, that there ought to be a training school established for officers, similar to those which already existed in Belgium and one or two other European countries. It would, they said, be a pointless extravagance.

But, by contrast, they were far from claiming that the behaviour of every warder was in every way unexceptionable, or that the warders exercised a positively reformative influence by their example. There was no obscuring the fact (for it was a matter of record) that during the year previous to the start of the Commission's inquiry, there had been 240 cases of prisoners being caught in possession of tobacco, and even the prison governors agreed that probably many more cases had gone undetected. The Commissioners readily acknowledged that tobacco in such large quantities could not have been smuggled into the prisons except by corrupt officers. They believed that the only way to halt the traffic would be to forbid warders as well as prisoners possession of tobacco, and to subject *them* to regular searches. But they refrained from recommending this remedy for fear of the damage it might do to staff morale.

Presumably, they would have been as pre-disposed to acquit the warders of dishonesty as they were to acquit them of "unkindness", if they had felt obliged to assure the public that penal servitude turned dangerous men into good citizens. But in fact they did not hesitate to explode that official pretence. The discipline, they frankly stated, "not only fails to reform offenders, but in the case of the less hardened criminals, and especially first offenders, produces a deteriorating effect from the indiscriminate association of all classes in public works."

This, the Commissioners implied, was the inescapable price of a "sufficiently dreaded" system of punishment, though they suggested that the position was possibly worse than it needed to be. For example, they criticized the corrugated iron cells, with which some of the convict prisons were provided, on the grounds that the partitions between these were so thin that the occupants of neighbouring cells could communicate with each other in whispers, and the silence rule was turned into a complete mockery. Again, they considered that more might be done through classification than was being done to offset the danger of contamination. Specifically, they recommended a division between first offenders (the "star" class) and recidivists (the "ordinary" class): a recommendation which was to be acted on in 1882, three years after the publication of their report, and is, of course, still operative.

But the Commissioners were not naïve enough to imagine that the separation of first offenders from recidivists would necessarily equal the separation of lesser from greater criminals. Indeed, they saw no positive way of preventing the corruption of minor offenders, who might otherwise never be tempted to offend again, by hardened criminals, short of substituting three years of separate confinement for all minimum (five years) sentences of penal servitude. That was an idea which they considered, but found to be inconsistent with "humanity."

On the other hand, they were opposed to any steps that might have the effect of reducing the severity of the discipline in the interest of making it more constructive. Thus they noted with approval that religious instruction and elementary education had been downgraded in the sense that classes no longer took place in lieu of labour, but only in the evenings, and they ignored complaints that even so prisoners were probably given much less opportunity for such "improvement" than was promised them under the regulations.

In short, though they didn't go quite as far as to say so, deterrence for the Kimberley Commission was all, and reform a totally lost cause. "Twenty years is such a long time," Du Cane told them in a reference to reprieved murderers, "that I think a man is almost a different man at the end of it; when one sees a very old man passing the latter years of his life in prison one cannot help thinking that there cannot be any great advantage in his being there." The Commissioners didn't agree. Life sentences, they said, especially in the case of those imposed on reprieved murderers, ought to be literally interpreted.

Though that recommendation was not to be accepted, it was none the less in tune with the temper of Parliament and public. The Kimberley Commission's inquiry coincided with the central government's take-over of the common gaols, and may be said to have set the final stamp of approval on the establishment of a single prison *system*, whose paramount, if not its only objective, was terrorization.

There remained, however, one important difference between penal servitude and ordinary imprisonment, despite the fact that both came under the same administrators and that these men, in their dual role as directors of the convict prisons and prison commissioners, were in effect pledged to make the one discipline no less deterrent than the other and the two as nearly as possible identical. The reason was contained in a speech which Lord Caernarvon addressed to the International Prison Congress of 1872:[22] "There is a school which holds—and I believe the opinion to be as dangerous as it is attractive," he said, "that all prison labour ought to be remunerative, and that the great, if not the primary objective of a prison is to make it self-supporting. But, as stated by the House of Lords' Committee in 1863, whatever may be the actual incomings from prison work, 'a profitable return from industrial labour ought not to be made the test of prison efficiency.' If, indeed, it were so considered, it must lead to a relaxed discipline, and an injurious influence on the mind of the prisoner. Where, indeed, the sentence is of sufficient length, it may have the happiest effects upon the offender; but it ought to follow upon the harder and more penal labour, and ought not to be made the equivalent for it."

That principle, which incidentally amounted to a rejection of the older (and since revived) reformative theory of "work as a cure for crime", was strictly applied by Du Cane. Consequently, labour in a local prison, when it ceased to be "hard" (i.e. calculatedly unproductive) meant some more or less useless and soul-destroying occupation, such as oakum-picking, which a man could perform in the loneliness of his cell. The whole of an ordinary prison sentence had to be served in separate confinement, and even if this had not been so, it would clearly have been impractical to provide workshops for the benefit of the comparatively few prisoners who were in for long enough to graduate from the crank or the treadwheel.[23]

Convict labour, on the other hand, could be genuinely productive. It continued for a while to be used for the manufacture of goods sold in the open market; for example, in 1878 the output of mats from the convict prisons (notably Brixton) exceeded the country's total remaining output of mats by nearly 24%. Moreover, penal servitude was traditionally equated with employment in public works, and as such could be a major undertaking.

During the '80s, for instance, five hundred supposedly able-bodied convicts were regularly engaged, under the auspices of the War Department, in the construction of fortifications for the defence of Chatham arsenal. This project had necessitated the erection of a purpose-built prison at Borstal, near Rochester, for which convict labour had also been used, and it posed a uniquely difficult security problem whose solution, according to Major Arthur Griffiths,[24] one of Du Cane's inspectors of convict prisons, constituted "an epoch in prison history."

"It was decided to lay down a narrow gauge railway along the whole line of front the forts were intended to cover, and send the prisoners to their work by train. Part of this plan was the invention of a special kind of railway-carriage, constructed with a view to safe custody. These carriages are small, open, third-class carriages, with a sliding-gate of iron bars; when the train is made up, a chain passes along the exterior of these gates, and it is padlocked at each end. The warders on duty with parties occupy raised seats also at each end of the train, and have the convicts under supervision continually. The compartments hold from eight to ten apiece, and a train-load is made up from eighty to a hundred convicts.

"The effectual guarding of the convicts when at work was a matter of equal importance. This, with the experience of many years gained in all varieties of outdoor employment, has been reduced almost to a science at Borstal. 'The site of the works is enclosed by a palisading ten feet high, with a ditch on the inner side, and wire entanglements on the inner side of the ditch' [Directors' Report—1885–6]. The convict-laden train runs within the palisading; but outside all, on a wide outer circumference, are sentries of the civil guard, on high platforms at regular intervals, and commanding the ground in between them. No fugitive from the works could pass them unobserved, and they are on such a radius that they must have him a long time under their eyes while approaching. In addition to this, an elaborate system of signalling has been devised by means of semaphores in the highest points. These are worked by good service convicts, men in the last year of their sentence, who can be trusted to use field glasses, and to communicate promptly any news that has to be sent on."

That description may suggest that convict labour under Du Cane was to some extent more imaginatively used than prison labour of any kind is being used at present. But although, as we have already noted, the idea of employing prisoners to build new prisons has recently been revived, it seems unlikely that there could ever be a reversion to the kind of imprisonment, which originated with the Hulks and was known generically as "public works." An obvious reason for this is the denial of jobs that it would be bound to entail for free workers, except during a period of over-employment. A less obvious reason has to do with the problem of security, and hence once again with the dwindling courage of deterrent theory.

No doubt, as Major Griffiths claimed, the "great works raised around Rochester" were "substantial, self-evident proof" of the "more positive results obtained by convict labour." But it is clear from his account that these results were achieved at the cost of exposing human beings to a greater degree of public shame than would be tolerated today. Though Major Griffiths spoke of their "alacrity", their "cheerfulness of aspect" and the "healthiness of their life", that, one may be sure, was just sales talk—of the kind which, regrettably, is still apt to emanate from the Home Office. These heavily guarded men, in their hideous dress with the broad arrows, had the aspect of brutes enslaved. In fact, the very sight of them was apparently so terrifying that no one who set eyes on a convict at work could ever be persuaded to give an ex-convict a job. The original purpose behind the intermediate prisons in Ireland, where the inmates wore plain-clothes, was to persuade the public that convicts due for release were, after all, human beings and fit to be treated as such. But there were no intermediate prisons in England.

All security (or what is obstinately held to be imperative in the name of security) entails a measure of degradation,[25] of course; and it may be that from the individual's point of view Mountbatten's police dogs represent something hardly less humiliating than Du Cane's armed civil guards did. But the police dogs are concealed behind prison walls; the civil guards were in the open. Society becomes more quickly revolted by penal practices which it can see than by those which it can't.

9
WOMEN AND CHILDREN

DETERRENT PRINCIPLE IS plainly compromised when either the youthfulness or the sex of the offender dictates mitigation of the punishment for the crime committed; and, in fact, under the exterminatory penal system of the 18th century and earlier children were as harshly dealt with as adults and women as harshly dealt with as men. But in both cases some differentiation of treatment began to develop as the prison system emerged during the 19th century.

In a book of memoirs[1] published in 1932, a former prison governor (Colonel Rich), who remembered Du Cane's immediate successor, Ruggles Brise, as an "absolute sahib" and who believed that "our best prison service in the world" had been "messed up" by "impractical idealists", described how one of his female charges had repeatedly smashed up her cell. "Naturally", he wrote, "such a woman is not 'right'. She is rotten through and through. Nobody could call her insane or anything approaching it. She is merely quite uncontrolled, has never practised any self-control and never will. The only thing that can cure such a case is fear, and prison instils no fear. Physical pain might do a lot, but it is against our custom to beat women, and I should be far from recommending that we begin to do so."

Colonel Rich forgot, if he ever knew, that it had not been "against our custom" to beat women until Parliament outlawed the practice in 1818. That action was no doubt chivalrously inspired—out of a dawning realization that even women malefactors belonged to the fairer and frailer sex; and the same consideration later insured them immunity from the crank and the treadwheel. Similarly, the reforms insisted on by their champion, Elizabeth Fry,[2] which resulted in their segregation from men in the common gaols and in the appointment of female instead of male officers to take charge of them, though perhaps more morally than chivalrously inspired, had to do with their physical identity.

But one may see in retrospect that the preferential treatment of women under the prison system, in so far as it exists today or ever has existed, is above all owed to their own peculiar emotional resistance to a male-made and male-administered punishment. "It is a well established fact in prison logistics", Major Arthur Griffiths wrote in his history of Millbank (1875), "that the women are far worse than the men."[3] Though that fact may still be "well established", it can now be stated rather differently. One may say without fear of contradiction from the Home Office that while female crime is a very minor problem by comparison with male crime, imprisonment is harder for women than for men to bear philosophically—to bear, that is, without losing whatever mental balance or emotional stability they may once have possessed.

Indeed, over thirty years have passed since it was officially admitted that conventional imprisonment behind high walls was something women offenders could and should be spared. In 1938, when the Prison Commissioners had plans in hand for demolishing Pentonville and selling the site to the London County Council, they intended to return the slightly younger fortress of Holloway to its pristine state as a men's prison. "Colonies for women and girls from Holloway" they announced, "are to be built outside London and the inmates will be housed in small groups."[4]

The letter of that promise remains unfulfilled, of course. But its spirit is alive and growing bolder. At the time of writing (February, 1970), it is little more than a year ago since the Home Secretary informed Parliament that Holloway is to be pulled down, and a secure type of hospital prison is to be erected in its place. Thereafter, so the Home Secretary stated, all female prisoners, apart from those in need of psychiatric care, are to be accommodated in open prisons.

However swiftly or tardily action may at last follow intent, the result will be an historically ordered development, not a revolutionary one. When "our best prison service in the world" was originally established, there were such means as the dark cell and the hobbles for instilling fear into fractious females, which, it is true, "impractical idealists" subsequently renounced. Nor was there any hesitancy about using them. "If a woman 'smashes' ", Mrs S. Gibson, Superintendent of the female convict prison at Woking told the Kimberley Commission, "you cannot make her punishment too severe."

Yet the fact remained that punishment could not be made severe enough to cope with the intractable disciplinary problem that women posed. Consequently, in the case of the convicts, i.e. those under sentence of penal servitude, certain concessions had to be offered to their obstinate femininity.

The most significant of these was introduced in 1864—in the very same year that conditions for male convicts were being systematically toughened. The Government built a so-called "refuge" at Fulham, a kind of minimum security institution, to which women who had earned a sufficient number of marks, and were otherwise considered suitable, might be sent to serve out the last nine months before they were released on licence.

The Fulham refuge itself had only a very brief history. In 1870 it was converted into an ordinary prison to replace Brixton (originally built for female convicts in 1853), which in turn became a men's prison. But the policy it had symbolized survived, with the responsibility for providing and administering refuges taken over by charitable organizations. By 1878, the year of the Kimberley Commission's inquiry, there were three such places available. Two of them, at Winchester and Streatham, were Protestant; the other, at Finchley, was Catholic.

The Winchester refuge was described to the Kimberley Commission by its superintendent, Miss Eliza Pumpfrey. One may gather from what she said that it was as little escape-proof as a modern open prison, for while the women worked indoors and were not allowed to leave the building, neither the front door nor the back door was ever locked. Moreover, though its regimen was probably more repressive, and its living conditions certainly a great deal more spartan, than one would expect to find in an open prison today, the basic purpose behind it would appear to have been no different. For Miss Pumpfrey used language that still has a progressive ring to it. It was her task, as she saw it, to rehabilitate the women committed to her charge, and she left no doubt that in her view this was largely a matter of healing the wounds, physical and psychic, that had been inflicted on them by punitive imprisonment, or, more exactly, by their resistance to it.

"They want a friend", she said. "They want someone to look after them. They are like a lot of little children. Some of them have no friend. I know the case of a girl who was brought up by an old woman. She never knew her mother, and was regularly dragged out of the slums. She behaved very badly in prison—at Woking. She came to me without any gratuity, but they have now sent her one pound, and she has gone on very well in our home and has never had anything against her, and has got to be a very strong woman . . . I attribute her bad health to bread and water punishment, and also to the hobbles, and being in dark cells."

The usual punishment for misbehaviour in the refuge, Miss Pumpfrey said, was a fine. In extreme cases, a woman would be locked up in her bedroom for a maximum period of three days, and fed on a restricted diet of bread and gruel. But since a staff member would be assigned to spend most of the time with her, acting as counsellor not guard, the punishment, Miss Pumpfrey assured the Commission, was not the equivalent of solitary confinement. (In 1967, the average population at Bullwood Hall, girls' closed borstal, was 91; 56 punishments of "confinement to room" were awarded.)[5]

There was a school attached to the Winchester refuge, which the children of the inmates might attend. Miss Pumpfrey made it her business to "place" all her charges before they were released—usually in domestic service. Some of the "placed", she said, made a habit of returning to the refuge for their "holidays." She estimated that 60% of them did well.

By the standards of today, sixty percent is accounted a high success rate for any form of institutional treatment; about as high as it ever seems possible to achieve. But at a time when penal policy generally was so little geared to reform, the refuges may be said to have existed less as experiments in rehabilitation than, to quote Du Cane—as a "valuable means of stimulating women to good conduct in prison."

And other such means were used for persuading these

obstinate prisoners to swallow their medicine with a good grace. Female convicts were offered a larger gratuity than the men, a maximum of £4 instead of £3 on their discharge, and they could start earning marks, as the men could not, during their probationary period of separate confinement. They were also entitled to a higher maximum remission of sentence—one third rather than one quarter. Thus if a woman under sentence of five years penal servitude earned her full complement of marks, and also qualified for transfer to a refuge, she would, as Du Cane told the Kimberley Commission, serve only two years and seven months of "actual imprisonment."

Moreover, the medicine itself was slightly more diluted in the female convict prisons than consideration of the physical identity of the inmates would alone have made necessary. Even during their probationary period, the prisoners worked with their cell doors open. After they had reached the second class or stage (after 18 months, that is, provided they forfeited no marks), they exercised in threes or fours rather than in single file, and in addition they were allowed an hour's daily period of recreational association (talking). Further, their schooling took place during working hours as well as in the evenings.

This is not to suggest that the female convict prisons were in any sense easy-going places. There were two of them at the time of the Kimberley Commission's inquiry—at Woking and Fulham—and they were run by lady superintendents who, to judge from their evidence before the Commission, were hardly less punitively inclined than their male colleagues. Mrs Gibson of Woking had great faith in the hobbles; she described them as a "most merciful restraint." Miss Susan Seale of Fulham noted that it was only within the last two or three years that the women had been permitted to work with their cell doors open, and she considered the change a "great mistake." Mrs Gibson said that though there had been a time when the women were allowed to walk in twos at exercise and to choose their own companions, she had put a stop to this practice on her own responsibility. The result was a mutiny. But that only convinced her that she had done "the very best thing."

Nevertheless, Du Cane and his associates plainly feared that unless some mitigation of the standard discipline were authorized in the female convict prisons, the mutinies would be too frequent and too big. Even in the local prisons, where the women weren't officially granted any similar dispensations, little attempt was apparently made to enforce the rule of perpetual silence on them. In 1884, a certain Mrs S. W. Fletcher, an American spiritualist, published an account[6] of a year she had served for alleged fraud in the gaol at Tothill Fields, Westminster. "Prisoners must not make a noise in walking," she wrote, "must not sing, or talk with their warders or each other. But no Home Secretary can absolutely govern the tongues of five or six hundred women." And on her very first visit to the exercise yard she discovered that communication could in fact be carried on with impunity. "It was a curious sight this regiment of women, from eighty-five years old to twelve, all dressed alike, but looking so different—a regiment composed almost entirely of drunkards, prostitutes, thieves. One aged prisoner had with her her daughter and grand-daughter, who, she proudly said, she believed were without exception the best thieves in London because she had learned it 'scientific' herself, and taught them the same way."

At this period, as we have previously noted, very young children were still being sent to gaol; and although the prison authorities disliked receiving them, there were no provisions made under the system for dealing with them as a separate group or for modifying the discipline in their case or for effectively segregating them from the adults. It is true that with the establishment of privately run reform and industrial schools,[7] to which young offenders might be committed by the courts, the move towards keeping children and adolescents *out* of prison had already begun before the government's take-over of the common gaols. But Judges were not always as willing to take advantage of this solution as they might have been, at least they frequently seemed to consider it necessary to prescribe a short dose of punishment preparatory to a longer dose of "re-education". In 1885, for instance, an eleven-year-old boy, convicted of *attempting* an indecent assault on a ten-year-old girl playmate in a field, was sentenced to six months' hard labour to be followed by six years in a reform school.

Apart from the *Euryalus* Hulk, the earliest effort to

differentiate between the responses appropriate to juvenile and adult crime is commemorated by Parkhurst, which stands today as possibly the most dismal example of how long a prison can outlast its original purpose and how soon that purpose is likely to be abandoned or found useless. Parkhurst, built in 1838, four years before Pentonville, was the second government-owned penitentiary, and the second of the government's experiments in reformative imprisonment. It was designed to give boys between the ages of nine and nineteen, who were under sentence of transportation, a specialized form of preparatory training based on teaching them a trade as well as attending to their spiritual and educational needs. One may say that the idea, like every similar development that has taken place since, was sentimentally inspired. For while juveniles were considered no less fitting subjects than adults for transportation, strong objections had been raised on humane grounds to making "seclusion" the basis of their preparation for leading good and useful lives in the colonies. Both Millbank, therefore, and Pentonville, after it had been built, were thought to be unsuitable.

Nevertheless, the discipline at Parkhurst was extremely punitive. The boys were required to wear "strongly marked prison dress", and an iron on one leg. They spent the first four months in separate confinement, and though they were afterwards placed in junior or senior wards (according to their age) they continued to sleep in individual cells; moreover, they were kept under uninterrupted surveillance, and the silence rule was strictly enforced "during all occasions of instruction and duty." Their diet was even sparer than the diet at Millbank, and while some of their training entailed working out of doors (on farmlands attached to the prison), there was a heavy emphasis, as in the modern detention centre, on drills and parades. One may also assume that the lash was very freely used, since this was commonly supposed to be an essential part of the cure for juvenile delinquency.[8] Indeed, Jebb believed that for all minor offenders a week's separate confinement, coupled with "one or two good whippings", would be the most effective treatment possible. Today, incidentally, faith in the instructive value of corporal punishment for the younger of juvenile offenders is not wholly lost. It is noteworthy that while borstal lads cannot be thrashed, and the flogging of adult male prisoners has recently been outlawed, the caning of boys in approved schools (or "community homes," as they are now to be re-named) is still permitted.

The reason why the Parkhurst experiment came to an end is obscure,[9] though presumably with the substitution of penal servitude for transportation and the arrival of the reform and industrial schools, it was believed to have outlived its usefulness. In 1863, at any rate, the boys, or as many of them as remained, were dispersed, and the penitentiary itself was turned briefly into a second prison for female convicts. Then in 1869, when the women were transferred to their new prison at Woking (built by the inmates of the already existing Woking prison for "invalids" among the male convict population), Parkhurst was occupied by men, and began a third chapter in its over-long history.

But an occasional juvenile offender might still be sent there, as indeed he might be sent to any of the other public works prisons, and if so he was subject to the full rigours of the discipline. Michael Davitt told the Kimberley Commission that at Dartmoor a sickly 18-year-old youth had been punished for "malingering" after being put through the galvanic battery test, and had subsequently died. The Commission learned that there were boys as young as 16 and girls as young as 14 serving sentences of penal servitude, and they considered it deplorable that these adolescents who might have been guilty of nothing worse than a "single act of folly," should thereby (so they believed) inevitably be condemned to a lifetime of crime and vice as a result of the corrupting influence of the older convicts.

Their distaste for denying the young offender any chance of salvation was one of the influences that hastened the move towards dealing with juvenile delinquency and adult crime as two separate problems. A parallel influence was exercised by such horror stories as the following which from time to time were reported in the Press (1898): "C.R., an emotional, nervous lad of only seventeen was sentenced to twelve months' hard labour. Taken to Wormwood Scrubs, he became depressed and cried for his mother. Two days after his admission he was found in his cell again crying, bleeding from a wound in his head supposed to have been caused by his having knocked himself against the wall. He was then taken to the infirmary and placed by himself in an observation cell. When a warder did look in, the boy was found in a half-sitting posture, hanging by a large handkerchief at the foot of his bed . . ."[10]

In short, before the century reached its close, a growing revulsion against cruelty to children and a corresponding social awareness that the young offender might be less far gone in "wickedness" than the old offender, had led to dissatisfaction with a system that dealt with both just as deterrently. But more than this, or partially perhaps because of it, society had begun to question whether terrorization was necessarily the best, or the whole, answer even to adult crime. The door to an allegedly reformative penal policy was re-opening.

10

THE GLADSTONE COMMITTEE

"IT WILL HARDLY be denied," Major Arthur Griffiths wrote (1894),[1] "that the prison system in this country can challenge comparison with any in the world. It may be no more perfect than other human institutions, but its administrators have laboured long and steadfastly to approximate to perfection..."

The justification for that claim ultimately rested on a set of statistics, which *appeared* to show that since the establishment of a central regime and a uniformly deterrent discipline the crime rate had steadily fallen. As Du Cane put it, "the remarkably ... sustained decrease in our prison population of late years must be considered to show that the recent legislation, with which it so remarkably coincides, has in principle and execution not only completely succeeded in its object of promoting uniformity, economy and improved administration, but also in that which is the main purpose of all—the repression of crime."

There was no doubt that Du Cane's system had promoted uniformity, economy and, in the sense of bureaucratic tidiness, improved administration. But had it also succeeded in "repressing crime" or at least had it come as near to achieving that objective as could reasonably be expected? That was the overriding question. And before the century was over Parliament answered it with a decisive 'no'. In other words, the deterrent policy, though it had been carried to as extreme lengths as "humane" considerations would allow and to extremer lengths than those same considerations would ever again permit, was pronounced a failure. This is an historic fact which, for the benefit of those who believe in "tougher" punishment as an answer to the problem of law and order, cannot be stated too emphatically.

In the same year that Major Arthur Griffiths loyally spoke

of the near-perfection of the system, the Rev. W. D. Morrison, chaplain at Wandsworth prison, published a sensationally disloyal article in *The Fortnightly Review*.[2] He challenged Du Cane's claim that the decrease in the size of the prison population justified the conclusion that crime itself was under control, and produced figures of his own to show that the rate of recidivism or re-conviction of ex-prisoners had alarmingly risen: from 70,864 between the years 1868/77 to 152,728 between the years 1883/92. He attributed this state of affairs to the dehumanizing discipline which, he charged, was calculated to drive men mad or destroy them mentally and physically, and he blamed the discipline in turn on centralization: "Prisons can never be successfully administered without a practical knowledge of the prison population, and an intimate acquaintance with the prison staff. Both of these requirements the country magistrates possessed, and as a result prisoners were never mechanized into mere pieces on a chessboard; and the prison staff was never rendered impotent as a reformative agency by a smouldering spirit of disaffection." (Those words may, perhaps, be instructively compared with the concluding sentence of a memorandum issued by the Prison Officers Association in November, 1963: "There is a common attitude among prison officers which reflects a bitter hopelessness, and which must be eradicated if the prison service is to function effectively.")

Morrison demanded an official inquiry: "We need it in order to see what can be done to diminish the steadily increasing burden which the repression of crime is imposing on the taxpayer. It is needed in the interests of social security. It is needed in the interests of the criminals themselves."

Though he was promptly sacked by Du Cane, Morrison had put the match to a bonfire of national self-doubt that blazed in the Press and could not be extinguished, except by parliamentary intervention. For at a time when society hoped it was on the way to eradicating poverty and ignorance, which were believed to be the root causes of crime, there could be no disputing the fact of a high and mounting rate of recidivism. As the Webbs were to write a quarter of a century later in a celebrated passage:[3] "Statistics varied from year to year under the influence of special circumstances; but the great stage army of offenders in all categories continued its unbroken array, with a monotonous regularity; and it seemed almost a mockery to talk of social progress, when in the background was the silent, ceaseless tramp of the multitude of men, women and children, finding no rest but behind prison walls, and only issuing thence to re-enter again."

The Home Secretary appointed a Committee under the chairmanship of Herbert Gladstone to conduct an inquiry, and in 1895 the Committee produced their report.[4] They described recidivism—"the compact mass of criminals in our midst", despite the spread of wealth and education—as "a growing stain on our civilization." And while they conceded that there might be some substance to Du Cane's claim that the discipline had proved its effectiveness as a general deterrent, they found that the drop in the prison population was also attributable to improved educational opportunities and other social and political causes. For instance, the Reformatory and Industrial School Acts and the Summary Jurisdiction Acts had reduced *prison sentences* by 29·5%.

In short, the Committee repudiated the stand that had been adopted as a result of the two separate inquiries into imprisonment and penal servitude by Parliament in 1864—namely, that a prison system could logically serve no other or better purpose than to "deter society." The case for adhering to that point of view had been very forcibly put to them by Sir Godfrey Lushington, retired permanent Under-Secretary at the Home Office. "I consider", Lushington said, "that a mediaeval thief who had his right hand chopped off was much more likely to turn over a new leaf than a convict who has had ten years penal servitude." And he continued: "I regard as unfavourable to reformation the status of a prisoner throughout his whole career; the crushing of self-respect; the starving of all moral instincts he may possess; the absence of all opportunity to do or receive a kindness; the continual association with none but criminals, and that only as a separate item also separate; the forced labour and the denial of liberty. I believe the true mode of reforming a man, or restoring him to society, is exactly in the opposite direction of all these. But of course this is a mere idea; it is quite impractical in a prison. In fact, the unfavourable features I have mentioned are inseparable from prison life."

The Committee quoted that passage from Lushington's evidence in order to reject it. "We do not agree", they wrote, "... We think the system should be made more elastic, more capable of being adapted to the special cases of individual prisoners; that prison discipline and treatment should be more effectually designed to maintain, stimulate or awaken the higher susceptibilities of prisoners, to develop their moral instincts, to train them in orderly and industrial habits and whenever possible to turn them out better men and women, physically and mentally, than when they came in."

That was a declaration of policy which Parliament in due course accepted, and upon which we have never since gone back. For this reason, no doubt, it is commonly described as a radically new policy, whose adoption marked the dawn (even if it proved to be a remarkably slow-breaking dawn) of our present "enlightened" penal era. But it was, of course, nothing of the kind. Essentially, it was no more than a re-dedication to the hopes which had first given birth to the concept of a prison system and which were expressed, for example, in the Act of 1779: "That whereas if many offenders, convicted of crimes for which transportation had been usually inflicted, were ordered to solitary imprisonment, accompanied by well-regulated labour and religious instruction, it might be the means, under Providence, not only of deterring others from like crimes, but also of reforming the individuals and inuring them to habits of industry ... " Those means were tried—at Millbank and then at Pentonville. They proved abortive. It is an historic fact, which, for the benefit of Home Secretaries, cannot be stated too emphatically, that before the wholly deterrent prison policy failed, the deterrent-cum-reformative policy had failed likewise.

What reason, if any, was there for supposing that it could now succeed? Or, to put this question as Mr James V. Bennett, a former director of the U.S. Federal Bureau of Prisons has put it, what better reason was there than there ever had been for supposing that imprisonment, "inherently a symbol of punishment", could now be used to achieve a purpose "almost completely antithetical to punishment—rehabilitation?"[5]

The Gladstone Committee were not disposed to put their faith in the old panacea of "seclusion". On the contrary, they admitted that separate confinement led to "moral and mental deterioration", and it was only from fear of destroying the deterrent value of the discipline that they refrained from recommending its total abolition. "I look upon those nine months", Lushington told them, "as part of the punishment, and as being something which was intended to make the punishment more deterrent; but I am not aware that it is too deterrent . . . " But the Committee decided it *was* a bit too deterrent, and recommended that both for convicts and in local prisons it should be reduced.

Yet did a more hopeful way exist in principle of reforming criminals than the original idea of isolating them from bad influences and exposing them to good influences? If so, what was it? If not, was there some different sort of prison, or form of imprisonment, radically different, that could prove the practical validity of a theory which both Millbank and Pentonville had in their time disastrously failed to prove?

These were basic questions which one may doubt whether the Committee ever faced and which they certainly left unanswered. What the Committee did do was to offer a number of proposals for making the system less *anti*-reformative than they realized it was. None of these recommendations was new in the sense of never having been made before by either an individual or official body, and though all of them may be considered obviously desirable, the majority, nearly a century later, have not yet been implemented or fully implemented. The most important of them were as follows:

1. The Committee referred to the provision under the Act of 1877 for the special treatment of unconvicted prisoners. "We cannot think," they said, "that this provision has been adequately carried out." Today, as has already been remarked, it is, if anything, being less adequately carried out.

2. The Committee proposed that special institutions should be established for the epileptic and "obviously weak-minded" offenders. "It is indeed a question," they wrote, "whether

[these people] should be sent to prison at all." Today, as has again been remarked, numerous epileptic and obviously weak-minded offenders are being sent to prison and no special institutions exist *within* the prison system for their custody.

3. The Committee recommended that alcoholics or "habitual drunkards," as they called them, should receive medical treatment, and should be dealt with as "patients rather than criminals." Apart from the probably very large number of prisoners (long-term as well as short-term) whose crimes are caused by or closely related to alcoholism, hundreds of short prison sentences are still being passed every year for the actual offence of drunkenness. Experimental attempts have recently been made to deal with the latter problem by making two of the open prisons (Spring Hill in the south and Appleton Thorn in the north) available for so-called "alcoholic communities"; moreover, in some of the closed prisons, notably Pentonville, there are arrangements for putting suitable prisoners in touch with Alcoholics Anonymous. But it cannot be said that anything approaching *every* habitual drunkard who is sent to prison receives medical treatment or any other sort of therapy; still less, that he is dealt with as a patient rather than a criminal.

4. Surprisingly, considering the supposed insistence on separate confinement and the diminution in the prison population, the Committee learned that local prisons, especially in London, were often over-crowded,[6] so that for awhile after their reception prisoners might have to sleep three to a cell. The Committee emphatically denounced this practice, and under the Act of 1898 that followed their report every prisoner was guaranteed a separate sleeping compartment, as he had been under previous Acts. Today, of course, local prisons are habitually and grossly over-crowded.

5. "The old and the young," the Committee wrote, "the good and the bad, men convicted of atrocious crimes, and those convicted of non-criminal civil offences, are all to be found in the same prison." The Committee demanded a system of classification that would segregate the "good from the bad" etc. by placing them in different prisons. Assuming for the moment that the possibility of preventing contamination

by a classification system, however apparently sophisticated, is not a mere pretence—is not the "mathematical *im*possibility"[7] that de Tocqueville called it—the position today, though in advance of what it was under the Du Cane regime, cannot be said to approximate the standard demanded by the Committee (or, for that matter, by the Act of 1823). Thus, as has been said, imbecilic prisoners share the maximum security blocks with the most resourceful of professional criminals; and, to take one example of the ubiquitous use to which a local closed prison may still be put, Pentonville "receives" convicted prisoners from the London area awaiting sentence (regardless, presumably, of how "atrocious" their crimes may be), ordinary class prisoners (in context, recidivists serving short sentences, including a considerable number of alcoholics and drug addicts, as well as professional criminals) *and non-criminal* prisoners. There are 842 cells at Pentonville, and the average population in 1967 was 1,323.[8] Even in the open prisons, the sort of segregation that the Gladstone Committee had in mind is blatantly incomplete. At Ford, for instance, with accommodation in dormitories for a total of 536 men, non-criminal prisoners mix with "Star" and ordinary class prisoners serving medium sentences as well as with "older prisoners" serving long sentences.

6. The Committee recommended an end to "unproductive labour" and included oakum-picking in this category. They wanted workshops built, and dismissed as "mere tradition" objections raised by Du Cane and others to work in association. Here one must distinguish between the convict prisons (the equivalent of today's central prisons for long-term men), where the work always had been productive, and the local prisons. Today, in the central prisons what is officially referred to as the "rationalization of industries" i.e. increasing their productivity is, as we have seen, a partial reversion to the more constructive ideas that were already being practised in the mid-19th century. On the other hand, the abolition of purely penal labour in the local prisons has led to an apparently insoluble problem. On average, there is still not a sufficiency of work available—even work of such an uninspiring kind as mailbag-sewing—to occupy a prisoner's time, so that he

spends at least a part of every working day locked up in his cell.

7. The Committee said that "scientific and more particularly medical observation and experience" were "of the most essential value in guiding opinion on the whole subject," and they proposed in effect that medical officers should not be appointed to the prison service, unless they had received special training in the diagnosis and treatment of mental illness. Although prison medical officers today frequently give evidence in court about the mental state of offenders, only a small minority of them hold a diploma in psychological medicine, and the number of qualified psychiatrists attached to, or employed part-time by, the prison service is smaller still.

8. The Committee found that cases of "gross ill-treatment by warders" were "very few in number." But they also found that due to the "minute regulations", the warders were harsh and inflexible in their attitude towards the prisoners, and due to want of proper training were generally incapable of exercising a positively reformative influence on the individuals in their charge. Hence, the Committee recommended that training schools should be instituted in "two or more prisons." Today, there is an Officers' Training School at Wakefield, and also at Leyhill, but though officers are officially encouraged to develop a "treatment relationship" with prisoners, their training is not primarily geared to that end. Moreover, under the existing disciplinary rules and regulations an officer has hardly less power or opportunity to deal "harshly" with a prisoner than the old warders possessed.

9. The Committee described the silence rule as "unnatural" and recommended that on certain days prisoners should be allowed to talk to one another "under supervision" as a reward for good conduct. They recommended certain other ameliorations of the discipline: an increased distribution of library books, which was limited to one a week; an increase in the penal diet (i.e.,) the diet during the first week of imprisonment, which was a daily allowance of one lb of bread and 1½ pints of stirabout); and the introduction of "gymnastics". In these and kindred respects the general improvement has today doubt-

less gone well beyond the point the Committee intended that it should or ever envisaged that it would.

10. Finally, the Committee emphasised the importance of education as a reformative technique. A prisoner, they learned, received no schooling at all until after he had served four months, and was then "instructed" in the solitude of his cell by a uniformed officer. They strongly recommended that all prisoners, regardless of length of time served, should be enabled to attend classes conducted by school-masters in plain clothes. The extent and effectiveness of educational facilities in prisons today will be discussed later.

The declared purpose behind all these recommendations was to end what the Committee called the "most striking inequalities of punishment" that existed in prisons under the guise of an "orderly equality." "It is comparatively easy", they wrote, "to mass [prisoners] together, to call each of them by a number, and by a cast-iron system to make them all go through the same tasks, observe the same hours, and lead the same lives." But, said the Committee, since "the great majority of prisoners are ordinary men and women amenable to all those influences which affect people outside", what was needed was "individual attention."

Though that was admittedly to state a hitherto unstated principle, the Committee's combined proposals did not add up to a workable plan for giving it effect. To ask for "individual attention" was, in fact, to ask for something that no prison had ever been equipped to provide and that was fundamentally inconsistent with the legal concept of imprisonment as an instrument of measured punishment to fit the crime. Hence what followed may be best summed up in the Webbs' later aphorism—"perhaps the most hopeful and practical of prison reforms is to keep people out of prison altogether."

There was certainly not much else that could logically be done about short-term imprisonment once Parliament had abandoned the idea of using it for exclusively terroristic purposes, and one may regard the 1907 Probation of Offenders Act as an inevitable consequence of the Gladstone Committee's report, even though an extension of the probationary principle was not among the Committee's proposals. That

Act marked the beginning of a legislative trend towards keeping people out of prison altogether, which has continued ever since and which has most recently been exemplified by the introduction of the "suspended sentence" under the 1967 Criminal Justice Act.

Due in part, however, to judicial and magisterial capriciousness, and in part to governmental parsimony, this policy has persistently fallen short of its potential effectiveness. For instance, according to Sir Lionel Fox, a former Chairman of the Prison Commission, the Mental Deficiency Act of 1913 "kept out of, or removed from, the prisons a large number of unfortunates for whom imprisonment was indefensible."[9] So, indeed, it was intended to, as was the previous 1909 Lunacy Act. The Courts were empowered, under these two pieces of legislation, to make a hospital order in the case of convicted offenders adjudged to be mentally defective or insane, and the Home Secretary was empowered to transfer defective or insane prisoners to hospitals. But these powers, which now exist in a reinforced form under the 1959 Mental Health Act, though not wholly neglected, have never approached being as fully employed as they should be. Even if the courts and the Home Secretary were invariably willing to invoke them in suitable cases, it would be a practical impossibility for them to do so, for not nearly enough hospital space has been provided to accommodate all the numerous certifiable defectives, psychopaths and psychotics who commit offences. Imprisonment for these people, therefore, "indefensible" though it was thought to be even in Du Cane's time, and useless though it undoubtedly is except as a means of putting a more or less dangerous person temporarily (often very temporarily) out of commission, remains closer to the rule than the exception.

The point of trying to save the "obviously weak-minded" from imprisonment was presumably to avoid *punishing* offenders who were not responsible for their own actions and whom punishment, therefore, could neither reform nor deter. But this consideration did not apply to juveniles. The purpose of keeping them out of prison was to protect them from being contaminated by adult criminals, and though probation was found to be part of the answer, punitive custody was not by any means to be dispensed with. The Borstal system, which was developed by Du Cane's successor, Ruggles-Brise, and was given statutory recognition under the Prevention of Crime Act, 1908, was another logical consequence of the Gladstone Committee's report. The higher courts were empowered to sentence young offenders between the ages of 16 and 21 to two or three years "borstal training" in cases where either a short-term of imprisonment or penal servitude would previously have been considered unavoidable.

On paper, this may have seemed a major advance towards using custody for reformative ends. But, significantly, the very first building to be used as a borstal was the old public works prison near Rochester, which had originally been called Borstal; and, physically speaking, all the early borstal institutions were prisons by another name. Moreover, though "training", which was aimed at inculcating a "team spirit" by methods borrowed from the public school system, represented a total breach with separate confinement, it was offered under highly regimented conditions. Supposedly, as one of the borstal governors put it, it was "impossible to deal with juvenile offenders without the most exacting discipline."[10]

In fact, from the point of view of the individual, borstal training was a severer and more dreaded punishment than a short term of imprisonment. Nor, of course, was this unintentional, since juveniles were assumed to be no less deterrable than adults and the need to deter them was considered just as imperative. But, on the Gladstone Committee's own premise, the borstal concept made little contribution to solving the problem of *how* deterrent and reformative aims could be reconciled.

For one thing, the system was in its own way as inflexible as the prison system, and as poorly equipped to provide "individual attention." Nominally, every inmate of a borstal institution had been found equally "suited" to the training, but the courts which had made this judgement possessed only very superficial means upon which to base it, and actually the individuals who received borstal sentences might be cut from quite divergent physical and psychological patterns. Yet they were all "massed together" and, by a system in its own way no less "cast-iron" than the system operative in prisons, made to "go through the same tasks, observe the same hours, and lead the same lives." That, after all, was what punitive institutional discipline meant, and was ultimately bound to mean. For that matter, it was what the public school system meant at the time. But public schoolboys weren't problem children.

Moreover, it was merely sentimental to imagine that there was less risk of contamination in a borstal institution than a prison, simply because it was reserved for a group of offenders legally classed as juveniles. The risk of contamination is inherent in locking up delinquents together, however young they may be or however slight the disparity between their ages may *appear* to be; and, obviously enough, the greater the opportunities they are allowed for corrupting each other, the greater the danger that they will do so. "What I didn't know when I went in, I knew when I came out," an old "lag" has recently written in a prison magazine about an Approved School which he entered at the age of 12. And in *Low Company* (1935), one of the classics of penal literature, Mark Benney has said of his experiences in a more advanced borstal than any that existed under the Ruggles-Brise regime: "Throughout the institution crime was meditated and discussed with all the zest of youth. Experiences were compared, technical tips passed on, introductions to fences arranged, future crimes plotted. Many of these lads, of course, talked crime in a spirit of bravado, with no clear idea of devoting their future to the craft. But many others were absorbed in crime as an artist is absorbed in art and devoted much time to improving their predatory proficiency."

In short, one must doubt if there *is* a way to prevent contamination in a *penal* institution unless the inmates are somehow isolated from one another, and, furthermore, that the early 19th century penologists were probably right in regarding this as a pre-requisite to reform. As we have previously suggested, the separate system, for all its cruelties and patent absurdities, might have developed constructively, if there had been as much emphasis placed on its positive side (exposure to good influences) as its negative side (isolation from bad influences). But parsimony forbade that; and parsimony was a concomitant of retributive deterrent principle—the conviction that desirable though it might be to reform criminals (to do them good), it was imperative to punish them (to make them suffer).

For the same reason, no doubt, all the Gladstone Committee's major proposals for re-shaping the prison system itself were, with one exception, ignored. The exception was a proposal, which has not been mentioned hitherto, since it deserves special consideration. The Committee decided that the repeated punishment of persistent offenders for each offence they committed was "almost useless." Accordingly, they recommended that "a new form of sentence should be placed at the disposal of the Judges by which these offenders might be segregated for long periods of detention during which they would not be treated with the severity of first class hard labour or penal servitude, but would be forced to work under less onerous conditions."

The recommendation was enacted in 1908, though with the addition of a deterrent element which the Committee had not wanted or at any rate had not asked for. The Prevention of Crime Act empowered the courts to tack on a sentence of preventive detention (minimum five years and maximum ten years) to a sentence of penal servitude in the case of anyone found on conviction to be an habitual offender.

The result of this legislation was manifestly objectionable in the sense that whether the point of preventive detention was to rehabilitate an habitual offender or merely to protect society from him for a longer period than the actual crime of which he was convicted would ordinarily warrant, there could be no sense or justice in condemning him to an advance dose of penal servitude. Nevertheless, the idea of preventive detention won the enthusiastic approval of liberal reformers, including the Webbs and Bernard Shaw, because it seemed to promise the development of a new and genuinely non-punitive form of custody.

Nor was this hope immediately seen to be illusory. The first and, as it turned out the only, special institution for preventive detainees was built at Camp Hill, Isle of Wight, after very careful consideration had been given to the choice of a suitable site. Though the discipline was by no means free of needless repression, it was at least designed to teach men industriousness in a reasonably humane way, and certainly the inmates were far better treated than ordinary convicts. Their labour, much of it agricultural or horticultural, was less arduous and humiliating; they were subject to fewer indignities and entitled to greater dispensations. How privileged an inmate might become depended on how well or badly he responded to a training programme supposedly intended to help him help himself, and so, too, did the date of his release, for within the maximum limit set by the court a preventive detention sentence was indeterminate. There were a number of pavilions at the perimeter of the prison, each with a bed-sitting-room and kitchen. A man might be allotted one of these pavilions after it had been decided he was fit for release. He would have his own key, cook his own meals, and go out to work by day. This, one may observe, was a somewhat more sophisticated version of the present-day hostel scheme.[11]

All persistent offenders are not alike, of course. A few are serious menaces to society, the majority mere nuisances. But it may well be that the only possible answer to the problem they jointly represent is an indeterminate sentence to treatment, with a number of special institutions of a more and less custodial kind established to suit their varying needs. A system of this sort was no doubt what the liberal reformers believed would eventuate from the introduction of preventive detention, and so in a more rational society it might have done. But again, as we shall see, the punitive obsession and the parsimony which it excuses, proved insuperable obstacles.

They were equally a barrier to other of the Gladstone Committee's proposals. For example, it would have been clearly impossible to make local prison labour "productive" in the Committee's sense, short of scrapping all the existing buildings, which had been designed on the separate plan, and replacing them with new buildings that contained properly planned and equipped workshops. But such a project was not so much as contemplated.

Though some ameliorations of the discipline took place as

an immediate result of the Committee's report, such as the limitation of separate confinement to the first three months of a prison sentence and the abolition of the crank and the tread-wheel, these cost nothing to implement. Besides, Ruggles-Brise, who had by now succeeded Du Cane as Chairman of the Prison Commission, was not the man to preside over the dismantling of his predecessor's system, and his concern to save juveniles from a "life of crime" was evidently unmatched by a conviction that adult offenders were salvageable. "Let us not be tempted in the goodness of our hearts, and in the strength of our human pity and sympathy," he was to write after his retirement, "to overlook the necessary foundation of punishment, which is the assertion of the system of rights by pain or penalty—not pain in its physical sense, but pain that comes from degradation and the loss of self-respect."[12]

Still, if to degrade a man and rob him of his self-respect was an eccentric way to rehabilitate him, rehabilitation was none-the-less a purpose which Parliament required Ruggles-Brise to pursue. And if this new emphasis on reform was little more than verbiage, it inevitably gave rise to protests—in particular from Judges who had never set foot inside a prison—that the discipline was becoming too lax. At the same time, attacks on the system for its reformative failings continued, and though these were mostly launched by educated ex-prisoners,[13] there was one that came from an unexpected quarter.

In a series of articles published in *The Nineteenth Century* in 1902, Sir Robert Anderson, former head of the C.I.D., recalled how during a professional visit to a prison he had accidentally been locked up with the prisoner he was interrogating, and all of three hours had passed before a warder came to answer his signal of distress. He had found the experience traumatic. It had convinced him that cellular confinement of any kind was utterly mistaken. "The treatment of prisoners in former times was barbarous," he wrote, "but it was at least intelligent. Its whole purpose was punishment, and punishment was thorough and drastic. But in this shallow and conceited age we pride ourselves that we are not as our fathers were. Our great aim in prison discipline is the reformation of the offender, and with a stupidity that would be amusing if the matter were not so serious, we wantonly deprive a prisoner of the good influences that God's world of nature is so well fitted to exert on him.

"Give a man useful work," he continued, "interesting work, remunerative work; why should he not be paid for his labour? Don't stunt the moral nature or intellectual being of the convicts. I would make their prison life much more interesting. Why not? Give them concerts, lectures, interesting employment, light and happy services, a greater selection of ministers to preach to them . . . I am confident that in the prison of the future cells like those in vogue will only be used as punishment cells."

But there were still only the prisons of the past, and although the totally dark cell had allegedly ceased to be used since 1884 even for punishment, the regular cells evidently weren't much lighter. "All that night," an ex-prisoner has written[14] of his introduction to Reading Gaol in 1896, "I lay awake tossing and turning on a thin mattress that seemed to be all lumps . . . Like a squirrel in a cage, my thoughts whirled round and round . . . I felt I wanted to scream out at the black, menacing darkness that enshrouded me like a pall—darkness so utter that not a single ray of light could be seen. It was like being buried alive in a vault . . . At last, however, faint streaks of light crept into my cell which gradually became a uniform grey . . . Suddenly a harsh, vibrant clangour filled the air. It was the prison bell clashing its strident summons to the weary prisoners to rise and face another day . . . "

Something could be and eventually was done to let more of God's light into cells that had been designed to exclude it. But this cost money and therefore took time. There is a footnote in Lady Constance Lytton's account[15] of her first imprisonment at Holloway which reads: "In the Report of the Commissioners of Prisons for the year ending March 31, 1911 (Part I), the Surveyor of Prisons tells that: 'The provision of opening panes and clear glass in cell windows has been continued . . . another two years' work (if funds are forthcoming) should complete the prisons.' Two years to wait—and for want of money from the richest exchequer in the world! But they would have waited much longer if it had not been for the Suffragettes."

Even so the continuing excesses of the system, which the suffragettes encountered in the female prisons and duly exposed, were not *as* excessive as those in the male prisons, because, for reasons previously stated, it had never been possible to make them so. In 1922, Dr Mary Gordon, who, though a former medical inspector of prisons, was very far from being an apologist of the system, wrote[16] that the death-like silence which was supposed to reign was "all a myth." "Every well-behaved woman who is employed in the prison kitchen, workshop, or laundry or in any other associated party between 9.15 and 12 or 1.30 and 4.30 certainly gets opportunities of talking if she does so quietly."

The men as certainly did not. Nineteen-twenty-two was also the year in which *English Prisons Today*[17] was published as a companion volume to the Webbs' work. This was a massively detailed report, compiled by a group of conscientious objectors who had suffered imprisonment during the war, and it revealed with what determination "minute regulations" were still being enforced. "Prisoners who do not keep the prison regulations are liable to punishment," the report said, "and, since the regulations are of such a character that no one can possibly keep them, prisoners never feel immune from punishment." Cases were cited to illustrate the point; among them, the punishment of "three days No. 1 diet (i.e. bread and water), one week separate confinement, one day remission lost, and letter and visit postponed a week" for the offence of "saying 'Good Morning' to a fellow-prisoner."

If there was some residual reformative point left to the silence rule, especially in view of the partial abrogation of separate confinement in local prisons, other regulations clearly belonged to the policy of calculated degradation and destruction of self-respect. Thus visits, which were now permitted monthly after a prisoner had served the first eight weeks of his sentence, were held under the most humiliating conditions. There were two alternative arrangements which, so one may learn from *English Prisons Today*, were "described in prison parlance as the 'meat safe' and the 'cage' respectively."

"The former consists of two small compartments similar to telephone boxes, partitioned from each other by two screens of thick wire gauze about a foot apart. The visitors stand in one box, the prisoner with an officer behind to 'censor' the conversation, in the other. The wire gauze so darkens everything seen through it that no clear impression can be obtained of the persons in the opposite box. 'When my wife visited me,' says an ex-prisoner, 'I was entirely unable to recognize what I afterwards found to be an excellent photograph of our child.'

"The second arrangement is a most literal example of the truth of the analogy which continually comes to one's mind when writing of prisoners—the analogy of caged animals. A room is divided by two parallel rows of bars, reaching from floor to ceiling, into two bare cages with a corridor between. The prisoner stands in one cage, the visitors in the other, and the officer sits in the corridor dividing them."

An ex-prisoner's wife described a visit she had paid her husband under this second arrangement: "I shall never thoroughly get over the shock which I had when I saw [him] through the bars. It makes me ill now to think of it. He stood pressing forward through the bars, clasping them tightly, his face dirty and unshaven, his eyes distraught, his body clothed in a rough ill-fitting way. Just for a moment I felt I was looking through the dim light at some fierce, uncouth animal at the Zoo. Then I forgot his looks. The only thing that mattered was that it was *he*. But after I left him the cruelty of the thing was a bitter persistent memory."

In a good many instances, repression was carried even further than the rules authorized it to be. For example, there was a Standing Order that while prisoners were not to be encouraged to request their friends to petition the Secretary of State on their behalf, a letter written for that purpose was permissible. But the evidence showed that many such letters were in fact disallowed. Generally speaking, too, the censorship of letters was carried to grotesque lengths. Since a prisoner was forbidden to complain, or to allude in any way to his treatment, he was reduced to writing letters of an inanely cheerful type, largely filled with questions rather than news about himself. Nor could the questions necessarily be answered, since any reference to public events in a letter he received might attract the censor's scissors. Thus the following words were deleted from a letter sent to Dartmoor in 1904: "One of our old favourites, Dan Leno, is dead and it was a splendid funeral. I think all the musical artists were present, and the flowers were splendid. The Lord Mayor's show was a good old-fashioned one this year."

Such pettifogging tyranny may by now have ceased to be imaginable. But although *English Prisons Today* was compiled without the cooperation of the Prison Commissioners, it was based on the testimony not only of ex-prisoners but of prison staff, and one may doubt if there is any longer the least inclination within the Home Office, or anywhere else, to deny its substantial accuracy. For, as we have said, apologists of the prison system are the first to admit to its past evils or deficiencies, provided these are long enough past.

Yet before one can safely conclude that during the half century since its publication *English Prisons Today* has lost all relevance, except as an historic document comparable with John Howard's exposure of conditions in the common gaols, it is well to compare some of its findings with those of a report issued in 1963 by a group of men and women who had recently been imprisoned for their anti-nuclear bomb activities.

For example, on the medical service: "... attention is frequently hurried and callous, and suspicion of malingering is very prevalent" (1922) and "Even the best people who go into the Prison Medical Service seem to become institutionalized and develop a callous 'don't care' attitude towards their patients after a while" (1963). Or on food: "Diet is inadequate for some prisoners, and is excessively starchy and lacking in green stuffs" (1922) and "The prison diet is said to provide calories equal to those in the average diet outside, but these are provided by the very cheapest foods and are therefore mainly starch. If a prisoner cannot tolerate all this stodge he becomes undernourished" (1963). Or on discipline: "The impossibility of anyone obeying all the multifarious and unnatural prison rules gives officers with a prejudice against any prisoner ample opportunity to report him. Governors almost invariably accept the evidence of a warder against that of a prisoner" (1922) and "... many prisoners are inarticulate by nature and most others are overwhelmed by the repressive attitude when brought before the Governor, so in fact they have no chance to defend themselves" (1963). Or on exercise: "The exercise grounds are generally depressing and are frequently unadorned with flowers or shrubs" (1922) and "Exercise in overcrowded yards is degrading, depressing and of little benefit to the prisoner" (1963). Or, finally, on punishment: "Punishment by lowering the diet is dangerous to health" (1922) and "the general practice of punishing prisoners by solitary confinement and semi-starvation is too brutal and senseless to be continued" (1963).

Admittedly, the 1963 report lacks the authority of the 1922 report in the sense that it is far briefer and less well documented, but even if its findings can reasonably be dismissed as mere echoes of outdated complaints, it is still necessary to mention certain ways in which conditions of imprisonment have positively retrogressed during the past half century. The most serious of these is the fact that thousands of men are now obliged to sleep three to a cell; a situation which is due, of course, to overcrowding and for which it is said, nobody can fairly be blamed. But there have been some other minor changes for the worse, which would appear to be indefensible, among them the failure, as a result of developments previously described, to provide appropriately considerate and individual treatment for non-criminal prisoners. Moreover, in 1922, although there was no earnings scheme for convicted prisoners, remand prisoners, if they elected to work, were entitled to remuneration for their labour. So they still are. But the actual payment they receive is even smaller today than it was then, whereas the rental demanded of them for a "special cell" has increased sevenfold—presumably to accord with the drop in the purchasing power of money!

It must be noted, too, that there were experiments in progress half a century ago which seemed to point the way to penal reform, but which eventually were to be abandoned and forgotten. In Birmingham,[18] for example, an investigating committee had advised the magistrates that many criminals were "unfit for prison life," that they were "to a large extent defective mentally and physically" and that "proper medical advice might remedy their defect and make them decent members of society." Consequently, the magistrates arranged for a qualified diagnostician to be appointed as medical officer at Birmingham prison to examine accused offenders remanded in custody; and a second doctor was appointed, with the concurrence of the city authorities, to examine accused offenders granted bail. Out of 151 cases kept under medical observation at Birmingham prison during the year ended 31 August 1920—a year when the crime rate was extremely low by comparison with earlier and later years—19 were found to be either certifiably insane or mentally defective, and 113 were held to be "unfit for prison life." The logical lesson to be learned from these figures was that crime is to a large extent a medical problem. Nor, indeed, does that lesson remain altogether unlearned. "It is . . . highly desirable," says a Home Office Report (1964)[19] "that a thorough psychiatric appraisal should be made of every offender received into custody for the first time." Highly desirable, but under existing circumstances quite impossible. Yet it might have been possible by this time, if the Birmingham experiment of half a century ago had taken root, and spread, instead of withering.

There were also adventures in prison reform going on abroad, and lengthy accounts of these were included in *English Prisons Today* as a guide to what could and should be done in this country. At Auburn (N.Y.), and latterly at Sing Sing, the illustrious American penologist, Thomas Osborne, had introduced a measure of self-government. Very possibly, this was a dreamer's plan that was bound in the end to prove unworkable. Allegedly, at any rate, the electoral process did not prevent the strong being given authority over the weak, with results uncomfortably reminiscent of those in the common gaols when selected prisoners were invested with the powers of officers. Just the same, it is no wonder that Osborne's idea appealed to the imagination of English reformers, for the faults in the system he condemned, and tried to correct, were identical with the faults they saw in the home system. "It endeavours," Osborne said, "to make men industrious by driving them to work; to make them virtuous by removing temptation; to make them respect the law by forcing them to obey the edicts of an autocrat; to make them far-sighted by allowing them no chance to exercise foresight; to give them individual initiative by treating them in large groups; in short, to prepare them again for society by placing them in conditions as unlike real society as they could well be made."

But, when all this has been said, it cannot fairly be suggested that prison conditions today are just as repressive as they were half a century ago. On the contrary, though society's punitive obsession is still very far from dead, there has possibly been a more marked decline in the courage of deterrent theory during the past fifty years than during any other comparable period in history. Many of the "improvements" demanded in *English Prisons Today* have, on paper at least, been effected, and if the editors of, and contributors to, that report were to trust to official assurances, they would probably feel satisfied that the entire system had been transformed. The thing that would certainly impress them most is the renunciation of Ruggles-Brise's belief in degrading prisoners and robbing them of their self-respect. The statutory rules have for a long while specified that the "treatment of prisoners shall be such as to encourage their self-respect and a sense of personal responsibility."

This seemingly fundamental change of attitude (or approach) was not one that the administrators were forced to adopt against their will or better judgement. It would be nearer the truth to say that they persuaded Parliament to accept it, or, rather that one among them in particular acted as the true policy-maker. In 1922, in the same year that *English Prisons Today* was published, Alexander Paterson became a Prison Commissioner.

II

ALEXANDER PATERSON AND AFTER

On 30 November 1938, Sir Samuel Hoare, Home Secretary, moved the second reading of his Criminal Justice Bill. "The House," he said, "will have seen the angles from which I am attempting to approach these problems. They will see that I am trying to approach them from the angles of prevention and reformation. In a scheme of this kind there is no place for the remnants of a period that looked at the treatment of crime principally from the angle of retribution and deterrence. I am, therefore, proposing to sweep away the remnants of former dispensations, now little more than the stage properties of Victorian melodrama: penal servitude, hard labour, ticket of leave, the name criminal lunatic . . . These are changes much greater than changes of name. They are the outward and visible sign of the new outlook upon the problems of crime and delinquency."

Sir Samuel's words were enthusiastically received. Mr Geoffrey Lloyd was lyrical: "I conclude by saying that I think this Bill will be remembered for many great reforms which will cast their beneficent influence down long years in the future, and will affect for good many men who will never know that the good has been caused by this Act, by this House and by the initiative of my Rt. Hon. friend." To which list Mr Lloyd might have appropriately added the name of Alexander Paterson, for the Bill was essentially an expression of Paterson's aspirations.

The war forced it into cold storage, but, with some modifications and additions, it was eventually enacted in 1948, a year after Paterson's death. If it should be regarded as his memorial, it also tells a great deal about the scope and limitations of his influence.

One thing the Act certainly did not herald was a penal revolution. The "stage properties of Victorian melodrama" may have retained a lively existence in the imagination of the Judiciary, but for Parliament to "sweep them away" was, Sir Samuel Hoare's assurance notwithstanding, no more than legislative recognition of what, for better or worse, had long since been accomplished administratively. The abolition of the crank and the treadwheel, for instance, had rendered it impossible (or at least inconvenient) to make any distinction between imprisonment with and imprisonment without hard labour, save for requiring those sentenced to hard labour to sleep on a plank bed for the first three weeks. As the editors of *English Prisons Today* had pointed out, "with the exception of the few first division offenders, the treatment of the existing classes is governed by the same repressive and demoralizing principles that characterize the regime of the third division hard-labour prisoners." Though by 1948 those principles were less depressing and demoralizing than they had been in 1922, they none the less applied to all convicted prisoners alike, apart from first division offenders. The propriety of abolishing that exception has already been questioned.

For the rest, the Act marked orderly progress along the road previously chartered by the Gladstone Committee's report and the legislation which followed it. The courts were given additional powers to make probation orders and to impose fines, while their powers of sentencing juvenile offenders to prison were further restricted and new alternative means of dealing with juvenile offenders were introduced, notably custodial detention centres and non-custodial attendance centres. These, and like measures, were intended, obviously enough, to further the policy of keeping people out of prison altogether. At the same time, a renewed attempt was made to deal with the problem of people who could not be, or at any rate were not, kept out of prison.

Most importantly, the Act introduced two special forms of sentence for persistent offenders. One of these was called "corrective training." It applied to anybody of 21 and over who was convicted of an offence punishable by two years imprisonment, and had twice before, since reaching the age of 17, been convicted of similarly punishable offences. The other special form of sentence was preventive detention, but its conditions differed from those of the original preventive detention sentence, which had fallen into virtual disuse. It applied to anybody of 30 and over, who was convicted of an offence punishable by two years imprisonment, who had since the age of 17 thrice been convicted of similarly punishable offences and had twice been sentenced to borstal training, imprisonment or corrective training. Minimum and maximum terms were fixed: in the case of corrective training two years and four years respectively; in the case of preventive detention five years and fourteen years.

Before a person could be sentenced to corrective training, the trial Judge had to be satisfied that it was "expedient with a view to his reformation and the prevention of crime that he should receive training of a corrective character for a substantial time, followed by a period of supervision if released before the expiration of his sentence . . . " One might reasonably deduce from this that corrective training was intended as an essentially non-punitive response to offenders whom punishment had clearly failed either to deter or reform. Even on paper, however, there appeared to be little difference between corrective training and prison training—or what prison training was supposed to be now that the idea of degrading prisoners had been foresworn. All that the Prison Commissioners were able to think up by way of describing the individualized form of treatment they proposed to offer corrective trainees was:[1] (I) the provision of work which will so far as practicable help to fit them to earn their living after release, with technical training in skilled trades for suitable prisoners; (II) special attention to education; (III) the exercise of personal influence on the character and training of individuals by members of the prison staff; and (IV) the provision of every opportunity for the development of a sense of personal responsibility. One may recall that every part of this programme, with the exception of the last item, had nominally been operative in prisons at one time or another during the 19th century, and though Du Cane had rejected "special attention to education," he had based his whole claim to running a "reformatory" system on "the exercise of personal influence on the character and training of individuals by members of the prison staff."[2] As for the "provision of every opportunity for the development of a sense of personal responsibility," how could a sense of personal responsibility be "encouraged" in ordinary prisoners unless they were given every opportunity to develop it? Indeed, how could ordinary prisoners be offered less than the entire programme drawn up for corrective trainees, if Rule 1 of the new statutory rules was to be honoured? "The purpose of training and treatment of convicted prisoners shall be to establish in them the will to lead a good and useful life on discharge and fit them to do so."

Clearly, there was never any chance that "corrective training" could be better than verbiage, short of a determined attempt to find out *why* imprisonment or borstal or in a word, punishment, had failed to correct certain offenders and then to devise some fundamentally different form of treatment, whether custodial or non-custodial. But no such attempt was made or contemplated. No special institutions were built for corrective trainees. They served their sentences in existing prisons, to which "selected prisoners of the Ordinary Class" were also sent: a fact which revealed corrective training to be no less punitive than prison training. Actually, it was more punitive, for while an ordinary prisoner was entitled to statutory remission of sentence, a corrective trainee was liable to serve his sentence in full, unless, after he had served two thirds of it, the Prison Commissioners agreed to release him on licence. In other words, he was in precisely the same position as a convict in Jebb's time, except that while out on licence he was under the supervision of the After Care Association rather than the Police. This was to "sweep away" a stage property of the Victorian melodrama only to rescue it from the dustbin.

Before a person could be sentenced to preventive detention the court had to be satisfied that it was "expedient for the protection of the public that he should be detained for a substantial time, followed by a period of supervision if released before the expiration of his sentence . . . " The original preventive detention sentence had fallen into disuse, because Judges, loyal to the principle of punishment according to deserts, and therein reflecting the view of the public at large, had revolted against the practice of responding to some petty offence with a lengthy period of imprisonment over and above what they might consider the appropriate term of penal servitude. Assuming that it was still necessary to protect the public from offenders who, despite deterrent sanctions, persistently broke the law to a more or less serious degree, the rational solution would surely have been (a) to make preventive detention mean what it said, i.e. detention for preventive, not punitive purposes (b) to make it as reformative as possible and (c) to make the sentence wholly indeterminate, since detention for a fixed maximum period, however "substantial", is at best a guarantee of only temporary protection for the public and is less than no protection if it results in exacerbating the offender's criminal inclinations. Only a small minority of habitual offenders could really be classed as "dangerous", and the power of imprisoning them for very long terms, if not for life, already existed. In the case of the great majority, neither the particular offence of which they were convicted, nor their previous record, added up to a sufficient moral justification for using a punitive form of detention against them. At the same time, they were persistent nuisances, and an indeterminate sentence might have been morally justifiable provided it did *not* lead to something indistinguishable from imprisonment and *did* lead to their being given a genuine opportunity to learn how to live lawfully in freedom.

But the revised edition of preventive detention, which was introduced under the 1948 Criminal Justice Act, proved less rational than its original. While it left as much room for outrages to the public conscience, on the grounds of "injustice" —in May, 1964, for example, a man got eight years for stealing fruit to a value of under two shillings—it marked a retreat from both the indeterminate principle and the principle of distinguishing between punitive and non-punitive custody. The hopes that had been aroused with the building of Camp Hill were finally dissipated. Preventive detainees served their sentence in two or, if they were lucky, three "progressive stages" (another property of the Victorian melodrama salvaged and given a re-paint). They served the first stage, which ordinarily lasted a year, in a local prison under the standard conditions. They were then transferred for the second stage to a secure central prison, where they "could become eligible to earn" special privileges; these included "association in common rooms for meals and recreation" and in sum amounted to no more than the privileges that, as time went on, came within reach of every prisoner serving longer than a year. One of the central prisons at first "set aside" for preventive detainees was Parkhurst which, as we have seen, had never been found unadaptable to a new use, but by 1967 Parkhurst had partially reverted to its old "invalid" days of the 1870's, for though it was receiving "Ordinary Class" prisoners serving long sentences, it no longer received preventive detainees unless they required "medical attention."

Entry to the third stage depended on the decision of an Advisory Board, and this in turn depended on the Board's estimation of a man's chances of staying out of trouble when he was discharged. Few, in fact, were chosen. Those that were might be transferred to an open or semi-open prison, and in November, 1953, the hostel scheme was started for their benefit (or, rather, for the benefit of as many of them as one hut within the walls of Bristol prison could accommodate), though this was not, as the Prison Commission claimed at the time, an innovation but a revival of the arrangement that had been instituted at Camp Hill forty years earlier. The hostel scheme idea originated, as we have seen, with Bentham.[3]

Preventive detainees who entered the third stage were eligible for release on licence after they had served two thirds of their sentence, whereas if they got stuck in the second stage, as the majority of them did, they were required to serve a minimum of five sixths. In this sense, they were worse off than Du Cane's convicts.

Both corrective training and preventive detention were abolished under the 1967 Criminal Justice Act. Twenty years experience had shown them to be what it is clear in retrospect they were bound to be from the beginning—not to mince words, fraudulent. Regrettably, however, they have not been replaced by anything more hopeful.

In 1963, a committee of the Home Office's Advisory Council

On the Treatment of Offenders issued a report[4] on Preventive Detention in which they advocated its abolition on grounds not wholly dissimilar from those which have been stated above, though differing from them in one essential. The Committee pointed out that the result of a psychiatric survey conducted by Dr D. J. West, Assistant Director of Research, Institute of Criminology, Cambridge University, showed that only 12% of preventive detainees were of "normal personality", whereas 52% were "passive inactive deviants." "... it is this last group", the Committee reported, "which presents a special problem in terms of treatment. Broadly speaking, the other groups can be provided for within the existing prison system, and such problems as they present are not peculiar to persistent offenders. It is the petty offender against property whose *criminal behaviour is the result of inadequacy rather than deliberate choice* who ... could with advantage be detained in rather more open conditions than are possible in a secure prison. In the first place, there would be very little risk to the public in removing this type of offender from closed prisons, since most of them are unlikely to abscond, or, if they did get out, to resort to serious crime. Secondly, they are less likely to continue preying on the public when released if during their sentence they are given more encouragement to form those habits of industry which are essential to their rehabilitation." (Author's italics.)

Note that expression "habits of industry" borrowed, though doubtless unconsciously, from the Act of 1779! However, the Committee went on to be less vague, than has been usual in such declarations, about *how* the "habits of industry" were to be fostered. "We have in mind that those who were fit might be allowed, at a comparatively early stage in the sentence, to work in ordinary jobs in the neighbourhood of the prison as the "hostellers" do at present in the third stage of preventive detention. For those who could not be trusted to work outside the prison, or as a preliminary to outside work, we hope that it would prove possible to provide a full day's work within the prison. We suggest, in particular, that consideration should be given to the setting up of one or two special establishments, possibly on the lines of the farming community at Ginevich in

Luxembourg, which some of our members visited, where the primary object, as we understand it, is to ensure that the prisoner does a full day's work and that in consequence the farm is, as far as may be, self-supporting, and where the prison staff work with the men and are *tradesmen rather than discipline officers*." (Author's italics.)

There the Committee would appear to have come close to clarifying the form, or at least one form, that non-punitive preventive detention might take. They were, however, thinking in terms of a fixed sentence, presumably of a comparatively short duration considering the type of petty offender to whom it was meant to apply. Though the result of this would be inequitable from the individual's point of view if "habits of industry" were in fact acquired before the pre-determined release date, and plainly wasteful from society's if they weren't acquired within the time allowed, the Committee had already rejected the indeterminate principle, and the reason why they had done so was implicit in their very next paragraph: "We have not overlooked the fact that a sentence imposed on a persistent offender must be a punishment for his past misdeeds as well as a preparation for his release. Partly for this reason . . . it may well be that the first part of the sentence should always be served in a secure prison."

But why, one may ask, *must* a man, whose "criminal behaviour is the result of inadequacy rather than deliberate choice", be punished for "past misdeeds", when presumably he has already *been* punished for all but the most recent of them? Not surely, to deter him, for if punishment had actually proved, or was potentially, a deterrent in his case, he wouldn't be a persistent offender. Nor, surely, to give him his "just deserts." Inadequacy is not a condition one wishes on oneself, or contracts through carelessness, any more than lunacy is. It is something one cannot help, and if a man's criminal behaviour is due to inadequacy, then, *ergo*, it is something he should not be blamed for.

One sees here a prime instance of the punitive obsession, and hence of the muddle-headedness, that has always bedevilled penal policy. This forces one to question whether anybody who elects to work within the prison system, and to accept its basic assumption that rehabilitation and punishment are necessarily reconcilable objectives, can really deserve the reputation of "great reformer", which Alexander Paterson achieved. He was certainly a humanitarian. As a young man, he had visited Dartmoor and had been deeply shocked by what he saw there. "The drab uniforms of the prisoners were plastered with broad arrows . . . their heads were covered with a sort of dirty moss . . . hair that a pair of clippers could not remove. The prison regime . . . determined to minimize the chances of violence or suicide . . . had succeeded in making human beings into objects of ugliness and contempt. As they saw us coming, each man ran to the nearest wall and put his face closely against it, remaining in this servile position until we had passed him by."[5]

It is, no doubt, largely owed to Paterson that such a prison scene was done away with sooner than it might otherwise have been—that prisoners were permitted to shave themselves, to associate, and so forth. On the other hand, when the present author visited Wormwood Scrubs in 1934 (as a matter of fact, at Paterson's suggestion) he was required to keep his hat on, because, so it was explained to him, if he took it off the prisoners would interpret the act as a mark of respect to which they were not entitled. Moreover, one may be sure that even today any such description of the evolution of the system as the following, which was written in 1952 by Sir Lionel Fox, Chairman of the Prison Commission, would give prisoners and a good many prison staff as well a very hoarse laugh indeed.[6]

"First, the old style, the powerful and perdurable Norman of Du Cane, ending with the South African war; second, the Transitional style of Ruggles-Brise, with the structural features modifying, though the feeling of the old style tends to persist; and third, after World War 1, the Early English of Alexander Paterson, releasing the true spirit of the structure in a 'first fine careless rapture' of seminal ideas, which his successors may not hope to recapture, but can strive to bring to full fruition, working out all their implications in a manner which may come, in the course of history, to be regarded as a 'Second English' style in its own right. Nor will the visitor informed with the spirit of this analogy be surprised, in looking at a building which the guide books tell him is Second English, to find here and there a feature of the earlier style, or even what he may suspect to be an original Norman wall."

When those words were written, every closed prison in the country belonged, architecturally, to Du Cane's "Norman" or earlier, so that Sir Lionel's analogy was, perhaps, unfortunately chosen. Seven years later, at any rate, in 1959, the Prison Commissioners decided that a new building programme was a matter of urgent necessity, and their reasons were spelled out in *Penal Practice in a Changing Society*,[7] which was presented to Parliament by the Home Secretary (R. A. Butler). "To have to work in prisons which are virtually unchanged since they were built in the nineteenth century or earlier, when the whole emphasis was on security and deterrence, does not invite constructive training which is necessary if they are to succeed. It is no more possible to train prisoners in these obsolete conditions than it would be to provide a twentieth-century system of education in antiquated schools or to carry out modern hospital treatment in the unimproved buildings of the pre-Victorian era. Nor can we hope to attract the sort of staff we need if their living and working conditions are below a normal modern standard, and if they lack the accommodation and the amenities which a good employer now regards it as his duty to provide. A building programme planned in relation to modern requirements is therefore a pre-requisite of progress."

But if this was indeed a "pre-requisite of progress", it is impossible to believe that it had suddenly become so. It must equally have been a pre-requisite to the execution of Paterson's "seminal ideas", all of which were aimed at resolving what he himself called the paradox of trying to train men for freedom under conditions of captivity. The demand for a new building programme in 1959 was tantamount to an admission by the Prison Commission that the paradox had been irresoluble; and this fact lends credibility to the evidence of educated ex-prisoners who, during Paterson's lifetime and afterwards, found little or no trace of the "Early English", despite what the guide books said. For example, Rupert Croft-Cooke, the distinguished novelist, who in 1954 spent nine months (less remission) in Wormwood Scrubs for an alleged homosexual offence, was emphatically disillusioned. "I came into prison," he wrote later,[8] "without preconceived ideas, without bitterness and wholly without fear . . . Had I not heard somewhere that prisons were enormously improved and their inmates really helped towards reinstatement after they were discharged. And I say that the thing is rotten throughout, a mosquito-swamp of evil in which crime breeds crime, in which minds fester and all hope of resurrection is lost. It cannot be saved by piddling improvements; it must be viewed with imagination, not with the squinting side-glance of a half-hearted reformer."

Now here one must be careful to avoid the implication that the Wormwood Scrubs Rupert Croft-Cooke knew was still just as "Norman" as Du Cane had originally designed it to be. Plainly it was not, if only because of the "association" that had been increasingly permitted since the formal and final abolition of the separate system in 1922 and, though a good many years later, of the Silence Rule. No doubt, Du Cane himself would have found the relaxation of discipline staggering—a massive submission to foolhardy sympathy for the criminal. Some of the more conservative old lags of his day might have been equally shocked. Indeed, one of them had told Colonel Rich back in the 'twenties, during the early days of this "first fine careless rapture", before the rot had gone nearly so far: "I must say I am surprised at the state of things in our prisons, but again I say, do away with 'Molly Colly'; do not be cruel, but be 'strick'. The dark cell was the only punishment that brought me up."[9]

The question to be asked, though, is not whether the improvements effected under Paterson's influence were in reality "piddling", but whether the change-over, or change-back, from separateness to association was, or ever could be, a change for the better. To be fair to Paterson, he did not, like the Gladstone Committee, dodge this question. In principle, he was opposed to the separate system, presumably because he believed it could serve only a negative purpose. "If a prison is merely a cloakroom in which the enemy of society is duly deposited," he wrote, "till called for after a fixed period, or a kennel in which he is safely caged until on the appointed day he is let loose on society again, then indeed the protection afforded is of a temporary nature, and it may well be that, after the security of a few months or years, society will be at the mercy of an enemy more bitter and implacable than before."

On the other hand, Paterson warned that "a sloppy and unthinking sentiment may rush us into forms of association far more injurious to those concerned than any evils of solitude." "We are not justified in herding some scores of weak and vicious characters together unless we can take such steps as will insure that the tone of the whole will be higher than the tone of the individual, so that each man may be raised rather than debased by his membership of the community. This is a stern proviso . . . "

Paterson had ideas for meeting the "stern proviso", though they were hardly "seminal". One of them was classification "according to both age and degree of criminality." Another was to furnish the prisoners with healthy topics of conversation (in place of their "criminal exploits" and the "indecencies of life") through the organization of "lectures, classes and debates and a measure of sport."

Actually, a suggestion that prisoners might benefit from lectures and concerts had been put to Du Cane by the Gladstone Committee, had surprisingly enough won his approval, and to a small extent was already being practised during Ruggles-Brise's "transitional style." However, Dr Mary Gordon, who served as Medical Inspector of Prisons under the Ruggles-Brise regime, regarded it as just another reformative smokescreen. "During my service," she wrote,[10] "I found nothing in the prison system to interest me, except as a gigantic irrelevance, a social curiosity. If the system had a good effect on any prisoner, I failed to notice it. I had no shadow of doubt of its power to demoralize or of its cruelty . . . When we adopt the puerile view that . . . an evening's pleasure, or any other such creation from *our* phantasies, will serve our turn with one crushed but untamable man or woman, we only cover up the root of our own failure. Nothing will serve us but to understand the laws that govern the prisoner's and our own psychology. As long as we give him no outlet, but foster in him those emotional states which lead to unreality and fresh crime, he will remain our manufactured article. He is as capable of taking our directions for his mind, or the food we provide for his soul, and weaving them into his criminal wishes as the man Tolstoy tells of was capable of being fortified by the beautiful Kreutzer Sonata to do his murder."

Those words, it should be emphasized, were published as long ago as 1922, in the same year that Paterson joined the Prison Commission, and one may suspect that, true or false, they were beyond his emotional comprehension. In essence, his ideas derived from the late 18th century and early 19th century reformers, with their faith in "good example", and if he hadn't happened to live at a time when the separate system was already discredited, he might have seen no reason to reject it. Nor was his understanding of what "good example" meant, or of how it was to be set, fundamentally different from that of his predecessors. He believed in imparting the supposedly Christian virtues which, idealistically, the public schools taught, and not surprisingly, therefore, he took a particular interest in the development of borstal training. There was no borstal boy, he claimed, without a latent capacity, to "respond to the appeal made to the British of every sort to play the game, to follow the flag, to stand by the old ship."

In *Gaol Delivery* (1946), Mark Benney has called the prison system a "religious experiment that failed and was left lying about." Paterson, by contrast, regarded it as a religious experiment that could be made to work, and he was able to inspire his fellow workers, in the office and the field, with the same conviction. One of them was Major B. J. Grew, who, in a book of memoirs[11] published in 1958, nine years after Paterson's death, assured the public: "Elizabeth Fry has been described as the prophetess of our penal system, for she envisaged separate cells for prisoners, and their employment on useful work; she wanted opportunities provided for education and rehabilitation, and she believed that prisoners should be treated not as objects of revenge but as human beings whose cooperation should be sought in the reformation of their own characters and that this should be achieved through personal example and influence . . . Elizabeth Fry would find all these things being carried out in Wormwood Scrubs and other English prisons today . . ."

Elizabeth Fry would doubtless also note with satisfaction the use made of volunteer prison visitors: a plan which she initiated and which, characteristically, was then dropped only to be revived, with a great flourish of trumpets, at the outset of the Paterson era in 1922. It may be fanciful to imagine that she would find everything exactly as she had wanted it to be, considering, for instance, the thousands of men sleeping three to a single cell. But that is not the point. The point is whether she, or anyone else, has ever discovered how to make punitive imprisonment reformative.

Major Grew happened to be governor of Wormwood Scrubs while Rupert Croft-Cooke was a prisoner there. But one does not have to disbelieve him in order to believe Croft-Cooke, or *vice versa*. Wildly divergent though their two accounts of conditions may seem, there is nothing basically irreconcilable in them. The difference is that while Major Grew assumed, and indeed had to assume, if he was to retain his professional self-respect, that the "useful work", the "opportunities for education" and so on were in themselves sufficient for the purpose of fitting men to lead good and useful lives on their discharge, Mr Croft-Cooke discovered that manifestly they were not.

Apart from the usual complement of imbeciles and psychotics among Croft-Cooke's fellow inmates, all of them first offenders, all of them, therefore, classified as "Stars", was a first-time-caught professional thief of great charm and long experience whom he calls "Mike" in his book. Mike "was an accepted leader among the tough and dangerous London screwsmen in the Scrubs," and, naturally enough, crime and the indecencies of life were the staples of his talk in association. "I remember thinking as I listened to him," Mr Croft-Cooke writes,[12] "how far I had come from my peaceful Sussex home, from the garden and the downs to the savage world he incoherently described. I was intensely interested and I could very easily see how his point of view could gain the sympathy of other young men in prison, how his predatory and anarchic creed could appeal to a sentimental or romantic nature. A man sent to prison unjustly or through an unjust law, smarting under his blows, feeling that he is already an outcast, could find in Mike's anti-social and wholly unscrupulous declaration the basis of a dogma of revenge."

That is another illustration of a point which need not be laboured further; namely, that classification is not, and never has been, other than a pretence method of isolating prisoners from corruptive influences. It is too arbitrary and mechanical to be effective, and given the present limits on prison accommodation and on the facilities for social and psychiatric investigation into an individual's background, so it is bound to remain. Even if this were not so, even if it were perfectly possible to segregate all the "good" offenders sentenced to penal institutions from the "bad", the result would merely provide a safeguard against contamination for those who aren't, anyhow, in need of reformative training and treatment.

Ironically enough, something of this sort actually seems to be happening, so far as the use found for open prisons is concerned, for the Home Office administrators have taken one of Mountbatten's security warnings even more seriously than he evidently intended it to be. "There will, no doubt," Mountbatten reported, "continue to be escapes, or abscondings, as they are better called, from open prisons. These represent a social nuisance and are an additional burden on the police, and everything possible should be done to reduce them. They should not, however, represent a threat to the life and safety of the population if chosen with care, and in regard to these prisoners I would not think it unreasonable for the authorities to take certain risks, always provided that the allocations are made with care and that no absconding is treated as a trivial matter." But apparently the "authorities" have decided it would be more prudent to take no risks at all, or at any rate, substantially fewer risks than heretofore, with the result that at the time of writing, despite the continued overcrowding of closed prisons, the open prisons are under-populated.[13] According to the Prison Department's 1967 Report, ". . . the growing tendency of the courts not to commit less sophisticated offenders to prison (a process since accelerated by the introduction of the suspended sentence) reduced the number found suitable for open prisons." That means, presumably, that in general only "less sophisticated offenders", i.e. offenders who might as well not be in custody at all, are now found "suitable for open prisons."

The first of the English prisons without bars was New Hall Camp. This was established in 1936 as a sort of country annexe to the old "separate" prison at Wakefield, which at the time was reserved for young "Stars" undergoing training. New Hall had accommodation for some fifty specially selected men from the main prison. They slept in dormitory huts, and by day were either employed outside the camp as agricultural labourers, or worked inside it at bootmaking and similar tasks. Conceptually, New Hall bore a close resemblance to the 19th century Irish intermediate prisons, and although its establishment in 1936 was both hailed and feared as a very bold new venture, it might more accurately be described as a tardy implementation of a subsidiary proposal made by the Gladstone Committee. For though Du Cane and his associates had been consistently opposed to the introduction of intermediate prisons in England, the Committee had recommended that the idea should be tried experimentally.

However, it can be fairly argued that the open prison, as it has been developed since the end of the second world war, and as we know it today, is less associated with the concept of the intermediate prison than with an experiment carried out six years before the appearance of New Hall. In 1930 a group of carefully selected and prepared borstal boys marched 132 miles from their converted prison at Feltham to build for themselves the first of the open borstal institutions at Lowdham, near Nottingham. Not one of them attempted to abscond on the way, although they were put under no form of restraint, apart from being accompanied by staff in plain clothes. This achievement, which was considered spectacular at the time, was owed to Paterson's initiative. Presumably, it led to a realization that there were adults as well as juveniles who could be trusted to serve the whole (or nearly the whole) of a sentence to captivity without being put behind bars. And this is one of perhaps two genuinely seminal ideas that have invaded the prison system during the present century.

Whether it equals an "advance" is another matter. It can, obviously enough, only be an advance to the extent that open prisons have actually replaced closed prisons; and that is still a very small extent which, as we have noted, is currently getting smaller. But, more importantly, one must consider what is meant by "advance", or, rather what objective prison administrators, since the beginning of the Paterson era, have supposed themselves to be advancing towards.

Paterson had a considerable gift of articulation. This could result in illuminating statements, as, for example, when he described a prison as a "monastery of men who have not chosen to be monks." But it could also result in compelling but none the less empty verbiage. Exaggerated claims and promises have been characteristic of the centralized prison administration throughout its history, either because the men at the top have been too high up to know what is really going on beneath them, or because they have persuaded themselves that the truth is what at any given moment they have thought it ought to be. "We may not have the best possible prison system," Paterson said as early as 1930. "But I do claim we have the best prison system in the world." Here he was being true to the traditions of his calling—in a sense, "standing by the old ship." But the fact that it *was* still the old ship might have been apparent to others, besides those forced aboard it, if Paterson had not been such a talented supplier of words for the construction of a new one. And those words have lost none of their power to bemuse his successors.

"Imprisonment *as* punishment, not *for* punishment," is, perhaps, the most famous of his slogans. "Its application means that a criminal pays off his debit account with society," Major Grew wrote in his memoirs.[14] "Society must then help him to avoid getting into trouble again by using that period of his loss of liberty, wherever possible, to help him to become a better citizen." The same principle, it will be recalled, was stated by Sir Joshua Jebb in regard to the objective and conditions of penal servitude.

But it is, of course, nonsense to pretend that society accepts, or ever has accepted, the equation of punishment with loss of liberty alone. If it were to do so, there would be no logical reason left for distinguishing between the treatment due to unpunishable people who may be deprived of their freedom (e.g., lunatics, whether or not convicted of offences against the law) and the treatment due to allegedly responsible criminals.

Logically, moreover, living conditions would have to be varied to suit individual needs, for those conditions which one prisoner will find up to the standard he is used to, another will find far below it. Diet is an example. A retired Chief Officer, L. W. Merrow Smith, has written (1962)[15] that whereas the prison dietary scale was at one time insufficient, both in quality and quantity to "maintain ordinary health", it is now "much better than that of many families in the lower wage groups . . ." So it may be, though incidentally there has never been a time when it wasn't represented to be as good as, or better than, the diet the poorer members of society were accustomed to. But even granted that the majority of prisoners find it perfectly satisfying, there must be the few who, because of their superior background, consider it penal.

This may be dismissed as a mere debating point. It may be said that a degree of standardization, particularly in regard to food, is unavoidable in any institution and is, therefore, a concomitant of loss of liberty, which consequently is bound to bear more hardly on some than on others. Nevertheless, the "pains" of imprisonment, as the American criminologist, Gresham Sykes has called them,[16] are undoubtedly far in excess of what custody by itself needs to entail. This being so, "Imprisonment *as* punishment, not *for* punishment" remains a meaningless slogan. It simply begs the question of what punishment is or should be.

"A Government", Paterson said, "would risk its reputation for being civilized if it maintained no prisons", and by prisons one must assume that he meant custodial institutions which were intended to serve a punitive as well as a reformative purpose. For a non-punitive prison is a contradiction in terms, just as a punitive mental hospital is a contradiction in terms—at least if and when it is not so, it is a recognized barbarity.

Moreover, the prisons which Paterson knew, and which he helped to administer, were as obtrusively "symbols of punishment" as their 19th century architects had known how to make them. To quote Rupert Croft-Cooke again:[17] "Look down a long interior street on each side of which are rows of identical cell doors. The floor of this street is of concrete, the doors are blank and painted a dull cream with formidable black iron bolts on each and a small eye-hole. The street is a hundred yards long, lit with naked not-too-powerful electric bulbs and running down to iron railings and a gated wall at the far end. Now begin to look upwards. Above these cells are others opening on to openwork iron-bound passages so that the long mean galleries run down the whole length of the hall. They are reached by two iron staircases which rise from the ground level. Above these is another identical iron landing and above that yet another . . . The roof which is almost invisible at night is of soiled and murky glass. At the level of the first floor is stretched wire netting to lessen the risk of suicide . . . A prison 'hall' realizes the highest hopes of its original architect, for it is probably the ugliest structure ever conceived by man."

So long as imprisonment means being locked up in such monstrously designed places—and that is what it still does mean in the great majority of cases—there can obviously be no validity to the claim that the punishment begins and ends with the loss of personal freedom. All the administrators can honestly claim is that, due to certain relaxations of discipline, the punishment is more bearable, or less unbearable, today than it was half a century ago. This, no doubt, is partly due to the inexorable retreat of deterrent practice before the humanitarian advance. But it is also reflective of the means by which Paterson believed it possible to resolve the paradox of trying to train people for freedom under conditions of captivity. Since Paterson infected his successors with his hopes as well as his illusions, they have carried on where he left off—or at least they did until, at the end of 1966, the Mountbatten report put this liberalizing policy (temporarily at least) into reverse.

In fact, penal reform has come to be almost wholly equated in in the public's mind with the idea of treating criminals more kindly, so that the question of whether one is against "reform" or in favour of it now appears to depend, not on an intellectual attempt to decide what sort of penal system might serve society's interests best, but on an emotional conviction that criminals are being dealt with too leniently or not leniently enough. Thus Mr John Sparrow, Warden of All Souls, has recently (*The Times*, 26 February 1970) accused reformers of "being more revolted by the thought of punishment than by the thought of crime." In the sense that the majority of the people to whom he was referring are not opposed to punishment as such, but only to punishments (e.g., the death penalty) which they consider cruel and excessive, this was a valid argument. But it was also based on the old unscientific assumption that punishment is more or less deterrent in accordance with its degree of severity, and since nobody's faith in this theory can be other than emotionally conditioned, Mr Sparrow, for all his intellectual eminence, was really just one more of the reactionary pots calling the progressive kettles black.

Still, assuming for the moment that the primary purpose of imprisonment should be to teach criminals to live lawfully in freedom, there is obviously a strong, if not an overwhelming, case for making the conditions of their captivity as like or as little unlike conditions in the free world as it is possible to make them: to offer prisoners as nearly as possible the same rights, joys and opportunities they would have as free citizens and, just as importantly, to face them with the same duties and responsibilities.

This has been the intellectual justification for the so-called "soft" policy: for such things as association, an earnings scheme, limited freedom of purchase out of earnings (tobacco,[18] newspapers and periodicals, confectionery and so on), increased facilities for keeping in touch with the outside world through visits and correspondence as well as access to television, radio and the printed word. But the policy has not been pushed nearly as far as rationally it should be and practically it could be. A prison is still a "monastery of men who have not chosen to be monks". A prisoner is still a person virtually without rights and without duties, except the duty of slavishly obeying the rules and regulations. He is still governed by fear. And, as for mere privileges, he is not yet as well off as the convicts aboard the dreaded Hulks were before Parliament took steps to end their "jolly life." So long as that "jolly life" lasted, a Hulk convict could earn more in real terms than the average prisoner can earn today, he could buy more, his correspondence was unrestricted and, unofficially at least, he might be permitted a conjugal visit.

Indeed, it is possibly true to say, as a generalization, that the total effect of the liberalizing measures introduced over the past half century has not been to make prison life less abnormal, but to make prison culture more criminal. The danger of contamination, as Paterson understood very well, is inherent in association. So is the danger of domination by the strong over the weak. Every Hulk community, as we have seen, had its exploiters who traded in food and tobacco. Today, every prison (or nearly every prison) has its tobacco "Barons." Thus, according to the retired Chief Officer, L. W. Merrow Smith, who has been quoted above,[19] "(they) illicitly advance 'snout' to other prisoners at exorbitant rates of interest. A return of three times the amount advanced is no uncommon demand, and payment is enforced by the barons' bodyguard henchmen. The unfortunate debtor has either to pay up from his next week's wages or else has to sham sickness in the hope of inducing the doctor to admit him to hospital, where for a time at least he is more or less immune from bodily attack. But if he cannnot 'work the dummy' on the doctor and is still unable or unwilling to meet his obligations to the 'baron' he will, sooner or later, be beaten up. If he is a powerful man, useful with his fists, he may avoid a frontal attack, but inevitably the day will come when something heavy is dropped on his head from an upper tier of cells, or he is otherwise 'accidentally' injured. Some men compromise with the 'baron' and repay the borrowed tobacco in cheese or margarine. In these cases they have to hand over the cheese and margarine as they receive them each day and content themselves with dry bread."

Another cause of violence in prison is the presence of effeminate types of homosexual—the "janes" as L. W. Merrow Smith calls them:[20] "Such men never lack protectors . . . Immediately one is received, the suitors pay court. Mostly the suitors are the vicious gangster type and, once accepted in their role, they act as unofficial bodyguards for the pseudo-ladies. Such 'friendships' which are revolting to all decent men, frequently lead to trouble. The 'lady' may tire of her protector and take another. This naturally leads to fights and sometimes serious incidents. Of course, the prison authorities do all possible to discourage these associations, but, despite this, homosexual acts take place."

Since the prison authorities know of only one way to "discourage" any form of activity—and that is to make it a punishable offence—one may assume that if and when homosexual behaviour is discovered the participants are ordinarily punished. But apparently this doesn't often happen. Officially speaking, homosexual behaviour is a comparatively minor disciplinary problem. Moreover, one is assured that the risk of a normally sexed man being seduced in prison, or of resorting to homosexual practices out of frustration, is very much slighter than might be supposed.

Still, to judge from the recorded experiences of a number of ex-prisoners, it would be unwise to assume that this risk is by any means negligible or that association has not exacerbated it. For instance, in *Walls Have Mouths* (1936), an account by Wildred Macartney of ten years penal servitude, one may read: "Masturbation is general in prison, and is referred to openly and indifferently. When I went to prison, the idea of becoming even temporarily homosexual never entered my head. There are many homosexuals in gaol, and for at least four years I took no interest in them. The first knowledge that the mind was being perverted by the unnatural existence of gaol came to me through my dreams. The imagery began to change. The persistent, sharply accentuated image of womanhood became clouded after about three and a half years. Even when awake I began to find that fantastic images were pushing the original normal image out of the way. Gradually a homosexual shadow obscured the normal picture, and I began to have definitely homosexual dreams. I do not propose to enlarge further upon my own sex life, but I shall assert that within my observation the beneficial effects of such contacts upon the mental and physical health were undeniable, and my experience was that of the average man. Of course, some repressed themselves terribly and never consciously entered into this life. Others went to extremes and developed perversions that would make Kraft-Ebing's hair stand upright.... That homosexuality should take place between convicts is inevitable, and so tense is the prison atmosphere with the vibrations of suppressed sex that the gaolers themselves are affected by it... Nora, a pansy of repute, gained a prestige, something like that of a great courtesan, by a long affair with a jailor known as S—, who was a very decent fellow."

Now if there were a wholehearted commitment to "normalizing" the conditions of imprisonment, the atmosphere could undoubtedly be made a great deal less violent and unhealthy than it is. "Baronage" thrives on a tobacco shortage, which is, in fact, a prerequisite to it. But this shortage is in a sense deliberately promoted, not by the "Barons", who step in to exploit it, but by the authorities who bewail and are evidently unable to control the consequences. For nicotine is a mildly addictive drug, and to permit a prisoner to smoke, while denying him the opportunity to buy sufficient tobacco to satisfy his needs, is to create a new and essentially abnormal form of starvation. Out of his still miserably meagre earnings the average prisoner cannot afford more than 20 cigarettes a week, and even so at the sacrifice of alternative purchases that might be of benefit to his body or mind. The solution to this problem is self-evident—increased pay, though that is not to say that if this were done, some other similar problem might not arise.

The solution to the sexual problem is hardly less obvious, for, as foreign example shows, there is no compelling reason why prisons should be run as monasteries. In so far as the conjugal visit has been discussed at all in this country, it has been represented as a means of maintaining family relationships, and the authorities argue that an extension of the "home leave" scheme, under which long-term prisoners are permitted to return home for a weekend near the end of their sentences, would be preferable for this purpose. But in Mexico and certain other Latin American countries, where attempts have been made to normalize the sex life of prisoners, the expression "conjugal visit" is frankly admitted to be euphemistic. Though it doubtless does help to maintain family relationships, its real point is to relieve sexual tensions in captive societies. At Ixtapalapa, outside Mexico City, for instance, every inmate is entitled to a weekly conjugal visit that lasts three hours and takes place in a kind of luxury hostel, which is accessible from both within and without the main prison. A man may choose his wife for his partner if he has one; but, whether he has a wife or not, he is allowed to choose a girl friend.

The known homosexuals at Ixtapalapa are segregated from the heterosexuals. If classification means anything at all, one may wonder why they are not similarly kept apart in this country. Equally, one may wonder why, now that homosexual behaviour between consenting adults in private is lawful in our free society, it should continue to be a punishable offence in our prisons; why, in other words, homosexual prisoners should not be allowed to satisfy their own sexual desires in their own way without fear of reprisals.

But that question is just a small part of the main question that provokes endless "whys". Why, if the objective of prison treatment is to encourage self-respect and a sense of personal responsibility, are many practices retained which are designed for precisely the opposite purpose? Why is a prisoner's correspondence read and censored? Why is it restricted, ordinarily to two letters a week? Why are his visits supervised and limited to one a month? Why is he given virtually no opportunity for initiative? Why is he locked up in a cell at nights and often for a good part of the day as well? Why is he deprived of all his everyday possessions—watch, fountain pen, and so on? Why is he none the less liable to periodic "naked searches"? Why is he allowed no freedom of movement behind the prison walls? Why is he obliged to wear prison dress which, though less ugly than it used to be, is still a "dress of shame"?

"Security" is the official pretext for these continuing degradations that make prison life so palpably remote from life in the free world. But what is alleged to be necessary for security purposes is simply a modified version of regulations that existed in Du Cane's time, when degradation was intended and individualization of treatment unheard of. "Moral supervision has, to a certain extent, replaced mere physical restraint," Major Arthur Griffiths wrote.[21] "It is found that prisoners can be more effectively guarded by warders than by huge senseless stones and purely passive chains, provided only there is above all the sleepless eye of a stringent systematic discipline."

To some extent, Mountbatten, particularly with his idea of a purpose-built prison for dangerous offenders, appeared to favour a reversion to the 18th century idea of strong perimeter defences. Whether such defences, however formidable they might be made, could equal total security is questionable. As Hablin Smith, a retired medical officer, pointed out in 1934:[22] "It was thought that a massive building with high walls, thick gates, and the like was the best method of keeping the prisoners in durance vile. Old Newgate appeared as safe as any place could be, from this point of view; yet escapes from there were frequent." Conceivably, the stronger a perimeter is made, the more provocative it is to a certain type of prisoner; the more determined it makes him to prove (to himself and the world) that there is no obstacle he cannot surmount. In any case very little is known about the psychology of escapes, or about what can best be done to prevent them, because no serious attempt has been made to find out. It is unfortunately characteristic of prison administration in this country that the Mountbatten inquiry was panic-inspired, that it was completed, within a matter of weeks, by a man who had no apparent qualifications for conducting it, and that nearly all its resultant recommendations have been uncritically carried out, with the exception, again characteristically, of the one which would have cost the most money to implement—the purpose-built prison.

One may be morally certain that most prisoners find the high surrounding wall of the closed prison a sufficient discouragement to escape, and do not need to be locked up in their cells like animals, to have their letters censored, their visits supervised, and so on. On the other hand, there may be a minority who could not safely be allowed a greater degree of licence than they already enjoy. Accordingly, the maintenance of a discipline, which makes nonsense of the promise to encourage self-respect, can be explained on the grounds that security arrangements in a prison must of necessity be designed to meet the case of the few determined trouble-makers, regardless of the consequences for the more or less docile majority. But that is another way of saying that classification is inadequate, and individualization of treatment still largely a myth. Besides, there are surviving regulations which cannot, by any stretch of the imagination, be regarded as necessary in the interests of security. The reception procedure, for instance, has hardly altered since Pentonville was built. It still includes the compulsory bath,[23] which may be an urgent necessity in some cases, but in others is a planned humiliation, even if the bath-water is neither as dirty nor as tepid as it was in Oscar Wilde's day.

One of the major degradations on reception has gone, it is true. Prisoners no longer have their hair cropped. When the Governor of Millbank was asked by the Kimberley Commission what purpose was served in doing this to women, since they were allowed to grow their hair again in prison, he was unable to answer; he supposed it was "just a tradition." Much of the prison discipline which continues to defeat the declared objective of prison treatment still has no more persuasive rationale than tradition, and it stems in particular from the principle of a standardized punishment.

"For four nights and three days . . . I found myself accommodated in an overheated and smelly cell with bare walls, a small, high window, red light in the ceiling and peephole in the door. There was a two inch thick straw mattress on the slightly raised wooden platform, a wooden shelf to eat from and a lump of concrete like a tree stump as a seat. I had bedding but no pillow. I was allowed out of my cell to slop out and taken for exercise . . . behind the detention block. After a day I was aching all over from the hard mattress." That is a description of one of the traditional prison punishments which one might suppose would today only be inflicted on unusually recalcitrant prisoners for unusually serious offences. In fact, the description comes (*Sunday Telegraph*, 9 April 1967) from William McConnachie, former Chief Constable of Southend. He was an inmate of Ford Open Prison, and was punished near the end of his sentence for the offence of absenting himself for a few hours from his outside employment without the governor's permission. During 1967, there were no fewer than 246 sentences of "cellular" (solitary) confinement passed on those "less sophisticated" offenders who are "suited to open conditions." At Ford, there were 60 by comparison with only 11 cautions and 16 stoppages or reductions of earnings. At Hollesley Bay open borstal (which one officially is assured is the most advanced of all the boys' borstals) there were 131 cases of solitary confinement (known euphemistically as "confinement to room") and 127 cases of solitary confinement on a "restricted diet" by comparison with seven cautions and 42 stoppages of earnings.[24]

One mentions these figures as an indication of how traditionally punitive imprisonment can still be, despite Home Office claims to the contrary.[25] The extent to which it can be non-punitive in this sense depends on the attitude of individual governors and, more particularly, on the cooperation they are able to win from their uniformed staff. It is instructive to note that at Blundeston, one of the new closed prisons, only 15 punishments of cellular confinement were awarded during 1947 compared with 76 cautions and 136 stoppages of earnings. Yet considering that Blundeston received in that year preventive detention prisoners and selected ordinary class prisoners serving long sentences, it is impossible to believe that its average inmate was so much easier to handle than the "less sophisticated" offenders at Ford. But it is not surprising to learn that Blundeston had one of the most progressive-minded governors in the country.

Theoretically, life can be made a great deal more "normal", or less hideously abnormal, in an open prison than in a 19th century closed prison, but not necessarily in practice, if the old authoritarian discipline survives, if the old terroristic methods of enforcing it are retained, if the old needless (and, indeed, contradictory) "security" regulations are imposed, and if, above all, the intention to degrade survives.

Phoebe Willets, who served a sentence for anti-nuclear armament activities, has written[26] of Hill Hall, which is possibly as liberally run an open prison as exists: "If a prisoner . . . when she is put in beautiful surroundings is made to feel that she is being looked down on to a greater extent than when she was in the old-fashioned prison, then a large proportion of prisoners will prefer the grimmer surroundings . . . When, at Hill Hall, we were greeted with an excellent meal, it seemed to harass the mind of every officer that we might, everyone of us, be under the illusion that this was the Ritz, so that throughout our sentence, the words were perpetually echoing through our ears: 'This is *not* a hotel . . . Willets . . . This is *not* a hotel . . .' " It is a typical punitive tradition to address prisoners convicted or unconvicted, even women prisoners, by their surnames without a prefix. This doesn't happen in any Scandinavian prison, and one may note, incidentally, that *The Times* newspaper has recently renounced the practice.

Phoebe Willets also says: "The real tragedy was to see a new bunch of women come in, quiet and subdued, no doubt by the fear of entering a new prison, but often genuinely good-tempered and homely women that I had made friends with at Holloway. Then to watch them deteriorate after two weeks, sometimes sooner . . . It just isn't possible to take ordinary human beings and ask them to live together, to sleep together, to work together. Not to be able to walk out of the room when you feel the atmosphere get tense, not to be able to go out for a walk when you feel your temperature rising, not to be able to say quietly, 'I am so sorry, I must go now' when someone is trying to provoke you . . ."

Those objections could be met if open prisons were equipped with single rooms instead of dormitories, and if the inmates were allowed to use their leisure hours as they pleased—had freedom to take a walk in the grounds if they felt like it. But the one reform would cost a considerable sum of money, though rather less, one may guess, than the implementation of Mountbatten's proposals for making the closed prisons "secure", while the other would add volume to such outraged cries as come from Mr Duncan Sandys: "Prisons are becoming more and more like rest homes."

Still, it must be re-emphasized that we are concerned here not with the question of whether or not imprisonment should be made more or less punitive, but with the quite separate question of what could be done in the way of honouring the promissory notes issued by the Home Office. To treat adult women like naughty schoolgirls, as they are evidently treated at Hill Hall, seems hardly the way to encourage their "self-respect", still less their "sense of personal responsibility." Indeed, so far as one can see, the only special responsibility with which the inmates of an open prison are entrusted is the responsibility of resisting the temptation (or invitation) to abscond. But that is not a responsibility they are taught to accept; it is one they are presumed capable of discharging *ab initio*.

One does not wish to underestimate the practical consequences of an officially liberal attitude. Even if the prison service is by no means purged of its traditionalists—its martinets and outright sadists—it undoubtedly attracts some staff today, particularly senior staff, of a far higher quality of both mind and heart than it did in the pre-Paterson era. There are men working as governors and assistant governors who, one may feel sure, could, if they chose, pursue an easier and considerably more lucrative career as personnel managers in industry. In other words, they do what they do out of a genuine belief in and dedication to a reformative penal policy.

Yet even in the most progressively run of prisons, where conditions are as little repressive as, or perhaps rather less repressive than, the rules permit them to be, one cannot say that much more has been achieved than a shift from an authoritarian to a paternalistic attitude. "What we try to do at Blundeston", a man is informed on his arrival there, "is based on the assumption that you want to go straight when you are released. To this end you will be expected to think for yourself, to discipline yourself, and to make an effort yourself. You can use the Staff as a sounding board to work out for yourself what has gone wrong in the past, what you can do while in prison, which should, of course, be in line with what you want to do on release."

The recidivist who reads that, and believes it, may be more alarmed than encouraged, especially if he has already spent long years in authoritarian types of prison, and is partially or wholly institutionalized. "Thinking for himself" and "disciplining himself" is not his idea of an "easy nick." He has learned to "slope through any ordinary sentence", as Sir Ian Horabin has put it (*The Observer*, 10 October 1965), through knuckling under to an imposed routine—doing no more nor less than he's told to do when he's told to do it.

But in fact he has less to fear than he may imagine, for the Blundeston system does not add up to a renunciation of any part of the routine to which he's accustomed—not even, as it happens, the slopping-out. The official description[27] of it, which it is worth quoting in full, reads as follows:

"Each wing of 76 prisoners is divided into eight sections of from 8 to 10 prisoners, each with a Section Officer responsible for developing an individual counselling relationship with each man on his section.

"He is expected to build up a case history for each prisoner who will attend a Review Board twice per week with his Section Officer, Wing Principal Officer, Assistant Governor or Deputy Governor.

"The Section Officer attends the Hostel Selection Board, presents a report to the Board, and is involved in the decision making.

"When a prisoner is released a summary of the case history is forwarded to the After-Care Officer. The Section Officers are expected to work in close liaison with the Wing Principal Officer and the Welfare Officer with on going situations concerning the men on his section.

"All sporting, social and recreational activities are run on a group or club basis with prisoners involved in the organization and administration supervised by an officer who acts as a Liaison Officer.

"Each Wing has a prison Wing Committee consisting of Chairman, a Secretary and representatives for Sports, Messing, Television and Education. There is an hour's meeting each Saturday which Staff attend in a support and guidance role.

"Each month the Chairman and Secretary of each wing attend a Central Council meeting, with the Governor as Chairman, at which available staff attend and prisoners may attend as non-participants. The function of this meeting is to facilitate feed back from the Wing Meetings. This allows for problems to be brought into the open for free discussion.

"The regime of the prison system is centred on shared responsibility, open communication and the development of positive relationships between staff and prisoners. There is an attempt to use the total human resources to aid to the development of a sense of community."

Here it should be said that the new closed prisons, of which Blundeston was the first, and in which millions of pounds have been and continue to be invested, are designed for association. This means, that while the cells in "model" Blundeston are considerably smaller than those in "model" Pentonville, the workshops, classrooms and recreational facilities are far superior, and the whole look of the place infinitely less grim. There is, for example, an airy and pleasantly furnished room for visits which may last two and a half hours instead of the twenty minutes allowed in the old prisons, and are not nearly so obviously supervised. Prisoners are allowed to smoke and tea and biscuits may be purchased, though the punitive rule which prohibits visitors from bringing in gifts of any kind, food and tobacco included, is strictly enforced.

Still one may readily see that the Blundeston system—assuming, for the moment, that it operates exactly according to specification—is an essay in benevolent paternalism, which has little or nothing to do with making conditions behind the two high surrounding wire fences of the prison (there was only one of these before Mountbatten reported) approximate as nearly as possible to conditions outside them. On the one hand, such needless "pains" of imprisonment as sexual deprivation are left unalleviated. On the other hand, the actual "share" of responsibility imposed on an inmate for running the institution or, more pertinently, for running himself is limited to the opportunity he has for making known his wishes (or complaints) about the arrangements for "Sports, Messing, Television and Education." If that can be called a responsibility at all, it is a responsibility of a very undemanding kind, and is anyway easily evaded. When the author had the opportunity of sitting in at a Central Council Meeting in Blundeston, he learned that one of the Wing Committees had resigned *en bloc*—because they had decided that their proposals were automatically ignored by the administration, and it was a waste of effort putting them forward.

Although the Governor was the only staff member present at this particular meeting, and no prisoners attended it aside from the Chairmen and Secretaries of the surviving Wing Committees the discussion did admittedly appear to be free and open, in the sense that the chief ruler and the ruled addressed each other pretty well as equals, and words weren't minced. But the idea of encouraging prisoners to express themselves rather than forcing them to adopt a posture of cringing respect is really the essence of paternalism, and the relevant question is not whether paternalism makes prison life more normal, which it doesn't, but whether under present circumstances it can be said to serve a reformative aim.

Prison magazines, where they exist, are an outlet for self-expression, though how far self-expression is allowed to go depends on the will of individual "Daddy" Governors, and ultimately, one supposes, on the Granddaddies in the Home Office. Possibly, *Con-Tact*, the Hull Prison Magazine, is the most outspoken of these publications—or at least it was until the Editor resigned in protest against the exclusion of certain material condemned as unsuitable for outside circulation. In the February (1969) edition, *Con-Tact* carried an interview with the Governor, in which he was faced with and answered the direct charge that Home Office talk of "training and treatment" is humbug. It may be instructive to reproduce an extract from this interview, because it is particularly revealing about what paternalism means or may mean in practice.

Con-Tact: There are 250 men in this prison and comparatively quite reasonable as inmates, you must have come across worse prisons, and I have been here three years now, and there hasn't been any sort of real motivated scheme or any plans to use this place as a pilot scheme to start anything here. Why is this?

Governor: This is a valid criticism. When you are in an establishment such as this where certain things concerning security must be observed—everyone is aware of this, I'm not telling them anything they don't know already—one of the first things to do before anything else is to have the staff and the inmates communicating. I don't mean agreeing, but communicating at a level that is agreeable to both. Now I could say I wanted to introduce all sorts of weird and wonderful ideas and grandiose plans. In this situation all I can say is I am giving everybody an order—this will take place. Now apart from anything else I don't think this is in any way a way to treat and train individuals in the sense that they are talking about. I've got to have assistants. I've got to have aids. I've got to have extensions of my personality, etc. These must become the staff. The first thing in prison you've got to create is an atmosphere where everybody begins to treat each other as human beings. Now I'm not necessarily talking about the staff treating prisoners in such a way but also about how inmates treat the staff. In other words, the way I see it is that you have got to create an atmosphere where there are certain allowances made for failings and shortcomings in our dealings with each other that we are all prone to.

Con-Tact: There is a barrier, but it is the system which draws the line between inmate and officer. It's a system that the officer trespasses over at the risk of condemnation from his fellow officers and his superiors and it's a system that the inmate daren't cross over because he is liable to be thought of as a grass or a slag. Would you agree with this?

Governor: It's perfectly true, there is a system and let's get this straight from the outset, that is that there will always be a barrier between different people. It may be great, it may be small; even in an ideal family life and marriage situation there will always be barriers. The problem here is how to make the barriers on a level that people can communicate across them without them being so high that everything isn't blocked out. You say there is a system in terms of the staff. There is also an inmate culture system, which I would hazard a guess, not necessarily from my experiences at Hull but from my experiences at a number of prisons up and down the country, that is a much more powerful influence than ever I or any member of the staff can hope to assert. And I would go further than that and say that I am surprised, and sometimes wonder, just how this system, the inmate system is allowed to operate. Very often you can see it operating to the disadvantage of a large number of inmates because a small number of inmates want to maintain this system for their own benefit. Now what are we talking about? We are talking about the barons, the strong arm men.

Interestingly enough, the *Con-Tact* editor strongly denied the existence of "barons", though he admitted that Hull was probably a unique long-term prison in this respect (its population includes offenders in Mountbatten's 'A' or dangerous category). Nevertheless, a fundamentally destructive inmate culture would, for reasons already stated, appear to be a concomitant of association; it is unavoidable short of such a sophisticated system of classification that there would be no room left for the concept of a "prison" as we know it today, whether ancient or modern.

Even if this were not so, it would still be something of a sophistry to compare the barrier that divides prisoners and prison officers with an emotional obstacle to communication in an every-day human relationship. For the one, unlike the other, is deliberately constructed and traditionally designed to be insurmountable. Theoretically, it might be possible to replace prison officers with social workers. But that is not the same thing as expecting prison officers to transform *themselves* into social workers, when they are neither suitably dressed for the part nor possessed, unless by chance in individual cases, of the qualifications to play it. Doubtless, a minority of them, possibly more than a minority, are enthusiastic about the paternalistic policy, and would rather treat prisoners as fellow human beings in need of help and guidance than as sub-human non-citizens fit only to be punished or ordered around. But this doesn't alter the fact that "screws" are "screws": men in uniform, who do the locking and the unlocking, and whose paramount duty, whether they like it or not, is custodial.

In these circumstances, it must be said that however much verbal encouragement prisoners and staff may be given to attain an "agreeable level of communication", neither side is in reality given much of a chance to succeed, for the simple reason that the traditional barrier has not been properly dismantled. On the contrary, it has inevitably been strengthened since the Mountbatten inquiry led to a terror-struck re-emphasis on security. "New tasks were defined for the prison service", says the 1967 Prison Department Report, "and staff trained in new duties. Staff who had long been encouraged to develop treatment relationships towards prisoners had little time left for this important work after discharging tasks arising from the need to concentrate on security." Incidentally, training as opposed to "encouragement" for "this important work" never was more than minimal. A neophyte officer, after a month's practical experience in a local prison, undergoes a two months' course at either Wakefield Training College or Leyhill, the purpose of which is largely, if not exclusively, to teach him routine duties and test his ability to carry them out. That may be the sum total of the training he receives throughout his career, though until they were "suspended" in 1967 there used to be brief "refresher" courses, which offered established staff an opportunity of instruction in such rehabilitative techniques as group counselling.

Here one sees another example of the chronic parsimony that frustrates reformative aims. To recruit and train social workers to staff the prisons would obviously cost a great deal more money than it costs to recruit and train turnkeys; and while one is not suggesting that the paternalistic policy would succeed if this were done, one *is* suggesting that short of its being done, paternalism is bound to remain a very half baked sort of idea, dependent, in so far as it can operate at all, on the will and ability of individual prison governors to persuade his officers to cooperate. There are governors, as has been said, of the highest mental calibre, and the governor at Hull is manifestly one of them. Maybe, he sincerely believes in the possibility of a prison staff that will be "extensions of his personality"—every man jack of them determined to lay the foundations of a progressive regime. One doubts it, if only because he is a personality in mufti and they are personalities in uniform. It may be recalled that the Gladstone Committee condemned the practice of using uniformed officers as teachers, and one must question whether, basically, it is any more sensible to use uniformed officers as "counsellors."

There is a second, and quite distinct reason for believing that parsimony or the punitive obsession which is responsible for it, largely defeats the objective of the Blundeston system and similar efforts being made elsewhere. This may be clarified by quoting a further extract from the interview in *Con-Tact*:

Governor: ". . . You say that what Governors say about treatment and training is humbug. I would say to you that when I or any other Governor tend to talk about treatment and training we tend to look at the individual case where there is a problem that we can see and understand and if we can get to that with one man, we can probably do something about it. The problem with prison is not so much that there isn't any training available but that there is such a diversity of needs and requirements that it is impossible to implement a training plan that would cater for everyone. Which isn't an excuse for not training anyone. What do you see as training—group work? Case work? What do you feel you need? You know that you could tell me this perhaps as an individual but no two individuals are alike.

Con-Tact: While I basically agree with what you say the Home Office nevertheless keeps turning out this humbug to the mass media that there is great rehabilitation, great reform and a great programme in process in prisons. This isn't true, is it?

Governor: Who trains who in this, eh? I don't think I have ever successfully trained or reformed anybody in my life, and I doubt if it is likely that I would be capable as an ordinary human being of either reforming or training anybody to be fit acceptable members of society. I don't think this is within the capabilities of any one or any number of human beings. What you can do is to make as many resources or as many choices available as you can and then encourage people to use them. This is the same outside as inside. Think about these choices, think carefully and clearly how you are going to use them.

Now to say that it is impossible to cater to every individual need in a prison is another way of saying that as reformative institutions prisons are and always have been fundamentally misconceived, and that may very well be true. On the other hand, if one excepts the imbeciles, the psychotics and the rest of the mentally deranged or seriously disordered people who get sent to prison, it may also be that the most hopeful way of discovering what Churchill called the "treasure in the heart of every man" is to give him the opportunity to find it for himself, and the freedom, once he has found it, to use it. This, presumably, is what the Hull Governor means by "choices" and "resources". The "treasure" is to be equated with some hitherto untapped capacity that a prisoner may have for immersing himself in a constructive as opposed to a destructive (or criminal) activity. It is exemplified in the story of the "Birdman of Alcatraz", who during years of solitary confinement became an ornithologist.

But the average prisoner cannot reasonably be expected to unearth his treasure, or, as the official account of the Blundeston system puts it, "take responsibility for himself", unless sufficient choices are open to him. To suppose that this is simply a matter of putting him to work, regardless of what sort of work he is put to, provided it can be called "productive" or "useful" is at best what Dr Mary Gordon described as a "creation of our phantasies", and at worst a disguised manifestation of a vengefully punitive spirit.

At Blundeston, there is enough work available to keep the men occupied for eight hours a day. It includes two vocational training courses—Bespoke Tailoring and Painting and Decorating. Otherwise, it consists of such traditionally enforced ways of passing the time in prison as tailoring production, laundering, boot and shoe making, printing and bookbinding, general administrative assistance and general cleaning. These hardly seem the kinds of activity that are likely to excite a recidivist prisoner's interest or teach him that there is more satisfaction to be got out of honest endeavour than crime. Moreover, apart from the two vocational training courses, for which an inmate may apply and may or may not be chosen, one detects no element of choice in the programme: not even the choice between participating in it or staying out of it. For though an inmate of Blundeston can earn as much as 10s a week (more than twice the average earnings in a local prison), if he is exceptionally productive, his labour is none the less forced labour.

In other words, there is no use pretending that even in the modern prisons, "choice" is anything like as wide as it might be made or that it begins to compare with the range of choice on the outside. Suppose a man has a latent interest in, or talent for, watch-making, say, or accountancy, or art, or motor mechanics, or canoe-building, or any other such constructive occupation, what chance has he of developing it? The answer is either none at all, or a limited chance dependent on how "privileged" he is.

As a matter of fact, possibly the biggest step towards the encouragement of "choice" has been taken at Wakefield, one of the first of the local gaols to be built in Pentonville's image and now a central prison which, though nominally reserved for "Stars", was selected for Mountbatten's special security treatment, including dogs and television cameras. Since the beginning of 1968 Wakefield has had a scheme under which prisoners may apply for enrolment in full-time business studies courses. These are conducted by a resident tutor, with the assistance of outside lecturers, notably from the Wakefield Technical College. At the end of 1968, 13 students were enrolled in the course for basic studies, such as Maths, English, Commercial Law and Book-keeping; another 13 were enrolled in the course for the Ordinary National Diploma (O.N.D.); and 11 were enrolled in the course for advanced examinations in subjects suited to a particular individual's hopes and future plans.

Wakefield has an average population of 700 inmates. There

are three permanent members of its education department: the tutor-organizer, the business studies tutor, and a teacher (a woman) of remedial English for men whose reading ages vary from eleven to nil. With outside assistance, the Department is able to offer an impressive number and variety of classes under the headings of handicrafts, recreational/social (e.g. Jazz Appreciation and Poetry reading and writing), Educational, and Classes related to Vocational Training such as engineering study. Since the beginning of 1968, the Business studies scheme has meant that daytime as well as evening classes are held; a development which may be seen as a reversion to the pre-1863 practice of permitting "instruction" to interfere with "work" on occasion and to be conducted at the expense of "punishment". Correspondence courses are also arranged, students are enabled to sit for examinations, and an attempt has been launched to find university places for suitable candidates on their release.

One may judge from all this that at Wakefield the Educational Department is unusually active and ambitious. Yet to read the Tutor-Organizer's report for 1968 is only to realize how much more might be accomplished than is possible under limitations imposed both by want of sufficient facilities and by the obsession with security. Thus although the total student attendance was 900 during the year, "including full-time, part-time and duplications," the potential, as the Tutor-Organizer pointed out, was much greater. One finds, for example, that in the case of both the leatherwork and the woodwork classes, there were so large a number of applications that a student was likely to be restricted to one class a week. In any case, the idea behind these classes is manifestly not to offer a handicraft as a "choice"—to encourage a man to become an expert potter, say—but merely to allow inmates an opportunity of "making" something which they can send to their family or friends. This is paternalism again, and characteristically the students are allowed an initial 30s—a "free gift" as the Prison Department calls it (what is an unfree gift?)—for the materials used. Thereafter, if they want to purchase the objects they produce, they are required to pay for the materials out of their earnings together with a 50% administrative charge.

There are, of course, educational departments at other prisons besides Wakefield, some of them doubtless just as ambitious and just as hopeful that the means for expansion will be forthcoming. But it must be emphasized that education even for a long-term prisoner is a privilege, not a right, and that, ordinarily only evening classes are held so that if he wants to attend them it is in lieu not of "work", but of playing ping-pong or watching television or doing whatever else is available for him to do during an association period. Moreover, education, even of the most elementary kind, is no longer an obligatory part of "training and treatment", as it was in Jebb's time, and hence, classes can be closed down at will, if it becomes convenient to do so for one reason or another. At Wormwood Scrubs, for example, and at a number of other prisons educational opportunities were virtually all sacrificed to alleged security requirements and in every closed institution prisoners are liable to be automatically denied the privilege of attending classes on security grounds.

"Security must be paramount", the Wakefield Tutor-Organizer wrote in his 1958 report. "I accept this . . . On the other hand, I can see why tradition has it that the average life of a tutor organizer is 3–4 years, and I can see that the inescapable difficulties are bound to increase in proportion with further educational developments."

He went on to discuss the special problem of the Category "A" prisoners at Wakefield, whose numbers are likely to increase. "I acknowledge this is a matter of high policy, and that it is presumptuous for me to pontificate on the basis of just over two years' experience; but I feel it may be of interest to clarify my opinions on the subject.

"Of the 'A' men I have met so far, two are moronic. They are also illiterate, completely and without reservation. If they are ever to improve, they need tuition, not just individual tuition in cell but some form of corporate study which could be of help to them psychologically.

"The remaining 'A' men are at the other extreme. They have very high intelligence quotients, and they have previously applied their intelligence in concentrated, nervous fashion. They are what I call 'restless minds', which must be occupied.

In ordinary manual or shop work, these minds are nowhere fully occupied. The danger is that they are concentrating their intelligence on one topic—escape, or some other deliberate disruption of routine. They need study, the more academic and more full time the better. I am not thinking of papier mache, or matchstick cathedrals. Our affiliation with the local Technical and Art Colleges, basically over the O.N.D Business Studies Course, has made available to us the most comprehensive and erudite library facilities and tutorial advice and I am sure we could accommodate and exercise the cleverest and wiliest of this selected and selective company.

"Once again, having made my recommendation, I cannot see at the moment how the necessary reconciliation with security could be made; but I am sure that my own practical incompetence does not invalidate the virtue of my suggestion."

One may feel sure that it does not. But equally one may doubt whether anything will be done about it, since the security obsession is in reality just an aspect of the punitive obsession. It is possible to see a practical point in taking no risks at all with security in the case of palpably dangerous men whom time alone seems likely to render harmless, and whom it is possible to hold for ten or twenty years or longer. But the "A" Categorization has gone far beyond this. Indeed, it has gone a long way beyond the limits that Mountbatten himself set, for it is evident that in his mind Category "A" prisoners were prisoners who would have to be held in the special security blocks until such time as a new maximum security prison could be built for them; nor did he place their total number above 120. But today nearly all the central prisons, however they may otherwise be classified, whether for "Stars", like Wakefield and Wormwood Scrubs, or for recidivists, like Hull, have inmates in the "A" Category, many of whom are due to be released very much sooner than later.

If there is a choice between setting an unregenerate professional criminal at liberty in a year, say, from now and making an attempt during the time that's left of his sentence to re-direct his energies and talents into a constructive channel, it is surely quite irrational to prefer the former course, even though the latter course entails an added risk of his escaping. But this is *our* irrationality, which the Home Office authorities obediently reflect. We would evidently rather a prisoner came out of prison unreformed and certain to do us further mischief, than take the slightest chance of his being able to "cheat the law" by so much as a month or a day.

To sum up, then, the following points have been made about the present state of prison reform in historical perspective:

A. The separate system has nominally been replaced or, more accurately, re-replaced by the associated system. Many local prisons, however, are still insufficiently equipped for the purpose, and men, whether one, two (as has recently been permitted) or three to a cell, are apt to spend considerably more hours in it than out of it.

B. Contamination and a destructive inmate culture appear to be inseparable from association, at any rate in closed prisons, and classification has so far proved a wholly inadequate means of dealing with this problem. The new building programme, which was initiated in 1959, in which millions of pounds have already been invested (nearly three million in 1967 alone) and for which millions more are earmarked, may, therefore, prove as misconceived as the building programme which followed the construction of Pentonville in 1842 and with which we are still encumbered. It seems certain that the new prisons are too large for "individualization of treatment" to be other than mythical or for classification to be better than nominal: e.g. Long Lartin for 492 men, Lockwood for 492 men and Low Newton for 500 men are among the new closed institutions which are at present either planned or in process of being erected, and even Blundeston, which is smaller, has a population of 240. Coldingley, the "factory" prison for 300 men, was opened in 1969.

C. The declared policy of restricting the punishment of imprisonment to loss of personal liberty, and hence of making the conditions of imprisonment approximate as nearly as possible to those in the free community, is defeated by the retention of palpably punitive practices. Some of these may be justifiable in individual cases, though by no means in every case, on security grounds; e.g. censorship of letters, supervision of visits, locked cells. Others are either merely traditional or bound up with fear of undermining the (assumed) deterrent effectiveness of imprisonment; e.g., standardized diet, deprivation of sexual freedom, low rates of gratuity for work which may bear little or no relation to the value of the work done.

D. The declared policy of "encouraging a prisoner's self-respect" is likewise defeated by the retention of traditional practices that were originally designed to humiliate him. These include the whole of the reception procedure, when he is deprived of his own clothes and all his personal possessions, required to take a bath, and issued with prison dress.

E. An attempt is being made in a few prisons to reconcile traditionally deterrent rules and practices with a reformative policy through the substitution of a paternalistic for an authoritarian regime. The aim is to end the natural hostility that exists between the rulers (who are, in effect, all-powerful) and the ruled who have virtually no rights. Officers, to use the official language, "are encouraged to develop treatment relationships with prisoners." This policy, in so far as it had gone, received a serious setback as a result of the Mountbatten report and the renewed emphasis on security. In any case it would seem unlikely to get very far unless officers discarded their uniforms and were trained as social workers. No such idea is contemplated.

F. The declared policy of encouraging a prisoner's sense of personal responsibility is defeated because he is in fact guaranteed no chance of assuming any responsibility for his own future. He may—depending on which prison he is sent to—find an opportunity to develop some latent interest through attending classes or taking a correspondence course, but education is a privilege, not a right, and is no part of the standard "training" except at Wakefield where a full-time business studies course has been instituted for the benefit of a few selected inmates. He may—again depending on which prison he is sent to—find an opportunity for vocational training in some form of manual work, such as bespoke tailoring or painting and decorating. But, generally speaking, prison training still means what it always has meant: forced labour. Though this labour may be technically useful and productive, it is unlikely to prepare a man for anything he can profitably do, or will want to do, after his release, and, as noted above, in most local prisons there is far too little of it to occupy his full time. The new "factory" prison at Coldingley may or may not prove an exception.

G. Open prison "training" would appear to be essentially no different from closed prison "training", apart from the facts that the inmates are entrusted with the responsibility of not absconding and that the great majority of them sleep in dormitories (a degree of association which would horrify Howard and which as late as 1898 Parliament said should never be allowed.) Open prisons are equipped with their punishment cells, and, like closed prisons, are run more or less paternalistically, according to the attitude of the governor and his ability to win the cooperation of his uniformed staff. In a sense, they are the descendants of the 19th century Irish intermediate prisons and of the women's refuges. Nevertheless, the idea of allowing selected prisoners to serve the whole or nearly the whole of their sentences under open conditions is one of two genuine innovations which this century can claim as its own.

The other innovation is psychiatric treatment, which has not been mentioned up to now, because it has been held in reserve as the prime illustration of the central paradox, or as one may prefer to think, absurdity of imprisonment as an instrument of reform: the paradox not of trying to train people for freedom under conditions of captivity, but of trying to train them for freedom under conditions of *prescribed periods* of captivity. That is where this history began. And where it remains stuck.

12
THE PENAL HERITAGE

It seems likely that in the public's mind, and certain that in the judiciary's mind, psychiatry has replaced religious instruction as the treatment means relied on for the rehabilitation of a considerable number of prisoners. He would be a very eccentric Judge today who justified a prison sentence on the grounds that he was giving the offender (man or boy) a chance to repent of his sins under the expert and devoted guidance of a chaplain. On the other hand, a person who commits some non-acquisitive and therefore apparently motiveless sort of crime, which is not so outrageous that the Judge compulsively and conveniently falls back on "wickedness" as its only explanation, is likely to be assured that the "best possible psychiatric care" awaits him in prison.

This is not to suggest that religious instruction has been abandoned. On the contrary, there is no penal institution in the country without the services of a full-time or part-time chaplain, whereas there are many more penal institutions than not without the services of a full-time or part-time psychiatrist. Ironically enough, too, there may be a better chance today of curing individual criminals of their criminality through the inculcation of religious faith than there ever was under the separate system. For one thing, the instruction is no longer enforced. Possibly, the only genuine choice a prisoner is permitted to make is whether or not he wishes to attend services, though it is typical of how hard punitive traditions die that if he elects to attend once, he must continue to attend throughout his sentence, no matter in how unrepentant or disillusioned a state he may find himself!

Moreover, the introduction of tutor-organizers, welfare officers, and other administrative staff, has relieved chaplains of a variety of duties that used to be imposed on them, and they, therefore, have more time to attend to individual needs among members of their flock. Finally, unlike their 19th century predecessors, who, with a few exceptions, were narrow-minded, punitive-minded bigots, modern chaplains are, with a few exceptions, men of understanding and broad sympathies.

Nevertheless, Home Office missives have become remarkable for their absence of emphasis on religious instruction as a reformative technique. For example, in *Penal Practice in a Changing Society* (1959), there was just one cursory reference to it: "On the more specialized professional and technical side, the influence of religion must still be brought primarily to bear by the chaplains and ministers of religion, though their work may be helped by the general atmosphere in the prison and among its staff."

But the same document, which may be said to have given birth to Sir Lionel Fox's *Second English in its own right*, devoted a whole page to a glowing account of the psychiatric foundations of the new structure. "Whether it be for diagnostic work for information of the courts and for purposes of classification, or for the mental care and treatment of inmates under sentence, a modern prison service requires an adequate and specialized service of doctors with psychiatric experience, psychologists, and such other qualified persons as go to make a psychotherapeutic team." There followed an account of what the "modern" prison service already had, which sounded a great deal. "Three psychiatric clinics, with a qualified medical staff, visiting psychotherapists, and psychiatric social workers have been set up for men and women at Wormwood Scrubs, Wakefield, and Holloway. To these are transferred any inmates who in the opinion of the Medical Officer would benefit by psychiatric treatment."

Even more was promised. "Work will be starting shortly on a psychiatric prison hospital, at Grendon Underwood, Bucks. When this is ready, the major psychotherapy now carried out at the three clinics will be concentrated in one place where, in proper conditions, it can be extended in scope and deepened in value. But the value of psychiatry is not limited to the treatment of those abnormal states of mind which require the kind of psychotherapy that will be given in the new establishment. A psychiatrically experienced doctor can do much to help disturbed prisoners not only to adjust themselves to prison life, but also to change their general attitudes so that they make a better adjustment to society after release. This kind of help ought to be available in most of the larger prisons at all times."

It is easy to deride psychiatry, if only because psychiatrists themselves, with their widely divergent theories and dogmas, are so given to deriding each other. It is none the less true that a considerable proportion of crime is, and always has been, attributable to, or at least closely associated with, mental illness, and therefore demands a medical response. To say this is not to endorse the theory, again very easily derided, that *all* crime is a disease and *all* criminals are ill people in need of treatment. On the contrary, it is to go no further than Du Cane went. Sir Norward East who, with Dr de Bath Hubert, drew up plans for a psychiatric prison twenty years before work began on building the institution at Grendon, told a Prison Commission in 1932: "Convicted prisoners fall into three groups: (1) Those whose mental condition is not abnormal (2) Those whose mental condition is abnormal but uncertifiable (3) Those who are certifiable under the Lunacy or Mental Deficiency Acts . . . All will agree that an offender who is insane or defective should not be imprisoned."[1]

Apart from the fact that large numbers in that third group have never ceased to be imprisoned, the medical response within the prison service still nowhere matches the size of the problem posed by the second group. Indeed, when a Judge tells some wretchedly unbalanced offender (a compulsive exhibitionist, say) that the best possible psychiatric care awaits him in gaol, he is giving an assurance that may turn out to be totally worthless, as he would know if he troubled to investigate the position for himself. The overwhelming majority of mentally disturbed prisoners who might benefit, or think they might benefit, from psychotherapy, or from any other form of psychiatric treatment, such as shock therapy, aversion therapy, hormone injections (temporary castration) or brain surgery, don't get it.

Imprisonment as a religious experiment failed, as we have seen, because, whether or not the idea of isolating criminals from bad influences and exposing them to good influences was valid in itself, the "good (i.e. religious) influences" were never afforded in sufficient quality or quantity to offset the inherent unhealthiness of cellular confinement, upon which, by contrast, money was willingly squandered. Imprisonment as a medical (or psychiatric experiment) seems all set to fail for a corresponding reason.

But there is also an in-built reason for believing that imprisonment cannot, under the most propitious circumstances imaginable, succeed as an instrument of reform, so long as it remains an instrument of punishment at the disposal of the criminal courts. And this brings us back to the point at which, so to speak, we came in.

When a doctor orders a patient a week in bed, he is making, as both parties understand perfectly well, an educated guess. That is to say, if the patient recovers before the week is over, he will be allowed to get up, and if he doesn't recover within the prescribed period, he will have to stay where he is. But a judicial sentence to imprisonment is not a guess in this sense. Nor, assuming its purpose to be primarily reformative, is it educated, for judges are not diagnosticians, psychiatric or otherwise. According to a distinguished contemporary lawyer, judicial sentencing is an art, not a science. A science it certainly isn't, but if it is an art it may often strike one as an art practised by philistines.

Grendon, which has accommodation for 274 inmates, though its average population does not appear to be much above half that number, was to some extent modelled on Herstedvester in Denmark, the world's first medically administered prison. Herstedvester, however, is called a preventive detention centre to distinguish it from an ordinary prison, and this is not a matter of mere semantics. For in Denmark if an offender is found upon conviction to be sane, but none the less "suffering from defective development, or impairment or disturbance of mental faculties, including sexual abnormality", he is held to be "unfit for punishment", and is committed directly for an indefinite period, either to Herstedvester or to Denmark's other preventive detention centre at Horsens in Jutland. It is then for a Medical Board to decide when he can safely be returned to the free community, and this decision depends wholly on an assessment of his response to treatment; theoretically at least, retributive and deterrent considerations do not enter into the question. The average time is two years, though it can be much shorter—or very much longer.

Now there is an obvious inherent threat to civil liberties in the indeterminate sentence, and one may not wish to see it introduced, without greater safeguards against its abuse than exist in Denmark or in other countries where it is operative. One may also think it morally indefensible to subject anybody to compulsory confinement for an indefinite period on the grounds that he is "unfit for punishment" but needs treatment, unless the conditions of his confinement are really as non-punitive as they can reasonably be made. This is not true of the Danish preventive detention centres, which, though paternalistically administered, are quite unmistakably prisons. Indeed, Dr Georg K. Stürup, the distinguished psychiatrist, who is medical director of Herstedvester and the true founder of the Danish preventive detention system, believes that abnormal offenders respond to a limited degree and kind of punishment. He has remarked to the present author that it is nonsense to speak of there being no "treatment" offered at any given prison, simply because there doesn't happen to be a psychiatrist or psychologist on the staff. Any form of prison training, Dr Stürup asserts, is treatment of a sort, and may have its proper place in a general therapeutic plan.

But equally Dr Stürup maintains that if any kind of treatment is to succeed, the indeterminate sentence is imperative, and in this surely he is right. As long ago as 1933, an illusioned author (Albert Crew) wrote:[2] "Today a prison may be regarded as a sort of hospital for social misfits, the chief aim of which is the reformation of the prisoner, so that when he goes out into the larger world again, he may have a fair chance of resuming life without loss of self-respect, and without any undue retention of bitterness." But it would be an odd sort of hospital that sent some patients out into the "larger world again" knowing full well they were going to collapse as soon as they got there, while it kept others confined long after the need for doing so was over and when the effect could only be debilitating. Yet that is precisely what is risked at Grendon, because, though the inmates there are called "patients", they are in fact prisoners who have to be held for as long as, and no longer than, a criminal court has decided is their due punishment. The same thing is true, of course, of every other penal institution, save in the case of the small minority of prisoners who are serving life sentences.

Though the administrators show some awareness that this situation is hardly as compatible as it might be with a reformative policy, they dare not, or at any rate will not, face up to the root cause of it. Thus in a departmental White Paper, *Treatment of the Adult Offender* (1966), it was said that there comes a time when many prisoners, especially long-term prisoners, reach a "peak in their training" and when, therefore, it is inadvisable to continue to hold them for fear that they will go downhill. If this is so, then the obvious answer is the indeterminate sentence or something like it. But this was not the answer the White Paper proposed. Instead, it stated the problem in order to justify the introduction of a parole scheme, although parole, as a means of guaranteeing that a person will not be confined for longer than is necessary to reform him, is, for three reasons, patently inept.

In the first place, it is purely arbitrary. Under the 1967 Criminal Justice Act, a prisoner may now be released on licence after serving one third of his sentence or one year whichever is the longer. But how can it reasonably be maintained that while a man sentenced to three years *may* reach the peak of his training after one year, a man sentenced to 30 years cannot possibly reach the peak of *his* training until he has served ten years?

In the second place, parole leaves the judiciary free to defeat its purpose (or such purpose as it can really be said to have, apart from its usefulness as a smokescreen) by passing proportionately longer sentences.[3]

Finally, the parole Authority, however it may be constituted and especially if it is politically vulnerable[4] (as it is in England, since the Home Secretary has the final word) is not and cannot be solely concerned with the question of fitness for freedom. It is also influenced, and as often as not decisively influenced, by retributive and deterrent considerations. To take an extreme example from the United States, where both Federal and State parole plans have been in operation for many years, there could have been no danger to the public in releasing Alger Hiss on the day that he was sent to prison. Yet he was consistently refused parole, and was required to serve his five years sentence (less time off for good behaviour) in full. One may feel morally certain that the fate of a similarly notorious offender in this country would be no different, even though the threat he represented to the public's safety was clearly over.

To put the point in a slightly different way, suppose as a result of some major advance in the science of genetics, guaranteed means were found to render all violent offenders harmless. In those circumstances, parole would doubtless be boldly recommended by the Licensing Board for numerous eligible prisoners of whom Press and Public had never heard. But would it be *as* boldly recommended for prisoners of whom Press and Public had heard a great deal—the Krays, for example? For that matter, would the Home Secretary be prepared to release every murderer serving a life sentence without discrimination or regard to the degree of odium his crime had incurred, including, say, Ian Brady and Myra Hindley?

One is not concerned here with the question of whether there are not, in fact, criminals who *deserve* to be punished or punished more severely than other criminals; that is a question of ethics outside the scope of this book. One is simply trying to demonstrate the muddle-headedness (or hypocrisy) in claiming that imprisonment is a reformative institution when, in fact, it is an instrument of punishment at the disposal of the criminal courts. To quote Dr Mary Gordon again:[5] "My complaint against our prison system is not that it punishes men who break the law, but that those who administer it persistently strive to conceal the reality of that punishment with a smoke-screen of cant, humbug, and hypocrisy." There has not been, nor could there have been, any fundamental change in the position since those words were written nearly half a century ago.

In principle, and provenly to a large extent in practice, a curative response to crime or to given criminals, is irreconcilable with a punitive response; and if as a society we wish to behave rationally, we must choose between the two. But there can be no choosing the former course until we get over our awe of the judiciary and our fear of interfering with its traditional prerogatives. For the truth is that Judges are simply not qualified by either training or temperament to exercise the sentencing power if its objective is to be reformative. It is remarkable that despite legislative attempts to keep as many offenders as possible *out* of prison, and in spite of persistent warnings from the executive that rehabilitative aims *in* prison are being defeated by overcrowding, the courts continue to send more and more people *to* prison.

Admittedly, this can be explained and excused as the inevitable result of an ever-mounting crime rate. Just the same, when the present Lord Chief Justice announced, as he did recently, that as a means of discouraging appeals "without merit" it would be proper and appropriate for Appeal Court Judges to tack on to a sentence the time (at present likely to be about five months) which an unsuccessful appellant has spent in gaol before his appeal is heard, one may pardonably conclude that the judiciary doesn't really care how overcrowded the prisons are and is disinclined to do any more than it can help doing to empty them. There is certainly no reason to believe that its sentencing policy invariably reflects a loyal devotion to the declared reformative aims of the executive. "Society has to be protected from a menace like you." When a Judge uses words to that effect, as Judges frequently do, he does not mean that ten years, say, is the minimum time which, in his carefully considered view, is needed to fit the offender to "lead a good and useful life" on discharge. He means just what he says, and it evidently doesn't worry him that at the end of the ten years the "menace" is likely to be a worse menace than ever.

But both the executive and the legislature habitually match any limitations they may place on the judiciary's powers with a kind of grovelling concern to pander to the judiciary's ego. Thus a "person who holds or has held judicial office" is assured of a seat on the Parole Licensing Board. Similarly, the Home Secretary is obliged to consult the Lord Chief Justice before releasing a convicted murderer on licence. Again, Judges have been empowered since the suspension of the death penalty to "recommend" the minimum term that a murderer sentenced to life imprisonment should serve, and now that the death penalty has been finally abolished there is the possibility that a much greater step will be taken along this anti-reformative road. For the Home Secretary, anxious presumably to appease public superstitions as well as judicial vanity, has set up a Committee, under the chairmanship of a Lord Justice of Appeal,[6] to consider, *inter alia*, whether it might be advisable to replace the mandatory life sentence for murder with a sentence as long or as short as the trial Judge may decide it should be.

It would, of course, be ludicrous to imagine that a Judge is capable of making a reliable prognosis of the chances of rehabilitating a murderer or anyone else, or of the time required for treatment. Indeed, the accepted idea that a Judge possesses by virtue of the office he holds some special knowledge or insight that makes his advice on penal policy worth having or seeking only serves to obscure the fact that a reconstitution of the *sentencing* system is an absolute pre-requisite to a non-punitive "prison" or custodial system.

This fact is equally obscured by each and every legislative and executive measure for making imprisonment more "reformative." The prime example is "after-care", a piece of jargon which creates the entirely false impression that prisoners, like hospital patients, are treated to a period of convalescence as soon as they are ready for it. Actually, it is the "care" prescribed by the courts which, in general, makes the administrative "after-care" desirable, and, in general, too, the few who get it are the least in need of it.

Parole is associated with after-care; that is to say, when the plan was instituted an already woefully understaffed and overburdened probation service was given the additional responsibility of supervising the parolees. One may doubt whether this can amount to more than token after-care, or nearly as much after-care as Philip Organ was able to give his ticket-of-leave men from Lusk.

The hostel scheme, designed to ease the "difficult transition from captivity to freedom" for men under sentence of four years and over, is another after-care technique. One may fairly assume that after a man has passed the "peak in his training", the longer he is required to stay in captivity, the more difficult the transition to freedom will be for him and the more likely, therefore, that once he is released he will pester or injure society anew. If the hostel scheme is really a way of easing this transition (and it may well be), then rationally there should be no delay in admitting him to it, but in fact he does not become eligible for admission until he has served all but the last six to ten months of his sentence (less the statutory remission, of course.) Even then, his chances of being admitted are very much less than even, for it goes without saying that not nearly enough hostel space has been built to accommodate all the prisoners who are entitled to apply for it. On the contrary, several hostels were closed down as a result of one of the more extreme of Mountbatten's requirements.[7]

Again, it would be rational to select the most difficult cases for hostel treatment—the prisoners who appear to be the most embittered or most institutionalized or the least purged of their criminal propensities—for slight though the hope may be that they will not immediately abscond or commit further offences, there is otherwise no hope at all of persuading them to live honestly and peaceably before they are discharged. All that society has to gain from declining to take the gamble is six to ten months additional respite from their predatory or violent activities.

But, as may readily be guessed, precisely the opposite considerations dictate the method of selection.[8] This is defended on the grounds that if "undue risks" were taken, the hostel scheme might fall into such public disrepute that its very existence would be jeopardized, and it is, in fact, true that there was a considerable outcry against it in 1963, when it became known that an inmate of the Pentonville hostel had committed murder and armed robbery. Doubtless, a comparable outcry will be raised against parole, if and when the Board grows incautious enough to place its trust in a man who commits a serious crime sooner than he would otherwise have the opportunity to commit it. But one cannot expect the public to react rationally while it is bamboozled by policy-makers, who in turn bamboozle themselves. Whatever the virtue and necessity might be under a genuinely reformative system of easing the transition from custody to freedom, under the existing system both parole and the hostel scheme are in reality methods of lessening a prescribed punishment where this can "safely" be done—and at the not altogether incidental cost of increasing embitterment and danger where it can't be. Like the liberalization of conditions within prisons, "after-care" belongs to a grand illusion: that it is possible to have a reformative prison system without divorcing it from a punitive system of criminal justice.

But while we cannot hope to make sense of reformative aims unless and until this divorce takes place, it does not follow that there is any certain way of reforming criminals whom society, in its own protection, is bound to deprive of their liberty. That is another question, and before considering it there is something else we had better be clear about.

Though the prison system has come to be represented by its administrators as an all-purpose system, dedicated in all cases without exception to rehabilitation, it is historically an ill-assorted amalgam of two quite separate systems with two quite distinct rationales. The one, which may now be described as local imprisonment (sentences of 12 months or less), descends from the common gaols; the other, central imprisonment, descends, a bit illegitimately, from Millbank and the Hulks. The Pentonville experiment helped to shape both systems, though in different ways.

Local imprisonment, a defence against minor crime, was never intended to be reformative. Deterrence and coercion were its raison d'être, and for a time, therefore, it was made as punitive as the public conscience would allow it to be. However, by the end of the 19th century a certain disillusionment had set in, for the system was clearly failing to frighten actual offenders into mending their ways (individual deterrence), while its effectiveness in scaring off potential offenders (general deterrence) remained a moot question. This gave birth to the idea of trying to reform minor criminals, but *by means other than imprisonment.*

Still, no serious thought was given then, nor has it been given since, to the feasibility of abolishing the system entirely. On the contrary, far more money continues to be spent on maintaining it than on the development of alternative resources, such as probation. Yet the system cannot be said to have taken on a rehabilitative function, for even if local prisons weren't overcrowded, and even if adequate training and treatment facilities existed in them, the great majority of the inmates would still be short-termers—in for six months or less. If deterrence were not the point of the system, there would be no point to it at all.

At the same time local imprisonment has presumptively become a less and less severe punishment during the past eighty years as a result of the policy of liberalizing prison discipline generally, which was initiated by the Gladstone Committee. According to deterrent theory, this should mean that local imprisonment has also become less and less effective. The facts, however, point to a more complicated conclusion. On the one hand, it is possible to argue that the system is working better as individual deterrence than it did in Du Cane's time, since it is apparently turning out many fewer recidivists. So far as is known or can be ascertained, the percentage of offenders who do not offend again after one taste of local imprisonment is high, though no higher than the percentage of offenders who do not offend again after being put on probation or fined or granted a conditional discharge.[9]

On the other hand, it can be argued that a short prison sentence is no longer "sufficiently dreaded" by people who would otherwise refrain from putting themselves in jeopardy of one. For while the rejection of Du Cane's uncompromisingly terroristic methods was followed by a fall, not a rise, in the incidence of minor crime, there has undoubtedly been a very steep rise in the incidence of all kinds of crime during the past quarter of a century.

Now assuming, rash an assumption though it may be, that both the drop in reconvictions of people who serve short prison terms and the increase in petty crime are a result of making the punishment of imprisonment as little severe as it is, we may seem to be caught up in a dilemma. But in fact our course is clear. It would be useless trying to go backwards, for if penal history has any lesson to teach us it is that punishment inevitably becomes less severe as time goes on, and cannot in any case be made severe enough to fulfil its presumptive potentiality as general deterrence. There is no need to retrace all the ground that has been covered in proof of this, but to recall just one piece of the evidence, the crime rate was mounting in 1785 despite the "severest exercise of justice" (i.e. wholesale hangings). If Parliament had decided then that the time was come to embark on a determined attempt to seek out and eradicate the causes of the mounting crime rate, instead of vainly persevering with measures to suppress it, we might be a great deal better off today than we are.

One is not suggesting that it is possible now, or that it necessarily ever will be, to dispense entirely with punishment as a means of deterring society. Though we do not *know*, we may very justifiably suspect, that if there were no legal penalties to be feared, there would be many more thieves than there are, many more motorists breaking the speed limit, and so on. Nevertheless, the present drug epidemic in the United States is happening in spite of draconian sanctions against drug-taking (an 18-year-old youth in Virginia was recently sentenced to 20 years' imprisonment for being in possession of a small quantity of cannabis), and the drug problem in this country will doubtless continue to grow if instead of going to the trouble and expense of attacking it at its roots, we lazily rely on the law to chop off bits and pieces of its spreading foliage.

In any case, to concede the necessity of retaining deterrent penalties as a defence against certain types of law-breaking is not the same thing as subscribing to deterrent theory which, by the test of its own assumptions, is inoperable. Ultimately, there can be no hope of eradicating crime until we are prepared to deal with its causes, and that, obviously enough, pre-supposes a determined effort to identify them. Meanwhile, granted that we are a humanitarian and a sensible society, we should ask ourselves not whether we need to make local imprisonment a more severe punishment, for that in the circumstances is an irrelevance, but whether we can afford to give it up altogether.

We should be aware that it is an extremely costly method of deterrence, and despite the fact that it evidently breeds less crime than it once did, it is still apt to be destructive to individuals and hence to society. To quote from a report of a European Working Group to the United Nations Congress, 1960: "Short sentences . . . have all the drawbacks of deprivation of liberty in any form with none of its advantages. In fact, habituation to prison life, the danger of moral contamination and the break with the family and the social and occupational environment are not offset by any constructive contribution provided by a sufficiently lengthy treatment."

There are two plausible objections to the idea of abolishing local imprisonment. The first is that there are offenders whom even a very brief taste of prison appears to deter after alternative methods of dealing with them have failed. One cannot, however, accept this objection as decisive so long as there is a possibility that the alternative methods *might* have succeeded, if they had been more effectively applied. For instance, a fine is rarely stiff enough to hurt, while the probation service is far too understaffed to offer individual offenders the sort of concentrated attention they may need.

The second objection is that without imprisonment as an ultimate sanction, there would be no way of enforcing court orders, fines included. But, again, one cannot be sure how true this is until more imaginative and less destructive alternatives have been tried. We have not gone as far as we might, for instance, in devising reliable methods for the collection of fines. The Yugoslav delegation told the 1960 United Nations Congress that in their country, when a fine is considered the appropriate penalty, an offender is never imprisoned if he refuses to pay: instead the money is collected from him forcibly. Presumably the Yugoslavs have ways and means of doing this which might not be unacceptable to us, if we troubled to find out what they are.

There are ideas, too, being practised abroad for avoiding the worst consequences of short sentences that we might do well to consider. One that originated in Western Germany, and has since been adopted in Belgium, South Africa and most recently in New Zealand, is to allow these sentences to be served over a series of weekends instead of continuously. But in any case, if the local imprisonment system were to be retained only as an ultimate sanction at the disposal of the courts, its running costs could be very considerably reduced. There would probably be no further need for any of the 19th century closed local prisons. There are 24 of these, and though some of them are admittedly also used as central prisons, during 1967 their "receptions" included no fewer than 9,857 sentences of a month or less. It might well be possible to replace them with labour camps, where conditions would be designedly punitive, but not more punitive than is necessary to fulfil the wholly deterrent (or coercive) purpose of maintaining this vestige of a deterrent prison system.

That, of course, begs the question of *how* punitive; and the answer is we don't know, just as we don't know whether we could or could not safely abolish local imprisonment. We have no idea what is the *minimum* amount of punishment required, if it is to deter any kind of crime or any kind of offender, because our blind faith in deterrent theory, the punitive obsession, inhibits us from making the slightest attempt to find out. One may remark in this connection that the grounds for deciding on maximum sentences for given offences are never by any chance stated. For example, a few years ago the radio "Pop" pirates were threatened with two years' imprisonment. But why? Why not one year or one month or ten years, if the purpose was simply to frighten them off, which it was, of course? For all the science that is used when decisions of this sort are reached, Parliament might as well dip its hand into a hat and draw out a lottery ticket.

There is not, and never has been, any science in deterrent practice. "We maintain our ignorance," Norval Morris, the distinguished criminologist, has written,[10] "either by not searching for knowledge or by searching by methods that cannot disturb our prejudices. Perhaps it is fanciful to suggest a deliberate suppression of the truth . . . "

Fanciful or not, a humanitarian society, if and when it has no choice except to punish, should be concerned to cause the individual as little pain as is consistent with a deterrent purpose. A sensible society should wish to invest as little of its resources as possible in punishment, in order to invest as much of its resources as possible in treatment methods that may be used as alternatives to punishment in cases where punishment is undesirable or manifestly unavailing. But so long as we do suppress the truth, deliberately or accidentally, our behaviour can neither be as humanitarian, nor certainly as sensible as it might be.

One has described deterrent theory as the punitive obsession, because in practice it often furnishes a rationalization of the urge to punish; that is to say, it is retribution in disguise. Thus the Labour Home Secretary (Mr James Callaghan) was able to persuade himself, and apparently the overwhelming majority of the electorate, that an appropriate, if not the only, answer to the growing menace of heroin addiction is to raise the maximum sentence for peddling the stuff from ten years to fourteen years. Pushing heroin is, of course, an especially reprehensible sort of crime, and one that understandably provokes keen hostility. Yet there is absolutely no evidence to support the conclusion that a threat of fourteen years imprisonment is more likely to deter a resolute offender than the threat of ten years, and commonsense may tempt one to be almost certain that it isn't. Indeed, Dr Desmond Curran, the psychiatrist, who may be assumed to have a deeper understanding of human behaviour than the average Judge or politician, dissented from his fellow members of the Wolfenden Committee when they proposed that the maximum punishment for a paedophiliac homosexual offence should be raised from two years to ten years.[11] "I see little reason to suppose," he said, "that the possibility of the maximum punishment of ten years as opposed to two years would have much, if indeed any, appreciable effect on deterrence. Only a small minority of the population know what is the maximum penalty for indecent assaults. Only a minute fraction of the population know their criminal statistics and what punishments are awarded; and if more did, they would know that the chances of getting more than two years for indecent assault would be small (about 1 in 18). Can it be seriously supposed that those who are guilty of indecent assault work out 'betting odds' of this kind before they indulge in their acts? And if they did, what deterrent effect would it be likely to have?"

Now if a man does, in fact, receive what is officially called a medium or a long sentence (over 12 months) he is ordinarily dealt with under the central prison system. This system may be said to have re-acquired its original reformative objective, which was abandoned after Cockburn and the Royal Commission of 1863 had drawn attention to the illogicality of employing a less severe punishment (i.e. a weaker deterrent defence) against major than against minor crime. Proponents of deterrent and, indeed, of retributive theory should recognize that the position, from their point of view, is once again as objectionable as Cockburn found it to be. For, if one excepts the inmates of the special security blocks, who are a special case, it is generally speaking true to say that, despite their presumptively greater culpability, medium and long term men are much better treated than the short-termers. It is for them, after all, that the modern prisons, like Blundeston, have been built and continue to be built; (there is no such thing as a modern *local* prison). Admittedly, many prisoners dealt with under the central system still have to serve their time (or most of it) in grim 19th-century establishments, but even so they are spared such characteristic features of local imprisonment as sleeping three to a cell, being locked up for much of the day as well as the night and being denied virtually all opportunity for recreation or a sight of the open air, apart from a half hour's exercise period in the prison yard.

From the reformative point of view, this is as it should be, since it is obviously logical to take the most trouble with those offenders who are the greatest danger to society. But here is another reason for perceiving that reformative intentions are incompatible with deterrent theory, and that to declare loyalty to both of them is to betray them both.

Unlike deterrent theory, an uncompromisingly reformative system would clearly not be inoperable, but we cannot know how effective or ineffective it might prove as a defence against crime until we are willing to try it. Broadly speaking, this pre-supposes the transformation of the existing central prison system into a non-punitive custodial treatment system. It also pre-supposes that criminals found to be uncontrollable by other means—criminals, that is to say, who had failed to respond to both probationary techniques and to whatever scientific research might show to be sufficiently severe penalties to deter anybody capable of being deterred—would be wholly or partially deprived of their liberty for as long as, but for no longer than, it might be considered necessary to fit them for freedom.

There is, one may note parenthetically, nothing very original in this concept. It was, for instance, advocated by *The Spectator* in its issue of 26 September 1842: "The criminal would be tried and convicted as at present: the change would begin with the sentence of the Judge, who would not say, 'You have been found guilty of this offence, and you are sentenced to so many years imprisonment', but 'You have been proved to have committed this wrong; you are unfit to remain at large; and you must be sent into seclusion to be disciplined until you can be properly and safely released'." Words like "discipline" and "seclusion" are, of course, unfashionable, but, if one forgets about them, one may find that what *The Spectator* said in 1842 is very closely echoed by what proponents of the so-called preventive school of penology are saying today. Thus Lady Wotton has written[12] (1959): "The legal process for determining who has in fact committed certain actions would continue as at present; but once the facts had been established the only question to be asked would be: what is the most hopeful way of preventing such behaviour in the future?"

Prevention can, of course, be achieved by punitive means, but only if it amounts, as transportation did, to extermination. There are at present some indications of a move in this direction under the old pretext of deterrence: for example, the gargantuan sentences passed on the train robbers and the proposal, supported by the present Tory Lord Chancellor among others, that murderers of policemen should serve a minimum of 30 years. This movement may be regarded, however, as a manifestation of momentary hysteria and seems unlikely to get much further, if only because history is against it. Its sponsors might be encouraged to think more constructively about problems of "law and order" if they would remember the warning uttered by Lord Wensleydale a century ago when he referred to perpetual imprisonment: "The criminal . . . would in course of time become an object of pity, and the public sympathy being excited, the sentence would ultimately be remitted." As indeed, the public sympathy already has been excited in the case of Rudolf Hess, who has not yet served thirty years and who may be thought to have been guilty of even worse crimes than killing a policeman.[13]

What Lady Wootton means by prevention is prevention through treatment and cure. To a degree this was what the pioneers of the Millbank experiment were after, and in the sense that that experiment while it lasted was *sui generis*, was not part of a penal system at the disposal of the criminal courts, it came nearer to achieving a preventive policy than anything that has happened since, however crude the administrative process of selecting offenders for salvage may have been. But retributive and deterrent influences foredoomed the experiment to failure. Because of them, judicial sentences of transportation were commuted to fixed terms of incarceration, a vast fortress of terrifying ugliness was erected and, worst of all, only a minimal sum of money was afforded for the moral and physical care of the inmates.

It has previously been pointed out that Millbank under its two clergymen governors, Whitworth Russell and Daniel Nihil, may logically be regarded as the forerunner of the Grendon psychiatric prison under its Medical Superintendent. If, as has also been suggested, Grendon is a very much more enlightened penal endeavour than Millbank, this is not because the recipe association plus work plus psychiatric attention is necessarily to be preferred to the recipe seclusion plus work plus religious instruction as a cure-all for crime, but because the actual proportion of treatment to punishment appears to be considerably higher at Grendon than it was at Millbank.

Nevertheless, Grendon is simply one of the institutions in which a person sent to prison *as punishment* may serve part of his sentence; and there are, therefore, two in-built limitations on its potential usefulness as an instrument of prevention. One is the want of any guarantee against the premature discharge of "patients"; the other is the danger that if criminals are locked up together, and permitted to associate, they will get worse, not better.

The indeterminate sentence would remove the first of these

two limitations. But, short of reverting to seclusion—and that would seem to be unimaginable—the only way of dealing with the second is to create a "therapeutic community" through breaking down the barriers between treaters and treated, and thus insuring a sufficiently powerful infusion of "good influences" to offset "bad influences."

For reasons already stated, one must disbelieve that this is possible in a prison. There may be a better hope of achieving it at Grendon than at other institutions where it is being attempted, if only because some, though by no means all, of the officers there are trained nurses. Just the same, they are custodians in uniform, while the patients are prisoners in prisoners' dress. If Grendon deservedly has the reputation among some criminals of being the "easiest" of all the "nicks" (and, therefore, among reformers as being the "most advanced"), a "nick" is none the less what it is, and there is no sufficient reason to believe that it doesn't have an impenetrable inmate culture.

The concept of the therapeutic community is owed to one of the very few genuine pioneers in penal history, an American of erratic genius named Homer Lane. In 1913, with the aid of a group of private citizens, Lane founded an establishment for delinquent boys and girls, which he called the Little Commonwealth. The children, some of them committed by the courts, others sent directly from their homes, lived and worked together on a Dorsetshire farm. They were called "citizens", and as nearly as possible were given both the rights and responsibilities of citizens in a free community. This was achieved through empowering them as a democratic body to make and enforce their own laws, and through dividing them into families, each with its own "mother", herself an inmate and a sort of Wendy figure. The material prosperity of a family—how well it ate and was clothed—depended on its industry, individually and collectively. Homer Lane himself was called "Daddy". But though he retained a residual power of command in serious emergencies, he was ordinarily a father who treated his children as equals; that is to say, he worked alongside them, ate with them, and attended their meetings as a citizen with one vote, and no more.

The Little Commonwealth came to grief after five years as a result of a scandal. Two girls robbed the office safe, absconded with the proceeds, and when they were arrested by the police accused Lane of having made indecent advances towards them. The story was duly passed on to the Home Office, which thereupon decided to order a private inquiry not only into the specific charge, which was almost certainly false, but into the whole conduct of the Little Commonwealth. The man chosen for this task was J. F. P. Rawlinson, K.C., M.P., a reactionary who, as Lord Lytton, the chairman of the Little Commonwealth's Committee of Management was subsequently to put it, "believed in evil with as much sincerity as Lane believed in good." Precisely what Rawlinson reported is still unknown, but the Home Office was persuaded to withdraw its certificate of approval, and the Little Commonwealth had to be closed down.[14]

But the idea and the faith which gave birth to it survived its demise. Apart from other comparable ventures in dealing with maladjusted or delinquent children which have followed, such as A. S. Neill's Summerhill, David Wills's Bodenham, Otto Shaw's Redhill and George Lyward's Tenterden, Lane's work may clearly be seen as an influence in the development of the treatment for psychopaths at Henderson Hospital. This programme was originated immediately after the Second World War by Dr Maxwell Jones, and in 1953 it served both as the inspiration and the model for the Van der Hoeven Clinic—a Dutch institution where offenders serving indeterminate sentences are confined.

Holland has what criminologists call the "double track" system. This means that mentally abnormal offenders (including the sexual deviants and the "inadequates") may be sentenced to a fixed term of imprisonment followed by an indefinite period of preventive treatment. The system is in itself a more deplorable attempt than has been made in this country to reach a compromise between deterrent and preventive aims, for apart from the palpable inequity of both punishing a man on the former ground and depriving him of his liberty indefinitely on the latter, the advance sentence of imprisonment militates against the chances of the subsequent treatment being successful. However, this does not alter the fact that the system has produced in the Van der Hoeven Clinic a custodial treatment centre which is genuinely distinct from a prison.

It is a privately endowed institution, smaller than Grendon, with accommodation for a total of 85 males and ten females housed in a separate part of the building. The patients wear their own clothes, and although, for want of sufficient space, they share small, bunk-type bedrooms, these do not resemble cells and are never by any chance locked. There are no uniformed officers or guards. Instead, thirty-nine trained social workers, including a number of quite young women, act as group leaders and counsellors, and take their meals with the patients. Only two concessions are made to conventional ideas of security. A low, easily scaled wall surrounds the building; and the front door, which is under the observation of a porter in his lodge, is kept locked, though not bolted. Even so, a patient may be given permission to go to a movie in town (unaccompanied) or to visit, from time to time, a local family that has volunteered to entertain him. As soon as it is thought safe for him to do so, he will be allowed to take a regular job in Utrecht or nearby.

The patients are required to participate in administering the institution. Each of them serves for a while on a policy committee which, with the staff, determines rules and regulations. They elect three of their number to serve with two staff members on a supervisory committee, which is responsible for deciding how offences against discipline should be dealt with. They have total responsibility for organizing their own sport, study and recreational activities.

Work is voluntary, but if patients decline to work, as they do from time to time, they find themselves on relief, so to speak, since they are denied access to any private funds they may possess. Within the clinic they are paid approximately the full rate for the job, though the choice is not wide and is more or less limited to such manual tasks as carpentry. They can probably earn much more as soon as they are allowed to accept outside employment, but from the beginning they are expected to buy their own clothes and to make a sizeable contribution towards their keep. Similarly, if they choose to take one of the educational courses on offer, they have to pay a small fee in advance, so that if they fail to complete the course they lose their money. Alcohol apart, no restriction is placed on their purchase of luxuries.

These arrangements, obviously enough, are designed to give the patients an understanding of both the rewards and the responsibilities of normal living. One does not wish to suggest that they are perfect. For example, though it may be therapeutically helpful to oblige captives to underwrite the cost of their own captivity, it is hard to consider it just in a welfare state that provides free citizens with free medical and hospital care. One may also question the propriety of denying a patient access to his private funds if he has any, for though this may save him from being indolent, it does so artificially, and likewise insures a state of economic equality within the institution that is not duplicated in the free society which the patients are being prepared to re-enter. But, generally speaking, conditions at the Van der Hoeven Clinic seem indisputably more conducive to the creation of a therapeutic community and a "normal" way of life than those at Grendon can conceivably be, with the cells, the bolts and bars, the surrounding wall, 18 feet high, and the other traditional prison features.

One is apt to be told that this comparison is unfair and unrealistic, inasmuch as the Van der Hoeven patients must be very carefully selected with a view to excluding potential trouble-makers and "security risks"; whereas far more difficult cases are received at Grendon. But the directors and staff of the Van der Hoeven Clinic strongly deny a safety first policy. They claim to have accepted some of the most dangerous criminals in Holland, among them murderers, rapists, arsonists and violent heterosexual and homosexual paedophiliacs. By contrast, one may doubt whether the Grendon administrators would seriously maintain that maximum security is necessary for all or even most of their patients. One should remember, moreover, that the men behind the high wall at Grendon are in any case bound to be returned to society within a comparatively short time. Six months is the average length of stay, and unless a man is to be sent back to an ordinary prison, at the obvious risk of undoing any good that treatment may have done him, this must be spent at the end, not the beginning of his sentence. Clearly, there can be no room at Grendon for anyone, however mentally disturbed, who faces a further ten, twenty or thirty years behind bars.

The truth is that the security risks which can be taken in the interests of treatment depend on the public's willingness to tolerate them, and consequently they will remain very much less than they might usefully be so long as the punitive obsession persists. In our present state of knowledge (or, rather, lack thereof) it would, of course, be foolish to suggest that strong perimeter defences are needless in every case without exception. There have admittedly been many hundreds of abscondings from the Van der Hoeven Clinic, though mostly of a technical kind: instances of patients leaving the building without permission and returning of their own accord. The most serious incident in the Clinic's history happened when a man who was legitimately in town (he had been allowed to accept outside employment) raped a girl. This, like the case of the Pentonville hosteller who committed murder and armed robbery, should be regarded as a failure in prognosis rather than security, and doubtless under a preventive system there could never be an iron-clad guarantee against occasional failures of a similar sort, short of pursuing so cautious a policy that it would be an intolerable invasion of civil liberties. Still, it might be a reasonable prognosis that a dangerous man was too likely to escape, unless he were very much more securely confined than is possible at the Van der Hoeven Clinic.

In the author's opinion, two basic questions would have to be asked before a case was disposed of under a preventive system. The answers would depend on the results of a thorough diagnostic pre-examination of the offender's background, record, and character. But since they would have to be wholly divorced from punitive considerations, neither the trial Judge nor any other member of the judiciary should be allowed a part in giving them.

First, it would have to be decided what degree of custody was necessary. This, as we have seen, might need to be very little in the case of the largest number of offenders who are apparently undeterrable by penalties and untreatable by probationary means, namely the "inadequates". On the other hand, it might need to be considerable in the case of a small number of resourceful professional criminals.

Secondly, it would have to be decided what form of treatment was the most likely to effect a cure. Here, of course, we are again in the realm of the unknown or, more precisely, of the hardly explored, for if it is true that at the moment next to nothing is known about how to use treatment (as opposed to punishment) as a defence against crime, it is also true that there can be scant hope of discovering the means unless and until a full and unqualified commitment is made to the end. One may feel sure, for instance, that psychiatry (or any branch thereof) is not the whole answer; and one may suspect that it is not as large a part of the answer as its own practitioners are prone to claiming that it is. But to say that psychiatry is no answer at all is, under present circumstances, like complaining that a watch won't work when it hasn't been wound up.

It seems certain that whatever the form of treatment decided on, it would have to be carried out under conditions that both precluded a division inmate culture and were as little remote as possible from the conditions of normal living. This means that although some high security institutions might be needed, they would have to be small, with ample opportunity for "choice" (of work, recreation, and so on) behind the periphery and a sufficient ratio of therapeutic staff to inmates (at the Van der Hoeven Clinic, this is about one to two). It also means that none of the modern prisons, built or planned, would be serviceable, and that the traditions of conventional imprisonment would all have to be done away with.

Whatever form of treatment might be tried, it would have to be unskimped. Today, at Grendon, there is a heavy reliance on group psychotherapy. The Van der Hoeven treatment programme, on the other hand, is largely, though not exclusively, based on individual psychotherapy of a more or less analytic kind. Though one is not concerned here with the question of which of these two techniques is the more effective, or whether indeed either of them is, one cannot help observing that group therapy comes very much cheaper than individual therapy.

Nor would it be permissible to write off any offender as incurable. Deep though the "treasure" might be buried, and though it might never be found, the search for it would have to be unceasingly made. One is thinking here in particular of the so-called "monsters"—the most aggressive types of psychopath and the sex murderers. In this connection, it is pertinent to remark on the wide gap that separates the thinking (if thinking is the appropriate word) of the pro-capital punishment lobby in the House of Commons and that of the mass of their supporters in the country. Mr Duncan Sandys, who bases his case on deterrent theory, is not so purblind as to suppose that the death penalty could have deterred Ian Brady and Myra Hindley, the Moors Murderers, for instance—and, in fact, it did not.[15] But the pro-hanging majority among the electorate are, to judge from the sounds of *Vox Populi* in numerous television programmes, plain avengers at heart; and it is above all to deal with the most psychically distorted murderers who commit the most horrific crimes that they want the rope restored.

A cure for these people may or may not be discoverable; and for as long as it is undiscovered they will obviously have to be securely confined. But that would be no reason, if a preventive policy were faithfully pursued, for holding them for years on end under the sterile conditions of imprisonment. Apart from the cruelty to the individual which this involves—a cruelty, it may be recalled, which liberal reformers at the end of the last century considered more intolerable than capital punishment—it is, from society's point of view, wasteful and senseless; and the reason why has been most movingly and eloquently stated by two bereaved fathers, one an American, Professor Anatol Hold, the other an Englishman, Mr Michael Whitaker.

In Philadelphia, in 1959, Professor Hold's daughter, aged three and a half, was murdered in a basement by a 15-year-old honour student. A few hours after the boy had confessed, Professor Hold wrote an open letter to the People of Philadelphia, which was published in *The Philadelphia Evening Bulletin.* The following is an extract:[16]

"I am sure that his parents have been god-fearing, upright citizens, too uneducated in matters of the human soul to have recognized the plight of their child during the years of his growth.

"They undoubtedly took naïve pride in his constant good behaviour, neat appearance, and good performance at church and school, never suspecting that this very goodness was a serious cause of worry in the light of what must have been left unaccounted for.

"It is, of course, worrisome, from the social point of view, that there are parents with such lack of understanding. It is, I submit, much more profoundly worrisome that it should have been possible for this boy to go through his whole fifteen years without anyone who was responsible for his upbringing—such as his school and his church—having taken note (out of uncaring or lack of understanding) of the danger signals before the tragedy.

"Beware, citizens. The human animal cannot be cheated forever. It will have to love, or kill.

"You will understand that I am not lecturing you for the pure joy of sounding wise. I am hurt to the depths of my being, and I cry out to you to take better care of your children.

"My final word has to do with the operation of the machinery of justice. Had I caught the boy in the act, I would have wished to kill him. Now that there is no undoing of what is done, I only wish to help him.

"Let no feelings of cave-man vengeance influence us. Let us rather help him who did so human a thing."

Perhaps, as Dr Karl Menninger has written (*The Crime of Punishment*, 1968), that last sentence "deserves immortality." One could certainly wish that the last three sentences were known to every Judge, politician and man-in-the-street who is tempted to utter the empty parrot-cry, "consider the victim", in defence of a merely punitive response to murder. The folly and essential inhumaneness of that argument is made even clearer by Michael Whitaker, whose eight-year-old daughter,

Fiona, was raped and strangled in a field at Batley in August, 1969. Her assailant was a telephone engineer, who subsequently committed suicide.

In an article in *The Sunday Times Magazine* (29 March, 1970), Michael Whitaker wrote "... our daughter is not the only child to die in this way; five other young girls were murdered in similar circumstances between the end of August and the end of November last year. Over the years many children have died thus, young boys as well as girls, many children missing, many murders unsolved, and many more raped and mutilated, though not killed. One reads of these disasters, one shudders inwardly, and, if we believe, we pray. But perhaps the time has come to do more than pray. For my part I believe that we know almost nothing about the state of mind of men who commit these crimes. The abolition of capital punishment would be right, for one reason alone, if the State, through the agency of the most knowledgeable men and women in the appropriate fields, would attempt to enlist the assistance of the men who are convicted of these murders to give us some kind of insight into their motives.

"Perhaps they were maddened by the influences of commercial pornography or by the conditions of life in our industrial society, perhaps they could never find normal sex. Who knows? But we should try to find out, *because only through knowledge can there be some hope of preventing these disasters in the future*." (Author's italics.)

That is the true way of considering victims, just as ultimately the only possible way of winning the "battle against crime" is to identify and uproot its causes. But the identification must be a matter of scientific research, not of hunch. We cannot, for instance, reasonably regard pornography as a cause of sexual offences, simply because some Home Secretary happens to consider it distasteful, or dismiss the possibility of its connection with sexual offences, if another Home Secretary happens to consider its distribution civilized. Similarly, the uprooting must be total, not partial. Thus because we have a Welfare State, it is fashionable to conclude that poverty is not, as it was once thought to be, a major cause of crime. But, Welfare State or not, the facts are that poverty is still with us, and that the great majority of crimes are still committed by the least privileged members of society.

Meanwhile, we have to combat effects as best we may, and the lessons which penal history teaches may be summarized as follows:

1. Even if punishments could be made sufficiently severe in theory to keep crime in check, in practice they could not be. A penal system based on deterrent theory is, therefore, inoperable.

2. We have in effect inherited two separate forms of imprisonment—local and central. The first exists as a defence against minor crime, and though we may pretend otherwise, its purpose is wholly deterrent. Though its deficiencies were already so apparent by the end of the last century that a move began, and has continued ever since, towards the development of alternative defences against minor crime, it is still by far the more widely used of the two forms of imprisonment. Granted the necessity of some system of penalties to deter certain kinds of offence and certain kinds of offender, the inclusion of imprisonment would appear to be highly irrational, unless it is unavoidable, if only because prisons are extremely expensive places to build and maintain. We cannot, however, know whether it is avoidable or not until (a) the alternatives have been fully developed and (b) we have ascertained who among the offenders at present liable to be sent to prison are in fact deterrable (this would certainly exclude the large numbers of mental defectives) and what is the minimum penalty required to deter them.

3. Central imprisonment exists as a defence against major crime. It is rooted in the idea that while criminals are deterrable by punishment and deserve to be punished, they are also reformable and are entitled to be reformed (rather than exterminated). Broadly speaking, the retributive-deterrent objective is pursued by the judiciary with its power of imposing prison sentences (usually for fixed terms), while the reformative objective is entrusted by the legislature to the executive, which has the responsibility of enforcing the punishment. However, the two objectives would appear to be mutually incompatible, and, to judge from the high rate of recidivism

among people who commit major crimes, neither has been achieved.

4. Since central imprisonment failed during the brief period when its purpose was exclusively deterrent, and when it was a far severer punishment than society could be expected to tolerate today, the only reasonable alternative left would be to replace it with a wholly reformative or preventive system even though we have no assurance that such a system would succeed and cannot have until we try it.

Will we try it? If we don't, it will not be because it would cost too great a sum in money and human resources to be practically possible. That will only be the pretext for *not* trying it; a hollow enough pretext, when one considers the millions and millions of pounds that have been abortively spent during the past two centuries on building prisons, and the millions more that will be spent unless we call a halt.

The final question to be asked and faced is whether we really *want* to try anything that might by chance put an end to crime. For though we speak of how imperative it is to be protected from it, only a very small minority among us have seriously suffered from it. Are we, the great remaining majority, as much in earnest about waging the battle against crime as we are about punishing criminals? Might we even prefer to drop the one if we discovered that it precluded the other? Is there, perhaps, significance in the fact, for instance, that it never occurred to one of the opponents of homosexual law reform, not even to the liberal-minded Lord Devlin, that it is perfectly possible to make an act illegal, and hence to register society's disapproval of it, without threatening to send its perpetrators to prison?

In his sadly beautiful article, Michael Whitaker said that he asked the Home Office to institute the sort of scientific inquiry that he believed should be made into the death of his own child and of the five other children who were the victims of sex murderers in October, November and December, 1969. "One must hope", he wrote, "that the intrinsic merits of this request will lead to a positive response."

One must hope that they will. And, formally perhaps, they may. But in the light of history, and against a present political background of rabble-rousing chatter about "law and order", one must fear that nothing effective will be done to implement this far-sighted proposal by a man who *has* suffered terribly from crime and whom punishment did nothing to protect from it.

FOOTNOTE

A PRISON ONCE built is, as we have seen, all too likely to stay put; and there are a greater number of survivals from the last century than may be commonly realized. Rochester (originally known as Borstal), Reading, Portland, Feltham, and Portsmouth, for example, all remain in use, though they are now listed as "closed borstals" for boys, and their cells are called "rooms".

Indeed, the wonder is that we are not still stuck with Millbank, first and most extravagant of the central government's ventures in prison structure. However, it was pulled down in 1892, and as an experiment the demolition of one of the five pentagons was entrusted to volunteers among the unemployed, who were paid 6½d. an hour.[1] Thou this venture presented considerable difficulties, the sale of the debris yielded a net profit of £1,060, whereas the other five pentagons, demolished by regular labour, yielded a profit of less than £1,000 each.

The original cost of building Millbank, it will be recalled, amounted to £450,000. That was exclusive of the site, part of which is now occupied by the Tate Gallery.

NOTES AND DOCUMENTATION

Chapter 1

[1] Since 1963, when the Prison Commission was abolished, statements of expenditure have been included in the annual Home Office reports on the work of the Prison Department. Prior to that, they were included in the annual reports of the Prison Commissioners. While increased costs are to some extent attributable to the present building programme, the figures show that between 1930 and 1967 the cost of maintenance alone rose from under £1,000,000 to over £28,000,000. It continues to rise.

[2] In Denmark, during the second World War, when the Germans disbanded the Danish police, there followed an immediate and huge increase in crime. This is one among several similar incidents that has been relied on as "proof" of the validity of deterrent theory. But to reject deterrent theory is not to hold that law could be maintained if *all* penalties for violating it were removed. It is to deny that any *particular* punishment is necessarily required for deterrent purposes or that the more serious the crime the severer the punishment needed to deter it.

[3] Mr Duncan Sandys's statement was reported on 26 September 1967.

[4] Lord Justice Greer's letter published on 22 November 1938 was among several similar letters provoked by the Criminal Justice Bill of that year.

[5] *Recollections of a Prison Governor* by C. E. F. Rich (see bibliography).

[6] Quotation from an editorial (12 February 1901) on an article in *19th Century* by a former Head of the C.I.D. It may be noted that the attitude of *The Times* towards penal matters throughout the years has on the whole been liberal. For example, on 24 October 1842: "It is the inevitable and invariable tendency of labour on the treadmill to create obstacles

to that which ought to be the grand end of all punishment—the moral reformation of the prisoners themselves." Or again, on 24 February 1877: "We cannot go back to the cruel system of rendering labour as useless as possible in order to render it deterrent."

[7] Royal Commission on Penal Servitude, Lord Cockburn's dissenting report (see bibliography), 1863.

[8] From his evidence before the Criminal Law Commission. Quoted by Lord Caernarvon in the House of Lords, 19 February 1863, when his lordship also said: "Prison Inspectors have recommended that corporal punishment should cease, and have triumphed over its disuse. Moreover, the whole course of Parliamentary legislation has been to throw every difficulty in the way of sentencing prisoners to corporal punishment."

[9] From the evidence of G. L. Chesterton to Committee on Secondary Punishments (see bibliography), 1831.

[10] Committee's Report Respecting Transportation of Offenders (see bibliography), 1785.

[11] Royal Commission on Capital Punishment (see bibliography), 1866.

[12] Royal Commission on Capital Punishment (see bibliography), 1952–53.

[13] A Select Committee, ten years earlier had come out strongly against public executions. The Committee learned, *inter alia*, that in one town a circus performance had been postponed for two hours in order that potential customers might not be obliged to choose between it and the spectacle of a scheduled public hanging (see bibliography under Parliamentary Papers consulted, 1856).

[14] First published 1922; re-published 1963 (see bibliography).

Chapter 2

[1] Report on Secondary Punishments (see bibliography), 1831–32.

[2] Report on Returns Respecting Convicts (see bibliography), 1779.

[3] This followed three Select Committee reports on the Laws Relating to Penitentiary Houses (see bibliography). The

first two, 1810–11, contain all the information about Bentham's plans; the third, 1812, is concerned with the Hulks.

Chapter 3

[1] *English Prisons Under Local Government.*

[2] In 1847 a ten-year-old boy was reported to have died at Millbank after a punishment of 21 days bread-and-water and three days in a dark cell. (See bibliography under Papers consulted Royal Commission on the Management of Millbank Prison, 1847.) This happened after Millbank had ceased to be used as a penitentiary dedicated to reform, but from the beginning of its history it received child offenders.

[3] For example, the matron, a certain Mrs Chambers, was shortly dismissed for stealing a Bible and employing prisoners for her own private advantage; the steward was dismissed for embezzlement.

[4] It should be added, however, that both in and out of Parliament there had been severe criticisms of the Committee of Management for feeding the prisoners too well. The "consider-the-victim" school had accused the Committee's chairman (C. P. Holford) of running a "Fattening House"—and had suggested that security measures at Millbank were pointless, since criminals wanted to get into the place rather than out of it. Select Committee's Report on the State of the Penitentiary (see bibliography), 1824; also Report of the Committee of Management, 1823; and the Report of the Physicians, 1823 under Papers consulted.

[5] For instance, in September 1826 a prisoner named Hussey, after a spell in a dark cell for insubordination, promptly emptied a pail of water over a turnkey's head.

[6] Report on Secondary Punishments (see bibliography), 1831–32.

[7] Memorials of Millbank (see bibliography), 1875; Griffiths served for a while as a Deputy Governor of Millbank before his appointment as an Inspector of Prisons, and had access to the Millbank archives, notably to the journals of the various governors, and much of the detail in this chapter is drawn from his book. During the same year that 100 lashes were

remitted to 50, a prisoner was sentenced to 300 lashes for a similar offence. Only 100 of these were "laid on" without "much severity."

[8] *The Times*, 26 February 1838.

[9] *Hansard*, Vol. XLI, 26 February 1838.

[10] Report of the Inspectors of Millbank (see bibliography), 1844.

Chapter 4

[1] Committee on the Laws Relating to Penitentiary House, third report, 1812. This report contains the history of the Hulks service up to that time.

[2] See bibliography, 1828.

[3] See bibliography, 1831–32.

[4] Report of the Inspectors of Millbank (see bibliography), 1844.

[5] The Norfolk Island Penal Settlement was finally closed down on 30 September 1846.

[6] It might be less. Men under life sentence, or under sentence of 15 years for such aggravated offences as burglary, arson, rape, forgery and robberies with violence, were required to serve a minimum of two years in Norfolk Island before being transferred to a probationary gang.

[7] June 1847; for report of subsequent inquiry, see bibliography, 1847.

[8] See bibliography, 1850.

[9] See bibliography, 1852.

Chapter 5

[1] Report of the Prison Commissioners (see bibliography) 1939–40.

[2] William Crawford's report (see bibliography), 1834.

[3] W. Hepworth Dickson (see bibliography).

[4] Select Committee on Prison Discipline (see bibliography), 1850.

[5] For example, Lord Mahon during debates on the Prisons Bill, 3 June 1847.

[6] Report of the Directors of Convict Prisons (see bibliography), 1852.

[7] Report by Lt-Colonel J. Jebb (see bibliography), 1857–58.

[8] As above.

[9] Penal Practice in a Changing Society (see bibliography), 1959–60.

[10] Report by Lt-Colonel Jebb, 1857–58.

[11] Lord Mountbatten's Report of the Inquiry into Prison Escapes and Security (see bibliography), 1966–67.

Chapter 6

[1] Clerkenwell, prior to its being rebuilt in 1834 as a remand prison, was known as a "great brothel."

[2] In his preface to *English Prisons Under Local Government.*

[3] *English Prisons Under Local Government* (see bibliography). This is a definitive work, and the detail in this chapter is largely owed to it.

[4] See bibliography, 1850.

[5] The Webbs estimate that between 1777 and 1844 the general population rose by 130%, the prison population by upwards of 1,000%.

[6] Report on the State of the Gaols in London (see bibliography), 1813–14.

[7] The figure has steadily risen over the past twenty years. By May 1970 it had reached 13,000.

[8] The Webbs record that between 1810 and 1820, the custodial staff at Gloucester consisted of ten officers and two dogs!

[9] From his evidence before the Select Committee on Prison Discipline (see bibliography), 1850.

[10] On Criminal Commitments and Convictions (see bibliography), 1828.

[11] See bibliography.

[12] Report of the Inspectors of Prisons (see bibliography), 1837–38.

[13] Jebb's evidence before the Select Committee (see bibliography), 1850: "The repressive elements of the discipline are hard labour, hard fare, and a hard bed. If these elements be made the basis of penal discipline for short periods, it affords the best opportunity for introducing gradations into the daily routine, in which, during longer periods of imprisonment,

instruction and industrial training may, to some extent, replace them."

[14] *The Punishment and Prevention of Crime* (see bibliography).

[15] Evidence before the House of Lords Committee on Prison Discipline (see bibliography), 1863.

[16] W. Hepworth Dickson, *The London Prisons* (see bibliography).

[17] See bibliography.

[18] From his evidence before the Select Committee (see bibliography), 1850.

[19] From his evidence before the Select Committee (see bibliography), 1850.

[20] From his evidence before the House of Lords Committee (see bibliography), 1863.

[21] Told by Perry to the House of Lords Committee (see bibliography), 1863.

[22] See bibliography.

[23] *The London Prisons* (see bibliography).

[24] Hepworth Dickson himself was scathing about this particular incident: "His madness was very mild. He wished to fraternise with the other prisoners; sang hymns when told to be silent; and when reprimanded for taking these unwarranted liberties, declared that he was the 'governor'. So they put him into darkness to enlighten his understanding; and alone to teach him how unbrotherly men are . . . They said he *pretended* to be mad; which seeing that his vagaries subjected him to continual punishments was very likely!" Nearly a century later, a similar point was made by Wilfred Macartney in *Walls Have Mouths* about a Parkhurst prisoner who was accused of "feigning" madness. "He did years of punishment in acute discomfort, lived in filth and appeared to find it congenial, lost twelve months remission, and at the termination of a full sentence of four years, was discharged to a county asylum!"

[25] Today, of course, the public may imagine that outright lunatics are never sent to prison. But, for example: "There was a woman I remember who was quite mental when she entered the hospital on remand. She told me that she was making a tour of H.M.'s Prisons, and if she took a fancy to Holloway she would have her holidays there. Most of the time . . . she was in a

hospital cell. For nearly a week she would scream all through the night. We could hear her yelling Holloway over and over again." From *Who Lie in Gaol* by Joan Henry, 1952.

[26] "There were 19 suicides, compared with 11 in 1966," Report of the Prison Department (see bibliography), 1968–69.

[27] From his evidence before the Select Committee (see bibliography), 1850.

[28] *A Cure For Crime* (see bibliography).

[29] *On Iniquity* (see bibliography).

[30] From his evidence before the Select Committee (see bibliography), 1850. The best (Class Four) dinner available at the Birmingham gaol consisted of three ounces of boneless meat and half a pound of potatoes, while bread and oatmeal gruel were all that could be had for breakfast and supper. If by present standards, however, Maconochie appears to have been a somewhat half-hearted liberal reformer, it is doubtless true to say that as the courage of deterrent theory has weakened, so the courage of reformative theory has grown stronger. "I am not a friend to undue indulgence," Elizabeth Fry told the House of Lords Committee (see bibliography under Papers consulted) that reported on gaols and houses of correction in 1835. And she said she would "decidely favour short imprisonments with strict discipline over long imprisonments with inferior discipline."

[31] See bibliography, 1854.

Chapter 7

[1] While prison administrators have always complained that the great majority of prison sentences are too short for reformative purposes, they have been indefinite about the minimum time needed. Though juvenile offenders could not be sent to Parkhurst for less than a year, both the Governor and Chaplain were soon protesting that this was insufficient. Thus the Governor wrote (see Report of the Directors of Convict Prisons, 1857–58): "The durability of their sentences will not be sufficient for the training requisite to reclaim them from idle and vicious habits." And the Chaplain wrote: "The time is far too short for reformation; and as to the deterring effects of a prison,

it is manifest that this desirable and wholesome object is not accomplished . . . Time, pains and expense are almost thrown away. I am unable to see the benefit of short sentences, either to the prisoners themselves or to the community at large." Years later, this same view was echoed by a former Borstal governor: "Nothing of value can be achieved with juveniles in under three years I am certain" (see bibliography, *Prison Governor*, by Wallace Blake). On the other hand, there has always been a conviction that sentences can be too *long*. The Select Committee that investigated the situation at Millbank in 1824 (see bibliography) reported: "Seven years is a term sufficiently long to answer all practical purposes of reformation or *example*." The use of that last word (author's italics) in 1824 may strike an ironic note in the 1970's.

[2] Rules Settled by the Secretary of State (see bibliography), 1877.

[3] Report on the Work of the Prison Department, 1968–69.

[4] *Prisons and Prisoners* (see bibliography).

[5] From Du Cane's evidence to the Departmental Committee (see bibliography), 1895.

[6] *English Prisons Under Local Government* (see bibliography).

[7] Notably at Risley, a remand centre for men, boys, women and girls. There were 19 punishments of restricted diets awarded in the male part during 1967. And the only such punishment awarded to any female prisoner during the same period was at Risley.

[8] *My First Imprisonment* (see bibliography).

[9] 28 January 1879. The letter from the other (anonymous) correspondent, giving the figures of maintenance cost in locally administered gaols, was published on the following day.

[10] *Paterson on Prisons* (see bibliography).

[11] Report of the Directors of Convict Prisons (see bibliography), 1871.

[12] *The Punishment and Prevention of Crime* (see bibliography).

[13] Under existing regulations, Home Office authorization to visit a prison is only granted on the understanding (*inter alia*) that the visitor will not speak to any prisoner, unless he receives the Governor's permission so to do. Moreover, all prison staff are bound by the Official Secrets Acts. Finally, documents

relating to prisons, unlike most official papers, are restricted, not for thirty years, but for a hundred.

[14] *The London Prisons* (see bibliography).

[15] As reported, August 1969.

[16] *The Punishment and Prevention of Crime* (see bibliography).

Chapter 8

[1] See bibliography, 1863.

[2] Figures provided by the Directors of Convict Prisons.

[3] E.g. quotation from a prison magazine (November 1968): "Having seen the pathetic results in most prisons, some prisoners just aren't prepared to go through the motions of what they believe to be a wholly fruitless exercise."

[4] *Prison Was My Parish* (see bibliography).

[5] "Excessive" by comparison with the sentences passed a century (and more) ago. In 1896, for example, "life" apart (which never meant over 20 years), no prisoner was in for more than 15 years.

[6] Report of the Directors of Convict Prisons (see bibliography), 1871.

[7] In accord with recommendations made by Dr Guy, Medical Officer at Millbank. Report on Dietaries in Convict Prisons (see bibliography under Papers consulted, 1864).

[8] Jebb gave the Royal Commission an example of a man who served 13 years of a life sentence, and left prison with accumulated gratuities of £29–5–6d.

[9] *The Punishment and Prevention of Crime* (see bibliography).

[10] Report of Directors of Convict Prisons (see bibliography), 1870.

[11] See bibliography, 1867.

[12] See bibliography, 1871.

[13] Nearly half a century earlier, the Gaol Act of 1823 had provided: "No prisoner shall be kept in irons except in case of urgent and absolute necessity."

[14] See bibliography, 1878–79.

[15] Straffen, the child murderer, provides a particularly disgraceful instance. Originally found unfit to plead, and committed to Broadmoor, Straffen was convicted and sentenced to

death when he escaped from Broadmoor and committed a second, palpably compulsive murder. The sentence was commuted to life imprisonment, and for some fifteen years he was locked up at Bristol prison. However, at the time of the 1966 security scare he was transferred to Parkhurst and from there, a couple of years later, to Durham in exchange for one of the Richardson brothers! Durham is notoriously the worst of the special security blocks.

[16] A full account of the Mitchell case is contained in Lord Mountbatten's report (see bibliography), 1966–67.

[17] Report of Royal Commission on the Penal Servitude Acts (see bibliography), 1878–79.

[18] *The Punishment and Prevention of Crime* (see bibliography).

[19] *The English Prison System* (see bibliography).

[20] *The Punishment and Prevention of Crime* (see bibliography).

[21] *The English Prison System* (see bibliography).

[22] As quoted by Du Cane in *The Punishment and Prevention of Crime* (see bibliography).

[23] Though Caernarvon's idea was by no means universally accepted. For instance, his 1863 Committee had been warned by the Governor of Wakefield (Edward Shepherd) that the treadwheel was anti-reformative, since it made "idlers hate work more than ever".

[24] *Secrets of the Prison House* (see bibliography).

[25] In Du Cane's time it was held to be an imperative measure of security in the convict prisons that prisoners' clothes should be stacked *outside* their cells at nights.

Chapter 9

[1] *Recollections of a Prison Governor* (see bibliography).

[2] For example, in her evidence before the House of Lords Select Committee on Prison Discipline (see bibliography under Papers consulted, 1835).

[3] *Memorials of Millbank* (see bibliography). Major Griffiths also wrote in the same context that whereas men could invariably be tamed by punishment, "there are instances known of women who have maintained for months, nay years, an unbroken war with authority, and have won the day in the

end." He attributed this to "obstinacy and a species of mania."

[4] Report of the Prison Commissioners (see bibliography), 1938–39.

[5] Report of the Prison Department (see bibliography), 1968–69.

[6] *Twelve Months in Gaol* (see bibliography).

[7] One of these philanthropic institutions was established as early as 1788, and in 1849 moved from London to Redhill. In the sense that it catered for both convicted delinquents and children who might be sent there by their parents or had been deserted by their parents, it foreshadowed the modern Approved School system.

[8] Later, after Parkhurst had ceased to be independently administered (by a Committee of Visitors) and, like Pentonville, became part of the Convict Prisons establishment, discipline was, officially at least, somewhat relaxed. The Chaplain, J. J. Spear, told a Select Committee (see Report on Criminal and Destitute Juveniles, 1851, under Papers consulted) that corporal punishment was never resorted to, except in "extreme cases", though then, he said, it "had a most beneficial effect." However, it seems a reasonable assumption that a good deal of unofficial beating still went on.

[9] Du Cane himself was unable to account for it in his evidence before the Kimberley Commission (see bibliography), 1878–79.

[10] Quoted by G. C. Ives in his *History of Penal Methods* (see bibliography).

Chapter 10

[1] *Secrets of the Prison House* (see bibliography).

[2] March 1894.

[3] *English Prisons Under Local Government* (see bibliography).

[4] See bibliography, 1895.

[5] U.S. Federal Prisons Report, 1947.

[6] Immediately following the Government's take-over, many local gaols were closed down. This was part and parcel of Du Cane's economy drive. There was at least one prophecy then of resultant over-crowding. John Lloyd, a magistrate, wrote to

The Times on 28 December 1878: "The *maximum* number of prisoners to be now provided for may be taken at 21,030, and the certified cell accommodation, after deducting the 2,123 cells now closed, at 22,217. Mr Cross [the Home Secretary] has, therefore, lost 1,183 cells as an available balance to enable him to keep the numbers at each of the existing 78 prisons within their proper number. Will this balance be found sufficient?"

[7] In his report as Surveyor-General of Prisons (see bibliography under Papers consulted, 1847) Jebb wrote: "It was believed [30 years ago] even by those who had given deep consideration to the subject and who influenced public opinion at the time, that if prisoners could be *classified* it would effect everything that could be devised in the way of punishment and reformation." By way of contradicting this, Jebb went on to quote from the account by MM Beaumont and de Tocqueville of U.S. Prison discipline: "*L'impossibilité d'opérer une classification positive des criminels a été prouvée avec une certitude si mathématique que l'on doit la prendre pour point de départ dans toute la réforme des prisons.*"

[8] Report of the Prison Department (see bibliography), 1968–1969.

[9] *The English Prison System* (see bibliography).

[10] Wallace Blake, *Prison Governor* (see bibliography).

[11] An account of Camp Hill by Laurence Housman is included in *English Prisons Today*, edited by Stephen Hobhouse and Fenner Brockway (see bibliography).

[12] *The English Prison System* (see bibliography).

[13] For example, H. J. B. Montgomery in *The National Review* (August 1904): "The English prison system is bad in every respect, but it is, I am convinced, past tinkering with... Only the man of refinement is punished in gaol; for him it is an exquisitely devised torture. For the ordinary larrikin, loafer, or habitual criminal there *is* no punishment." That last sentence may be instructively, if depressingly, compared with Sir Ian Horobin's conclusion (*The Observer*, 10 October 1965): "Prisons don't even punish in any sensible way. Provided you are dirty enough, lazy enough, selfish enough and cunning enough, you can slope through any ordinary sentence as a 'good' prisoner without more than the minimum torment."

[14] Stuart Wood, *Shades of the Prison House* (see bibliography).

[15] *Prisons and Prisoners* (see bibliography).

[16] *Penal Discipline* (see bibliography).

[17] Ed. Stephen Hobhouse and Fenner Brockway (see bibliography).

[18] An account of the Birmingham experiment is included in *English Prisons Today*.

[19] *Organisation of the Prison Medical Service*.

Chapter 11

[1] As provided under the 1949 Prison Rules (see bibliography).

[2] *The Punishment and Prevention of Crime* (see bibliography).

[3] And at Wakefield in the mid-19th century there was an establishment attached to the prison for the employment of discharged prisoners at mat-making.

[4] See bibliography.

[5] This, and all other quotations from Alexander Paterson's speeches and writings, are to be found in *Paterson on Prisons* (see bibliography).

[6] *The English Prison System* (see bibliography).

[7] See bibliography.

[8] *The Verdict of You All* (see bibliography).

[9] C. E. F. Rich, *Recollections of a Prison Governor* (see bibliography).

[10] *Penal Discipline* (see bibliography).

[11] *Prison Governor* (see bibliography).

[12] *The Verdict of You All* (see bibliography).

[13] To the extent (May 1970) of some 2,000 unfilled places.

[14] *Prison Governor* (see bibliography).

[15] *Prison Screw* (see bibliography).

[16] *The Society of Captives* (see bibliography).

[17] *The Verdict of You All* (see bibliography).

[18] Tobacco is a privilege that prisoners have regained, rather than won. It was condemned by a House of Lords Select Committee in 1835 (Papers consulted) as a "stimulating luxury", and for over a century thereafter was denied even to untried prisoners.

[19] *Prison Screw* (see bibliography).

[20] *Prison Screw* (see bibliography).

[21] *Secrets of the Prison House* (see bibliography).

[22] *Prisons And A Changing Society* (see bibliography).

[23] This pre-dates Pentonville. In 1790, the rules of the newly built gaol in Manchester provided: "On admission of a prisoner he will immediately be washed in a bath." By contrast, it may be observed that provisions for personal cleanliness during a sentence are no better today than they were a century and a half ago at Millbank: one bath and one change of linen weekly!

[24] Report of the Prison Department (see bibliography), 1968–69.

[25] For example, the extent to which starvation continues to be used as a method of penal discipline may be judged from the fact that no fewer than 3,814 punishments of restricted diet were awarded in men's and boys' prisons during the year ended 31 December 1967.

[26] *Invisible Bars* (see bibliography).

[27] See bibliography under Other Official Papers.

Chapter 12

[1] See bibliography, 1933–34. Sir Norwood East was himself a Prison Commissioner.

[2] *London Prisons of Today and Yesterday* (see bibliography).

[3] It should be said, however, that the present Lord Chief Justice (Lord Parker) has declared himself opposed to any such policy. Still, this does not alter the fact that the judiciary retains the power to defeat the purpose of parole, if it chooses to use it. Here an opinion expressed in a prison magazine by an inmate may be worth quoting: "I was arguing against the view, widely held in con-circles, that the judges are now simply giving longer sentences to balance the possibility of parole. I said that I did not believe this to be true. Now I'm not so sure. What has made me change my mind? It's the case of Regina versus Langan in the Court of Appeal (Law Report, 7 October 1968). Langan got four years and appealed against severity of sentence, but their Lordships dismissed the appeal on the grounds of the appellant's eligibility for parole in due course. I

conclude that if the Appeal Court can take account of a man's eligibility for parole when assessing the suitability of his sentence, so may an assize court or quarter sessions in giving it to him."

[4] Lord Hunt, Chairman of the Parole Board, has maintained that the Board is politically independent. But, for two reasons, this simply isn't true. A. The Board is not empowered to consider recommending any prisoner for release on parole unless and until the Home Secretary requests it to do so. B. The Home Secretary is not obliged to accept a recommendation for release by the Board. (See the Criminal Justice Act, 1967.)

[5] *Penal Discipline* (see bibliography).

[6] Lord Justice Edmund Davies who, it will be remembered, tried and sentenced the train robbers.

[7] Report of the Prison Department (see bibliography), 1968–69: "There was some curtailment of prisoners' activities, a reduction in the number of outside working parties, and of educational classes. Hostels at Cardiff, Chelmsford and Wandsworth were closed."

[8] In an account of the existing Prison System, *Prison* (see bibliography), Michael Wolff writes: "The greatest care is taken in the selection of prisoners for hostels. At Dartmoor, for example, only seventy-eight out of 273 men considered were selected in one year . . . Such care has to be taken . . . because both prospective employers and the public deserve to be as fully protected as possible and these men and women, as their long sentences indicate, have bad criminal histories."

[9] Thus Leslie Wilkins in a study comparing the results of probation with those of other penal measures, including prison, found no significant difference in reconviction rates. And in a report to the Council of Europe (1964) Dr Roger Hood summarized the conclusions of comparative studies of treatment results with the words: "Overall results are not much different as between different treatments." (See *The Honest Politician's Guide to Crime Control* by Norval Morris and Gordon Hawkins, Chicago, 1970.)

[10] Essay *Prison In Evolution* in *Criminology In Transition* (see bibliography).

[11] See bibliography, 1956–57.

[12] *Social Science and Social Pathology* (see bibliography).

[13] Though a more enlightened view might be that Hess should clearly not be held responsible for his actions (see an article by Trevor Roper on Hess's mental state in the *Sunday Times*, 24 May 1970).

[14] *Homer Lane* by David Wills (see bibliography).

[15] The Moors Murders were actually committed, though not detected, before the abolition of the death penalty; and because they were a case of multiple murder Ian Brady and Myra Hindley rendered themselves liable to capital punishment under the 1957 Homicide Act.

[16] Quoted by Karl Menninger in *The Crime of Punishment* (see bibliography).

Footnote

[1] Report of Surveyor (see bibliography), 1893–94.

BIBLIOGRAPHY

1. Parliamentary Reports and Papers (available in the State Paper Room British Museum as listed).

A. Direct Reference to, and/or quotation from in text:

Session	
1779	Report on Returns Respecting Convicts, House of Commons Journals, Vol. XXXVII.
1785	Report Respecting Transportation of Offenders, House of Commons Journals, Vol. XL.
1810–11	Two Reports from Select Committee on the Law Relating to Penitentiary Houses, Vol. II.
1812	Third Report as above, Vol. IV.
1813–14	Select Committee's Report on the State of Gaols in the City of London, Vol. IV.
1824	Select Committee's Report on the State of the (Millbank) Penitentiary, Vol. IV.
1828	Select Committee's Report on Criminal Commitments and Convictions, Vol. III.
1831	Select Committee's Report on the Best Mode of Giving Efficacy to Secondary Punishments, Vol. VII.
1831–32	Second Report as above, Vol. VII.
1834	William Crawford's Report on Prison Discipline in the United States of America, Vol. XLVI.
1836	First Report of Inspectors of Prisons (Home District), Vol. XXXV.
1837–38	Second Report of Inspectors of Prisons (Home District), Vol. XXX.
1843	First Report of the Commissioners of Pentonville Prison, Vol. XXIX.
1844	Second Report of the Commissioners of Pentonville Prison, Vol. XXVIII.

First Report of the Inspectors of Millbank, Vol. XXVIII.

1845 Third Report of the Pentonville Commissioners, Vol. XXV.

1846 Fourth Report of the Pentonville Commissioners, Vol. XX.

1847 Fifth Report of the Pentonville Commissioners, Vol. XXX.

Report of an Inquiry (by Captain Williams) into the General Treatment and Conditions of the Convicts in the Hulks at Woolwich, Vol. XVIII.

Report from House of Lords Select Committee on Discipline in Gaols, Vol. XXIX.

1847–48 Sixth Report of the Pentonville Commissioners, Vol. XXXIV.

1849 Seventh Report of the Pentonville Commissioners, Vol. XXVI.

1850 Final Report of the Pentonville Commissioners, Vol. XXIX.

First Report from the Manager (Voules) of the Hulks, Vol. XXIX.

Select Committee's Report on Discipline in Gaols and Houses of Correction, Vol. XVII.

1852 First Report from the Directors of Convict Prisons and the Hulks, Vol. XXIV.

1854 Report of Royal Commission's Investigation of Conditions at Birmingham Prison, Vol. XXXVII.

1854–55 Report of the Directors of Convict Prisons, including Report by Lt-Colonel Jebb on the Substitution of Penal Servitude for Transportation, Vol. XXV.

1857–58 Report of the Directors of Convict Prisons, including Report by Lt-Colonel Joshua Jebb on Discipline and the Ticket-of-Leave Scheme, Vol. XXIX.

1863 Report of House of Lords Committee on Discipline in Gaols and Houses of Correction, Vol. IX.

Royal Commission Report on Acts Relating to Transportation and Penal Servitude, Vol. XXI.

1866 Royal Commission's Report on Capital Punishment, Vol. XXI.

1867 Report of Home Office Commission's Inquiry into the Treatment of Treason-Felony Convicts, Vol. XXXV.

1870 Report of the Directors of Convict Prisons, Vol. XXXVIII.

1871 Royal Commission Report on the Treatment of Convicts, Vol. XXXII.

Report of the Directors of Convict Prisons, Vol. XXXI.

1872 Report of the Directors of Convict Prisons, Vol. XXXI.

1877 Prison Rules Settled by the Secretary of State, Vol. LXIII.

1878–79 Royal Commission Report on the Working of the Penal Servitude Acts, Vols. XXXVII and XXXVIII.

1893–94 Report of the Surveyor (i.e. Millbank), Vol. LXXII.

1895 Departmental Committee's Report on Prisons, Vol. LVI.

1931–32 Report of the Prison Commissioners and Directors of Convict Prisons, Vol. XII

1933–34 Report of the Prison Commissioners and Directors of Convict Prisons, Vol. XV.

1937–38 Report of the Prison Commissioners and Directors of Convict Prisons, Vol. XIV.

1939–40 Report of the Prison Commissioners and Directors of Convict Prisons, Vol. V.

1949–50 Statutory Instruments: The Prison Rules, Vol.

1952–53 Royal Commission Report on Capital Punishment, Vol. VII.

1956–57 Departmental Committee's Report on Homosexual Offences and Prostitution, Vol. XIV.

1959–60 Penal Practice in a Changing Society.

1966–67 Report of the Inquiry into Prison Escapes and Security by Admiral of the Fleet, the Earl Mountbatten of Burma.

1968–69 Report on the Work of the Prison Department.

B. Consulted:

Session

1778 Report of the Select Committee on the Punishment of Convicts by Hard Labour, House of Commons Journals, Vol. XXXVI.

1784 Report from Select Committee Respecting Laws for the Punishment of Offenders, House of Commons Journals, Vol. XXXIX.

1819 Report from Select Committee on the State of Gaols in England and Wales, Vol. VII.

An Account of all the Gaols in England and Wales, Vol. XIX.

1822 Select Committee's Report on Laws Relating to Prisons, Vol. IV.

1823 Report of the Committee of Management on the State of the (Millbank) Penitentiary, together with the Report from the Physicians, Vol. V.

1831–32 Annual Report of the Committee of Management, Millbank Penitentiary, Vol. XXXIII.

1835 Two Reports from House of Lords Committee on Prison Discipline, Vol. II.

1839 First Report from the Visitors of Parkhurst Prison, Vol. XXII.

1840 Second Report from the Visitors of Parkhurst Prison, Vol. XXXVIII.

1847 Second Report of the Surveyor-General of Prisons, Vol. XXVIII.

1847 Royal Commission Report on the Management of Millbank Prison, Vol. XXX.

1847–48 Report of the Inspectors of Prisons (Northern and Eastern Districts), Vol. XXXV.

1852 Select Committee's Report on Criminal and Destitute Juveniles, including Rules and Regulations in Convict Prisons, Vol. VII.

1852–53 Select Committee's Report on Criminal and Destitute Children, Vol. XXIII.

1856 Select Committee's Report on Public Executions, Vol. VII.

Return of Convict Licences Granted and Revoked, Vol. LXIX.

Home Department Report on Separate Confinement in Prisons in England and Wales (whether used, partially used or not used), Vol. XLIX.

1864 Return of Convict Licences Granted and Revoked (1856–1862), Vol. XLIX.

Report of Dr Guy's Committee on Dietaries in Convict Prisons, Vol. XLIX.

Ibid County and Borough Gaols, Vol. XLIII.

Correspondence with Inspectors of Prisons Respecting House of Lords (1863) Committee's Report, Vol. LXIX.

Correspondence between Home Department and Directors of Convict Prisons on Recommendations by Royal Commission (1863), Vol. XLIX.

1878 Select Committee's Report on Prison Dietaries, Vol. XLII.

1896 Report of the Prison Commissioners and Directors of Convict Prisons, Vol. XLIV.

1931–32 Report of Departmental Committee on Persistent Offenders, Vol. XII.

1933–34 Report of Departmental Committee on the Employment of Prisoners, Vol. XV.

2. Other Official Papers:

Blundeston Prison, Home Office booklet for visitors, London, 1968.

Organization of the Prison Medical Service (Home Office Report), London, 1964.

Preventive Detention, Report of the Advisory Council on the Treatment of Offenders, London, 1963.

Short-Term Imprisonment, United Nations Report, New York, 1960.

Treatment of Criminals in Denmark, Bulletin of the Ninth International Course in Criminology (Société Internationale de Criminologie), Paris, 1960.

3. Newspapers and Periodicals (referred to and/or quoted from in text):

Fortnightly Review, March 1894.

Nineteenth Century, January to December, 1902.

The Spectator, November 1842, March 1877.

The Times, 3 March, 26 June, 1817; 10 May, 22 October, 1821; 13 May, 26 May, 7 July, 13 August, 1835; 27 February, 27 April, 1838; 24 October 1842; 27 January, 28 January, 3 April, 1878; 12 February 1901; 22 November 1938.

4. Books

A. Direct reference to, and/or quotation from, in text:

Ball, B. P. H., *Prison Was My Parish*, London, 1959.

Benney, Mark, *Low Company*, London, 1935; *Gaol Delivery*, London, 1948.

Blake, Wallace, *Prison Governor*, London, 1927.

Grew, Albert, *London Prisons of Today and Yesterday*, London, 1933.

Croft-Cooke, R., *The Verdict of You All*, London, 1955.

Dickson, W. Hepworth, *The London Prisons*, London, 1850.

Du Cane, E. F., *The Punishment and Prevention of Crime*, London, 1881.

Fletcher, S. W., *Twelve Months in Gaol*, London, 1884.

Fox, Sir Lionel, *The English Prison System*, London, 1952.

Gordon, M. L., *Prison Discipline*, London, 1922.

Grew, B. D., *Prison Governor*, London, 1958.

Hobhouse, Stephen and Brockway, Fenner, (Eds.), *English Prisons Today*, London, 1922.

Horsley, J. W., *Prisons and Prisoners*, London, 1898.

Howard, John, *The State of the Prisons in England and Wales*, London, 1780.

Johnson, Pamela H., *On Iniquity*, London, 1966.

Lytton, Lady Constance, *Prisons and Prisoners*, London, 1914.

Macartney, Wilfred, *Walls Have Mouths*, London, 1936.

Menninger, Karl, *The Crime of Punishment*, New York, 1968.

Morris, Norval, *Prison in Evolution*, essay contributed to *Criminology in Transition*, London, 1965.

Paterson, Alexander, *Paterson on Prisons*, London, 1951.

Rich, C. E. F., *Recollections of a Prison Governor*, London, 1932.

Ruggles-Brise, Sir E., *The English Prison System*, London, 1921.
Smith, Kathleen J., *A Cure for Crime*, London, 1965.
Smith, L. W. M., *Prison Screw*, London, 1962.
Smith, M. Hablin, *Prisons and a Changing Society*, London, 1934.
Stead, W. T., *My First Imprisonment*, London, 1886.
Sykes, Graham, *The Society of Captives*, Princeton, N.J., 1958.
Webb, Sydney and Beatrice, *English Prisons Under Local Government* (with a preface by Bernard Shaw), London, 1922.
Willets, Phoebe, *Invisible Bars*, London, 1963.
Wood, Stuart, *Shades of the Prison House*, London, 1932.
Wootton, Barbara, *Social Science and Social Pathology*, London, 1959.
"Zeno", *Life*, London, 1968.

B. Consulted:
Adshead, Joseph, *Our Present Penal System*, London, 1847.
Anon., *Twenty Five Years in Seventeen Prisons*, London, 1903.
Behan, Brendan, *Borstal Boy*, London, 1958.
Benney, Mark, *The Truth About Prisons*, London, 1938.
Bentham, Jeremy, *Panopticon Versus New South Wales*, London, 1803; *Panopticon or the Inspection House*, London, 1771.
The Rationale of Punishment (Tr. R. Smith), London, 1830.
The Rationale of Reward (Tr. R. Smith), London, 1825.
Blagg, H. M. and Wilson, C., *Women and Prisons*, London, 1934.
Burt, J. P., *Pentonville Prison*, London, 1852.
Buxton, Jane, *Gate Fever*, London, 1962.
Carter, Lady M., *A Living Soul in Holloway*, London, 1938.
Chesterton, G. K., *Utopia of Usurers*, London, 1917.
Chesterton, G. L., *Enquiry into Prison Discipline*, London, 1857.
Collins, Philip, *Dickens and Crime*, London, 1962.
Douglas, Lord Alfred, *Autobiography*, London, 1928.
Dyer, D., *Impressions of Prison Life*, London, 1862.
Elkin, Winifred, *The English Penal System*, London, 1957.
Grygier, T., Jones, H. and Spencer, John C. (Eds.), *Criminology in Transition*, London, 1965.
Hart, H. L. A., *Law, Liberty and Morality*, London, 1963.
Heath, Carl, *A Modern View of the Rational Treatment of Crime*, London, 1913.
Henry, Joan, *Who Lie In Gaol*, London, 1952.

Howard, D. L., *The English Prisons*, London, 1960.
Hyde, H. M., *Oscar Wilde, the Aftermath*, London, 1963.
Ives, G. C., *A History of Penal Methods*, London, 1914.
Jones, Howard, *Prison Reform Now*, London, 1959.
Jones, Maxwell, *Social Psychiatry*, London, 1952.
Maconochie, A., *Secondary Punishment; the Mark System*, London, 1848; *Prison Discipline*, London, 1856; *Crime and Punishment; the Mark System Framed to Mix Persuasion with Punishment*, London, 1846.
Martyn, Frederick, *A Holiday in Gaol*, London, 1911.
Maudsley, H., *Responsibility in Mental Disease*, London, 1872.
Mays, John Barron, *Crime and the Social Structure*, London, 1963.
Morrison, W. D., *The Treatment of Prisoners*, London, 1904.
Morris, Norval and Hawkins, Gordon, *The Honest Politician's Guide to Crime Prevention*, Chicago, 1970.
Morris, Pauline, *Prisoners and Their Families*, London, 1965.
Morris, Terence, *The Criminal Area*, London, 1958.
Morris, Terence and Pauline, *Pentonville*, London, 1963.
Mountain, T. W., *Life in London Prisons*, London, 1930.
Norman, Frank, *Bang to Rights*, London, 1958.
Phelan, Jim. *Jail Journey*, London, 1940; *Tramp at Anchor*, London, 1954.
Playfair, Giles and Sington, Derrick, *The Offenders*, London, 1957; *Crime, Punishment and Cure*, London, 1965.
Radzinowicz, Leon, *A History of Criminal Law*, Vol. 4, London, 1968.
Rhodes, A. J., *Dartmoor Prison, 1906–32*, London, 1932.
Rylander, Gösta, *Forensic Psychiatry in Relation to Legislation in Different Countries*, Berlin, 1961.
Size, Mary, *Prisons I Have Known*, London, 1957.
Stock, A. G., *A Prison Anthology*, London, 1938.
Sykes, B., *Prison Life and Prison Poetry*, London, 1881.
Sykes, Robert, *Who's Been Eating My Porridge?*, London, 1967.
Wills, David, *Homer Lane*, London, 1964.
Wilson, Margaret, *The Crime of Punishment*, London, 1931.
Wines, E. O., *The State of the Prisons Throughout the World*, London, 1880.
Wolff, Michael, *Prison*, London, 1967.
Wood, S., *Memoirs of a Prison Chaplain*, London, 1955.

INDEX

"A" Category prisoners, 215–17
After-care, 177, 228
After Care Association, 180
Alcoholics, 160; Alcoholics Anonymous, 160
American colonies, convicts sent to, 23, 25
Anderson, Sir Robert (former head of the C.I.D.), 169–70
Appleton Thorn open prison, 160
Arrowsmith, Miss Pat, 108
Associated system, replaces the separate system, 217
Auburn (N.Y.), 175
Austin, Lieut. (Governor of Birmingham gaol), 88–92
Australia, convicts sent to, 23, 26, 42–3, 51–2, 61, 117

Baker, Colonel Valentine, 106
Ball, Rev. B. P. H., 122
Bayley, Mr Justice, 33
Beer allowance, 124
Belgium, 233
Bennett, Hon. H. G., 33
Bennett, James V., 158
Benney, Mark, *Low Company*, 166; *Gaol Delivery*, 189
Bentham, Jeremy, 26–9, 31, 32
Bethlehem Hospital, 39
Birmingham gaol, 88, 90, 174–5
Blackstone, Sir William, 74
Blundeston, 203, 218, 236; conditions and administration, 205–8, 212–13; vocational training courses, 213
Bodenham, 240
Borstal system, 143, 144, 165–6, 192
Bossy, Peter (surgeon on hospital vessel at Woolwich), 53, 56
Brady, Ian, 226, 245
Bramwell, Lord Justice, 133
Bramwell, Baron, 16–17
Brandish (convict), 53–4
Brett, William, 49
Bridewells, *See* Houses of correction
Bright, John, 16
Bristol prison, 95, 182
Brixton prison, 143, 148
Broadmoor, 137
Bulwood Hall (girls close borstal), 149
Burdett, Sir F., 87
Butler, R. A., 68, 186

Caernarvon, Earl of, 92, 93, 96, 142–3; his Committee, 92, 93–7, 110–11, 115, 117, 124
"Cage", the, 171, 172
Callaghan, James, 235
Camp Hill preventive detention centre, Isle of Wight, 167–8, 181–2
Campbell, Duncan, 23–6, 43
Capital offences, 15
Capital punishment, 245, 247; commuting of death sentences, 15; abolition considered by Royal Commission of 1865, 15–17; the case for retaining it for murder, 18–19; Gowers Commission on, 19; weaknesses of retentionist argument, 19–21
Capper, J. H. (Superintendent of the Hulk Establishment), 46–7, 50, 54–6
Capper, Robert, 47, 54
Categorizing prisoners. *See* Classification
Censorship of letters, 172–3, 200
Chatham public works prison, 66, 123–4, 131
Chattenden, an annexe of Chatham prison, 134, 136
Chesterton, George Laval (Governor of Coldbath Fields prison), 78–9, 84

Children. *See* Juvenile offenders
Cholera, 57
Churchill, Winston, 20–1; the Churchill Rule, 106–8
Classification of prisoners, 73, 77–8, 80, 125, 188, 190–1, 201, 217; Gladstone Committee's recommendations, 160–1
Clay, W. L. (Chaplain at Preston gaol), 83
Cockburn, Lord Chief Justice, 13, 118–19, 121, 123–4, 236
Coldbath Fields prison, 78, 84
Coldingley prison, 114–15, 218
Common gaols: traditional role, 71; conditions in, 71–2; administered by private contractors, 71; Howard's ideas of reform, 72–3; Government and local action, 73–83; general belief in punishment, 83–7; public conscience stirred about punishment, 87–8, 91; suicide at Birmingham gaol, 88–9, 91; reformers, 89–92
Commuting death sentences, 15
Complaints by prisoners, official attitude to, 99, 112, 208–12
Congreve, Sir William, 33
Con-Tact (Hull Prison Magazine), 208–10, 211–12
Contamination, problem of, 166, 197, 217
Convict labour, 143–5
Convicts, and the Hulk system. *See* Hulk system
Corporal punishment, 36–8, 48, 53, 55, 78, 87, 91, 93, 122, 124, 146, 152–3; of women, 30, 146; of juveniles, 152–3
Corrective training, 178–82
Crank, the, 88, 93; abolished, 169, 178
Crawford, William, 59, 60
Crew, Albert, 224
Crime rate: decline in decade after introduction of penal servitude, 117; in 1920, 175; rise in 1785, 232
Criminal Justice Act (1948), 107, 177–8, 181
Criminal Justice Act (1967), 164, 182, 225
Crofton, Sir William (head of the Irish convict service), 140
Curran, Dr Desmond (psychiatrist), 235
Custodial detention centres, 178

Dark cell, 61
Dartmoor, 70, 132–3, 136, 153, 185; prison envisaged at, 50–1; public works prison opened, 57; an "invalids" prison, 68, 125
Davies, Rhys, 107
Davitt, Michael, 132–6, 139, 153
Death penalty. *See* Capital punishment
Debt, imprisonment for, 105–6
Defence Hulk, 58
Debman, Lord, 13
Denmark, 223, 224
Denning, Lord, 19
Deterrence: the theory, 11; validity of the theory never tested scientifically, 12; a rationalization of the urge to punish, 85; the policy a failure, 155; the raison d'être of local prisons, 230–1; and punishment, 230–6, 248–9
Deterring agency, Charles Pearson's theory of, 86, 90–1
Devlin, Lord, 249
Devon, Lord, 128; his Commission, 128–31
Dickens, Charles, 59
Dickson, Hepworth, 62–3, 86
Diet, 34–5, 74, 94–5, 123–4, 152, 162, 173, 194
Dietary punishment, 85, 99–100, 123, 174
Double track system, in Holland, 240–2
Drug problem, 232, 235
Du Cane, Edmund (a Director of Convict Prisons, later Chairman of the Prison Commission), 81, 104, 108, 110, 146, 155, 161, 169, 185–6, 200, 231; his centrally controlled system, 98, 102, 105, 112–13; repressive ideas, 100–1, 112; and debtors, 106; and sanitation, 111; his terroristic discipline, 115–16, 125, 155, 187; and the prisoner/officer relationship,

139; and life sentences, 142; and hard labour, 143, 144; and women prisoners, 149, 150; attacked by W. D. Morrison, 156; and recreation, 188; opposed to intermediate prisons, 192
Duncombe, Thomas (M.P.), 53, 54

Earnings by prisoners, 32, 68, 82, 114, 124–5, 150, 196
East, Sir Norwood, 222
Eastchurch open prison, 100
Eden, Sir William, 74
Education: and rehabilitation of women prisoners, 149–50; emphasised as a reformative technique by the Gladstone Committee, 163; vocational training courses at Blundeston, 213; the Education Department at Wakefield, 213–15; a privilege and not a right, 215
Eichmann, Adolf, 19
Ellis, Havelock, 11
Ellis, Mrs Ruth, 19
English Prisons Today, 171–6, 178
Escapes, 12, 201
Euryalus (juvenile convict's hulk), 47–8, 151
Everlasting staircase. *See* Treadwheel

Factory Prisons, 82, 115
Farquarson, Major J. C. (Governor of Chatham prison), 131
Feltham, 192
Field (Chaplain of Reading Gaol), 96
First Division imprisonment, 105–7
First offenders. *See* "Stars"
Fletcher, Mrs S. W., 151
Flogging. *See* Corporal punishment
Ford Open Prison, 202, 203
Fox, Sir Lionel (former Chairman of the Prison Commission), 139, 164, 185–6; *Second English in its own right*, 221
Fry, Elizabeth, 36, 146, 189–90
Fulham refuge, 148, 150

Galsworthy, John, 20, 21
Gambier, I. W. (a Director of the Convict Prisons), 122
Gibson, Mrs S. (Superintendent of the female convict prison at Woking), 148, 150
Ginevich, Luxembourg, 183–4
Gladstone, Herbert, 157; his Committee, 157–63, 165, 167–9, 178, 187–8, 192, 231
Gloucester county gaol, 74, 78
Gaol Act (1823), 76–7
Gordon, Dr Mary (former Medical Inspector of Prisons), 171, 188–9, 213, 226
Gowers Commission on Capital Punishment, 19
Gradation principle. *See* Progressive stages
Graham, Aaron ("Inspector of Vessels"), 43, 44
Graham, Sir James (Home Secretary), 94
Gratuities. *See* Earnings by prisoners
Greer, Lord Justice, 12
Grendon-Underwood psychiatric prison, 37, 221–3, 225, 238–9, 242–4
Grew, Major B. J. (Governor of Wormwood Scrubs), 189–90, 193
Griffiths, Major Arthur (Inspector of convict prisons), 37, 144–5, 147, 155–6, 200

Habitual offenders. *See* Recidivists
Hair, cropping of, 202
Hanging, drawing and quartering, 14
Harcourt, Henry, 132–3, 135
Hard labour, 80–1, 88, 143; authorized by an Act of 1776, 23
Henderson, Colonel E. G. W. (Chairman of the Prison Commission), 110
Henderson Hospital, 240
Heroin addiction, 235
Herstedvester prison, Denmark, 223
Hill, Mr Justice, 16
Hill Hall open prison, 203
Hindley, Myra, 226, 245
Hiss, Alger, 226
Hoare, Samuel (Chairman of Prison Discipline Society), 46, 47
Hoare, Sir Samuel (Home Secretary), 177–8
Hobbles, 147, 150

Hold, Professor Anatol, 245–6
Holland, "double track" system in, 240–2
Hollesley Bay open borstal, 202
Holloway prison, 147, 221
Home Department, later Home Office, 77, 80, 89, 113, 136, 145, 147, 191, 203, 208, 212; takes over Hulk system, 43, 99; Justices obliged to submit quarterly reports to, 76; and treatment of imbecilic prisoners, 137; and reformative aspect of imprisonment, 139; Report of 1964, 175; and preventive detention, 182–3; inquires into the Little Commonwealth, 240
Homosexuality, 197–9, 200, 235
Horabin, Sir Ian, 205
Horsens, Jutland, 223
Horsley, Rev. J. W. (Chaplain at Clerkenwell prison), 100
Hostel scheme, 182, 228–30
Houses of correction, 30, 71, 74
Howard, John, 71–4, 77, 173
Hubert, Dr de Bath, 222
Hulk system, 62, 64, 66, 99, 145, 196, 197; birth of, 23; operations of Duncan Campbell, and transport of convicts to America, 23–5; observations of 1785 Committee on, 25–6; overseers appointed, and the Home Department takes over, 43; attempt to make the system reformative, 44–6; special training hulk for juvenile convicts, 46; a Superintendent appointed, 46–7; Government inquiries into conditions, 47–56; drastic reorganization, 56–7; the establishment under a directorate, 57; end of the system, 57–8
Hull prison, 100, 208–10, 211–12, 217
Hutchinson, Dr Copland (Medical Superintendent of Millbank), 34, 35, 38

Imbecilic prisoners. *See* Psychotics and mental defectives
Incorrigibles, extermination of, 20, 21
Indeterminate sentence, 224, 237–9
Industrial schools, 151, 153
Intermediate prisons, in Ireland, 120, 145, 192,
Invalid prisoners, 125
Ireland, intermediate prisons in, 120, 145, 192
Irish treason-felony offenders, 127–9

Jebb, Colonel (later Sir) Joshua, 60, 62, 75, 80, 84, 95–6, 110, 111, 123, 125, 193, 215; Surveyor-General of Prisons, 52–3, 54; Chairman of Hulk Establishment Directorate, 57; chairman of Directors of Pentonville, 64; and the ticket-of-leave scheme, 67–9; belief in the separate system, 69; and juvenile offenders, 152
Jenkins, Roy, 107–8
Johnson, Miss Pamela Hansford, 90
Jones, Dr Maxwell, 240
Journalists, and access to prisons, 113
Juries, their former reluctance to convict capital offenders, 15
Juvenile offenders: in Millbank, 39–40; in convict hulks, 24, 48; most of them kept out of prison, 102; treated much the same as adults, 151; earliest attempt at differential treatment, 151–3; some sent to public works prisons, 153; penal servitude sentences, 153; move towards more humane treatment, 153–4; Borstal training 164–6; custodial detention centres and non-custodial detention centres, 178; Homer Lane and other pioneers' work in treatment of, 239–40

Kimberley, Earl of, 131; his Commission, 131*ff*., 148–50, 153, 202
Knight, Thomas, 49
Kray brothers, 226

Labour Party, and political prisoners, 107
Lancaster Castle Gaol, 88
Lane, Homer, 239
Latham, Dr, 35

Leyhill, Officers' Training School at, 162, 210
Little Commonwealth, Homer Lane's, 239–40
Lloyd, Geoffrey, 177
Lloyd, John, 108
Lockwood prison, 217
Long Lartin prison, 217
Low Newton prison, 217
Lowdham open borstal, 192
Lunacy Act (1909), 164
Lushington, Sir Godfrey (retired permanent Under-Secretary, Home Office), 157–8, 159
Lusk, near Dublin, intermediate prison at, 120, 228
Lyons, Dr (member of Devon Commission), 129–30
Lytton, Lady Constance, 170
Lytton, Lord, 240
Lyward, George, 240

Macartney, Wilfrid, *Walls Have Mouths*, 198
McConnachie, William (former Chief Constable of Southend), 202
McGrigor, Sir James (Head of Army Medical Board), 34
Maconochie, Captain Alexander (Governor of Birmingham gaol), 89–91
Mad prisoners. *See* Psychotics and mental defectives
Magazines, prison, 208
Marks system, 89, 90
Maryland, 23
"Meat safe", 171–2
Medical service. *See* Prison Medical Service
Melbourne, Lord, 40
Menninger, Dr Karl, *The Crime of Punishment*, 246
Mental defectives. *See* Psychotics and mental defectives
Mental Deficiency Act (1913), 164
Mental Health Act (1959), 164
Merry, William (of Reading gaol), 81–2, 84–5, 124
Mexico, 199–200
Millbank penitentiary, 29, 60, 62, 64, 69, 73, 77, 86, 132, 152, 158, 159, 238; the building, 30–1; a rehabilitation centre, 31; Committee of Management, 31, 34, 35, 41; staff, 31; seclusion, 31–2; unhealthiness, 33–4; disturbances, 34, 35–6; food reduced, and outbreak of scurvy, 34–5; daily routine, and prisoners' earnings, 32; religious instruction, 32; the first inmates, 33; Select Committee's recommendations, 35; discipline tightened, and associated work abolished, 36; Rev. Whitworth Russell's administration, 37, 42; Rev. Daniel Nihil's administration, 37–9; child prisoners, 39–40; Committee of Management abolished, 41; becomes a reception centre for convicts, 41, 49, 51
Mitchell, Frank, 138
Monk or Taylor, George, 53
Moors Murder case, 90, 245
Morris, Norval (criminologist), 234
Morrison, Rev. W. D. (Chaplain at Wandsworth prison), 156
Mountbatten Report, 27–8, 70, 98, 109, 111, 123, 191, 195, 200–1, 204, 207, 209, 210, 216, 218
Mulcahy, Denis, 128–9
Murder: the case for the capital penalty, 18–19; weaknesses of retentionist argument, 19–20
Mutiny, in women's prison's, 150–1

Neill, A. S., 240
New Hall Camp open prison, 192
New York, Wall Street Prison, 84
New Zealand, 233
Newgate, 36, 76, 78, 79
Nicholas, Grand Duke, 33
Nihil, Rev. Daniel (Chaplain and Governor of Millbank), 37–9, 238
Non-custodial detention centres, 178
Norfolk Island penal settlement, 52, 89, 90
Nowers, Rev. J. H. (former prison chaplain), 139–40

Oakum-picking, 143
Official Secrets Act, 113

Open prisons: under-populated, 191; the first one, 192
Organ, Philip, 120, 228
Osborne, Thomas (American penologist), 175–6

Panopticon, the, 26–9, 31
Pantilers, 38
Parkhurst prison, 40, 41, 70, 134, 137; riot at, 137*n.*; juvenile reformative prison, 152; turned over to men, 153; preventive detainees at, 182
Parnell, C. S., 106
Parole (release on licence): a re-introduction of ticket-of-leave scheme, 68; present-day practice, 117–18, 225–30
Paul, Sir George, 74
Paternalism, in prison administration, 207–13, 218–19
Paterson, Sir Alexander, 189, 197; Prison Commissioner, 109, 176; influence, 177; on Dartmoor, 185; his "seminal ideas", 185–6, 188–9, 194–5; opposed to the separate system, 187–8; and open prisons, 192
Pearson, Charles (Chairman of 1850 Select Committee), 88; his deterring agency plan, 86, 90–1
Penal labour, abolished in local prisons, 161–2
Penal Practice in a Changing Society, 186, 221
Penal servitude, 69–70, 97; introduction of, 66; inquiry by the Royal Commission of 1863, 117–125; minimum sentence raised by Act of 1864, 120–1; treatment of invalid prisoners, 125–6; treason-felony offenders, 127–31; Devon Commission inquiry, 128–31; sanitary arrangements, 130–1; Kimberley Commission inquiry, 131–7; prisoner/officer relationship, 137–40; corruption of minor offenders, 141–2; convict labour, 143–5; juvenile offenders sentenced, 153
Penitentiary Act (1779), 23, 73, 74
Pentonville, 80, 95, 110, 114, 135, 146, 152, 158–61, 206, 213, 217; building of, 42; its original purpose, 52, 60, 61–2; the separate system at work in, 59–64; loses independent status, 64; slight reforms introduced, 64–6; structural model of local gaols, 75; hostel scheme, 229, 230
Perry, J. G. (Home Office inspector), 84, 85, 93, 96, 110
Persistent offenders, *See* Recidivists
Personal responsibility, prisoner's sense of, 207, 218–19, 241
Philadelphia, Eastern Penitentiary in, 59–60, 64
Political prisoners, 106–8
Portland public works prison, 51–2, 57, 127, 129–30
Portsmouth gaol, 135, 136
Prerogative of Mercy, 15, 121
Press, the. *See* Journalists
Preston gaol, 82, 83, 95, 113–15
Prevention of Crime Act (1908), 165, 167
Prevention of Crimes Act (1871), 121
Preventive detention, 167–8, 178–182; abolished, 182–4
Preventive extermination, 20, 21
Preventive school of penology, 237, 243–5
Prison Act (1877), 99, 105
Prison Medical Service, 173. *See also* Psychiatric treatment
Prison officers: untrained to deal with mental afflictions, 137–8, 162; ill-treatment and violence by, 138–40, 162; and tobacco smuggling, 141; poorly paid, 138; prisoners' attitudes to, 138; Training Schools for, 162, 210–11
Prison Officers Association, 156
Prison security: Bentham's Panopticon, 26–9; supervision of convict labour, 144, 145. *See also* Mountbatten Report
Probation officer, 117–18
Probation of Offenders Act (1907), 163–4
Probation orders, 178
Productive work, 82–3, 143–5, 168
Progressive stages, system of (gradation principle), 101, 124

Psychiatric treatment, 162, 219; replaces religious instruction, 220; an innovation, 221–2; chances of failure of imprisonment as a psychiatric experiment, 223–5
Psychotics and mental defectives: punishment of, 87–8; failure to keep them out of prison, 102; convicts as, 125–6; Du Cane's recommendation, 100–1; Home Office policy, 137; Gladstone Committee's recommendations, 159–61; attempts to keep them out of prison, 164
Public executions, 14, 25
Public works prisons, 145; the first to be built, 51; liberal regime of earlier days, 68; progressive stages system, 124; daily routine, 127–8
Pumpfrey, Miss Eliza (Superintendent of the Winchester refuge), 148
Punishment(s): for women, 30, 33, 36, 39, 146–9; dark cell, 61; corporal (*see* Corporal punishment); at Coldbath Fields, 78; the treadwheel, 81, 169, 178; general belief in, 83–7; dietary, 85, 99–100, 123, 174; public conscience stirred, 87–8, 91; the crank, 88, 93; reformers and, 89–92; observations of the Caernarvon Committee, 93–4; under Du Cane's regime, 98–100; Kimberley Commission inquiry into, 132–7; the hobbles, 147, 150; for juveniles, 152–3; conscientious objectors' experiences, 171; and deterrence, 230–6, 248–9
Purpose-built prison, 201

Race Relations Act (1965), 108
Rampton hospital, 138
Rape, ceases to be a capital offence, 18
Rationalization of industries, in central prisons, 161
Rawlings, John, 87–8
Rawlinson, J. F. P., 240
Reade, Charles, *It is Never Too Late to Mend*, 88
Reading gaol, 72, 81, 84, 170
Reception procedure, 74, 201–2
Recidivists, recidivism, 141, 156, 157, 205, 217, 231; preventive detention, 167–8, 178–9, 180–4; corrective training, 178–80
Redhill, 240
Reform schools, 151, 153
Reformative imprisonment: beginnings of, 14–15; transportation (*see* Hulk system); Bentham's Panopticon, 26–9; Millbank penitentiary (*see separate heading*); a full reformative system as yet untried, 236–7
Reformatory and Industrial Schools Acts, 157
Rehabilitation, 31, 109, 149, 169
Release on licence, *See* Parole; Ticket-of-leave system
Religious instruction, 29, 32, 33, 45, 65, 81, 82; still in use, 220–1; failure of imprisonment as a religious experiment, 222–3
Remand prisoners, 77, 102–4
Remission of sentence, 66, 119, 121, 150
Retributive theory, 18–19, 119
Rich, Colonel (former prison governor), 146, 187
Roguet, Dr, 35
Ruggles-Brise, Sir Evelyn (Chairman of Prison Commission), 139, 146, 165, 166, 169, 176, 185, 188
Russell, Rev. Whitworth (Chaplain and Governor of Millbank), 36, 42, 60, 238

Salisbury gaol, 74
Sandys, Duncan, 12, 204, 245
Sanitation. *See* Slopping out
Seale, Miss Susan (Superintendent of Fulham refuge), 150
Second Division imprisonment, 105–106
Security. *See* Prison security
Segregation of the sexes, 74
Self-determinate sentence, 90
Separate system, 42, 52, 59–65, 69, 74–8, 80, 83, 95–6, 159–60, 166–7; abolished, 72, 187, 217
Sexual problem, 199–200, 207
Shaw, Bernard, 20, 21, 72, 167

Shaw, Otto, 240
Sherwin, Rev. Ambrose (Chaplain at Pentonville), 123, 135
Short-term imprisonment, abandoned for purely terroristic purposes, 163
Silence rule, 36, 78, 80, 124, 125, 151, 162, 171, 187
Sing Sing, 175
Slopping out, 59, 109–12, 205
Smith, Hablin (former Medical Officer), 201
Smith, Miss Kathleen J. (former assistant governor of Holloway), 89–90
Smith, L. W. Merrow, 194, 197
Social workers for prisons, 211
Solitary confinement, 174, 202–3
South Africa, 233
Sparrow, John, 195–6
Spectator, The, 13, 237
Spring Hill open prison, 160
"Stars" (first offenders), 190, 192, 213, 217
Starvation. *See* Dietary punishment
Stead, W. T., 105–8
Stephen, James Fitzjames, 17
Streatham, 148
Stürup, Dr Georg K. (psychiatrist), 224
Suffragettes, 170–1
Suicides in prison, 88
Summary Jurisdiction Acts, 157
Summerhill, 240
Suspended sentence, introduction of, 164
Sykes, Gresham (American criminologist), 194

Tenterden, 240
Therapeutic community concept, 239–42
Ticket-of-leave scheme, 52, 66–9, 117, 118, 120–1
Times, The, 12, 33, 40, 42, 54, 108, 204
Tobacco, smuggled into prison, 141
Tobacco "Barons", 197, 199, 209
Tothill Fields gaol, 151
Transportation, 15, 16, 22–6, 41–2, 67, 238; virtually replaced by penal servitude, 66, 117
Treadwheel, 81; abolished, 169, 178
Treason, death penalty for, 14, 21
Treason-felony offenders, 127–30
Treatment of the Adult Offender (White Paper), 225
Treatment relationship, 38, 162

United Nations Congress (1960), 233,
United States: parole system in, 226; severe penalties for drug taking, 232. *See also* Auburn; New York; Philadelphia
Unproductive labour, its abolition recommended by Gladstone Committee, 161
Untried prisoners, *See* Remand prisoners

Van der Hoeven Clinic, 240, 242–4
Violence in prisons, 197
Virginia, 23
Visitors. *See* Voluntary prison visitors
Visits by relatives, 171–2
Voluntary prison visitors, 190
Voules, Herbert P. (Manager of Hulk Establishment), 56–7, 93, 95

Wakefield gaol, 72, 75, 82, 83, 115, 192, 217, 221; Officers' Training School at, 162, 210; its Education Department, 213–15; "A" Category prisoners, 215–16
Wandsworth prison, 72
Ward, Stephen, 104
Warders. *See* Prison Officers
Webb, Sidney and Beatrice, 20, 30, 74, 82, 91, 102, 115, 156–7, 163, 167, 171
Wensleydale, Lord, 17, 20, 237
West, Dr D. J. (Assistant Director of Research, Institute of Criminology), 183
Western Germany, 233
Whitaker, Michael, 245, 246–7, 249
Wilde, Oscar, 100
Willets, Phoebe, 203, 204
Williams, Captain (Inspector of Common Gaols), 54–5, 56, 83–4
Wills, David, 240
Wilson, Charles, 12

Winchester refuge, 148, 149
Woking: invalids prison at, 125, 127; female convict prison at, 148, 150
Wolfenden Committee, 235
Women: punishments for, 30, 33, 36, 39, 146–9, 150; in Millbank, 30, 33, 36, 39; segregated from men in common gaols, 146–7; in open prisons, 147; the Fulham and other refuges for, 148–9; education and rehabilitation, 149–150; discipline and mutiny, 150–1; conditions in Hill Hall, 203–4; necessity of single rooms for, 204
Wootton, Lady, 237–8
Wormwood Scrubs, 72, 110, 114, 185–7, 189–90, 217, 221
Wortz, Manniston, 49

York, Duchess of, 33